Social Science in America

The First Two Hundred Years

Social Science in America

The First Two Hundred Years

Edited by
Charles M. Bonjean
Louis Schneider
Robert L. Lineberry

University of Texas Press · Austin & London

International Standard Book Number 0-292-77530-X (cloth);
0-292-77531-8 (paper)
Library of Congress Catalog Card Number 76-14080
Copyright © 1976 by University of Texas Press
Printed in the United States of America

Previously published as the special Bicentennial issue of
Social Science Quarterly 57, no. 1 (June 1976).

Contents

Social Science in America

The First Two Hundred Years

Introduction

CHARLES M. BONJEAN

The University of Texas at Austin

Plans for the United States Bicentennial year were on the drawing boards long before 1976. All segments of American society were encouraged to participate in the "celebration" and to contribute in various ways to an understanding and appreciation of our society's past, present and future. The contributions have been many and varied, ranging from major historical renovations to mass produced T-shirts. Perhaps not surprisingly, the Bicentennial crusade has involved very few academicians. Maybe this is because much of it has been profiteering rather than provocative, long on zest but short on ideas, faddish rather than durable and ritualistic rather than rational. Some social scientists would say that it has been typically "American."

Still, the event has offered us a special opportunity to reexamine our society's first two hundred years—to assess our progress, to rediscover our mistakes and to look for trends. The belief that we can better understand the present and more adequately chart the future by identifying regular and recurrent patterns in the past is also typically "American" and a product of several of our society's dominant value orientations—progress, science and secular rationality, and achievement and success (Williams, 1970: 438–504). By definition, social scientists should be in a uniquely well qualified position to engage in this type of assessment. Thus, two years ago, the editors of the *Social Science Quarterly* felt that they could best make a Bicentennial contribution by publishing a special issue of the journal which would attempt to answer the following questions:

1. What have been the distinctive major contributions made by United States social scientists?

2. What impact have these contributions had on our understanding of American society?

3. What is the relationship of these contributions to the character or nature of life in the United States? That is, is our society any different because of the nature of this understanding and/or has the development of the social sciences been influenced in any way by the nature of life in American society?

Each contributor to this volume was asked to write an essay applying at least two of these questions to his own discipline. In fairness to the authors, it should also be mentioned that they were limited by a deadline and by space constraints. In fairness to the reader, it should be pointed out that a different panel of contributors would probably have emphasized some different contributions and been more or less critical of those included in this volume. While the editors of this volume have no disagreement with the achievements (and shortcomings) highlighted by each author, the list would obviously be a longer one had more scholars been invited to participate. Still, our intention was not to produce an abridged encyclopedia of the social sciences with a focus on the United States. Rather, it was to offer a brief and readable summary and assessment by outstanding scholars also known for their ability to synthesize.

The editors of this volume solicited advice and information from colleagues in their own and related disciplines and the following scholars were invited and agreed to participate in this written symposium: William H. Goetzmann, Stiles Professor of History and Director of American Studies at The University of Texas at Austin; Joseph J. Spengler, James B. Duke Professor of Economics at Duke University; Robin M. Williams, Henry Scarborough Professor of Social Science at Cornell University; Heinz Eulau, Professor of Political Science at Stanford University; Walter Goldschmidt, Professor of Anthropology and Psychiatry at the University of California, Los Angeles; and Kevin Cox, Professor of Geography at Ohio State University. Their essays were originally published in the June, 1976, issue of the *Social Science Quarterly*.

While each reader may be likely to have a particular interest in the chapter dealing with his or her own discipline, the relative absence of technical material and the scope of the issues discussed should make the others equally interesting. There are insights that are to be gained by comparing issues, trends and contributions and shortcomings in one discipline with those of another. Some of these are elaborated and evaluated by Louis Schneider in the final chapter of the volume.

The truly interdisciplinary nature of the social sciences is in some sense intimated in each of the essays and is clearly to the fore in most of them. Anthropology, for example, borrowed theoretical perspectives from sociology, economics, and psychology. Sociology, in turn, borrowed methodology from anthropology, economics and psychology. The quantitative movement in geography was spurred by previous developments in economics, sociology and the other social sciences. The impact of historiography was pervasive in political science until the behavioral revolution, which was stimulated by previous developments in sociology and psychology. Along the same lines, one can see the same theoretical and methodological issues recur in the various social sciences at different points in time. Taken together, the six essays will probably instill more respect for the impact of cross-disciplinary stimuli and a better understanding of the need for interdisciplinary contact.

Reference

Williams, R. M. 1970. American Society: A Sociological Interpretation. (New York: Alfred A. Knopf).

Time's American Adventures:

American Historians and
Their Writing since 1776

WILLIAM H. GOETZMANN

The University of Texas at Austin

Appropriately enough, virtually the entire two hundred year span of America's national existence falls within a period in which men and women characteristically oriented and interpreted their experiences historically. The Revolution itself might be described as a product of historical thinking. Lawyers talked about the evolution of the British Empire. Latter day Puritan ministers projected the Revolution as the millennium their typologies had predicted. Colonial observers in Britain wrote of the inevitable decline of society in Gibbonesque fashion. Tom Paine saw the break with England as the climactic moment of freedom towards which all history had been aiming. And Thomas Jefferson justified independence by means of an analogue with the historic migration of the Anglo Saxon peoples out of the forests of Germany into Britain, then to America.

By the same token in 1976, despite valiant Bicentennial efforts and striking commercial successes, history no longer seems central to American thought or even to that of western Europe. Recently, the transAtlantic historian, J. H. Plumb (1970), has written its epitaph. History has been replaced by new journalism, structuralism, psychology, systems analysis and the urgent felt need for contemporary problemsolving. In the anxious modern world the task that the historian performs appears to many to have little "work value"—either in predictive terms or in the area of moral imperatives. Policy makers steeped in history are said to be "preparing for the last war." And has it become true that "those who neglect the past are not necessarily condemned to repeat it"? Certainly time itself has become so relative and multiplicitous that the historian, who once saw his role as that of its keeper, stands, in the words of Henry Adams, "sorely perplexed." Why all this is so now, and why it was not apparently so for almost two hundred years, form the underlying questions of this essay which briefly surveys American historical writing and its role in the culture since 1776. This essay seeks generally to ask what have American historians been doing for two hundred years and how and why, and finally to look at the ways in which contemporary historians are facing up to reports of the death in their family of knowledge. In short, I hope, insofar as historians really have had anything to do with it, to trace time's American adventures.

Time is, of course, the essence but not the only subject matter of history. Traditionally the historian has been concerned with telling a story—the story of human ideas and behavior as it unfolded through time past. This has meant that the historian has had to be concerned with the discovery and relationship of facts or events out of which he creates the mosaic of his story. In turn this has raised important questions of validation especially as history moved from myth-making and the edifying moral tale to pretensions of scientific accuracy. In an age increasingly dominated by science since the seventeenth century, any serious historian has had to submit his facts to his peers for verification as well as present a story whose interior logic is in some sense convincing to his audience. There can be no fantasizing or a "history of the absurd." This has meant that, by and large, history itself has become dependent on science and thus rightly deserves to be numbered among the social sciences though it appears to lack some of the attributes of a true science. Predictability is one of these. Yet there is a sense in which the historian predicts—not about the future but about the past. Characteristically the historian works not only inductively from archives, printed materials and even objects, but he also develops an hypothesis about the past which he seeks to verify. Sometimes this can be done with precision through the location of incontrovertible documentary evidence attesting to an event. On other occasions he is working with trends, situations and complex personalities where the evidence can never be more than persuasive and colored by the historian's own point of view or interpretation.

History, particularly in America, has gone through an evolution from the conviction that absolute truth is scientifically attainable to an awareness of the relative position of the historian as interpreter. Much of this theory has been borrowed from European thinkers such as Von Ranke, Croce and Collingwood. The most recent original contribution has been made, however, by the American, Morse Peckham. Peckham (1970: 202-225) has argued essentially that there is no past at all. The historian lives only in the present and his story or research is merely a set of signals alerting his reader to the existence of surviving pieces of evidence out of which, if one chooses, one can fashion a story; and if the reader follows the author's directions in his intellectual Easter egg hunt, that story is likely to be a convincing if not satisfying story that provides insight into human behavior at the present time. History can say nothing about the past. It can only speak to the present because the existing present materials are all we have. Peckham's position inevitably leads to the conclusion that history is not science at all but a mode of social inquiry sparked by present day concerns and at the same time an interesting means of self-expression—interesting because of its mimetic qualities. It forms a kind of *trompe l'oeil* landscape with figures in it, but it can never be the real thing because that is past and gone forever. In short, for Peckham history is a form of art but a very special form dependent upon verifiable directional signals as to the existence of physical evidence that will make the art more convincing to the scientifically conditioned mind.

Perhaps this interpretation is extreme, but it puts the historian's current situation rather clearly. On the one hand he is engaged in a scientific enterprise and thus subservient to the canons and criteria of science. He cannot go back to myth-making or even the currently chic "advocacy history" if it is false to the tests of verification. For better or for worse, history is a scientific discipline. On the other hand, it is clearly subject to interpretation, configuration, insights, even the idiosyncratic language and means of presentation commanded by the historian, to the point where it becomes an art form and probably demands an underlying philosophy, or at least a logic, as well. Perhaps it is this very tension—so overt in the writing of history—that makes it *sui generis* as a discipline. Very likely it is this dual lens capacity, this binocular approach to human behavior, that gives to history its peculiarly human and hence compelling power as a means of organizing and judging one's experience.

Though it rests upon scientific principles, and often borrows scientific models, history, unlike science and most social sciences, does not deal in abstractions. Along with the phenomenon of change through time its essence lies in the concrete, the specific and the artistically convincing. It presents a satisfactorily verified world into which one can enter and lose himself. In some ways it is the dramatization of the scientific mind in action. Indeed one recent commentator (Winks, 1968), perhaps thinking of Hercule Poirot or Sherlock Holmes, has seen the historian as a kind of hero-detective. Clearly, then, history is tragedy as well as trends, and it can be farce with the historian in some subtle way always the hero. But the practice of history in America did not spring full-blown with self-awareness. Appropriately enough it evolved—historically.

The New World and History

The full bibliographical story of the development of American historiography is much too extensive to recount here and can be found in numerous book-length works.[1] It is important to note that from the beginning—even in the colonial period of American history—Americans were self-conscious about their role in history. Puritan writers saw themselves and their people as participants in a great cosmic drama that had been unfolding since the days of Adam. American history was cosmic history and it was part of a typology carried over from Medieval tradition. The Franciscans at the outset of the Age of Discovery, inspired by the twelfth century mystic, Joachim of Fiore, saw the discovery of the New World as the beginning of the last phase of converting the world's heathen, after which would come the Christian millenium and the reconstitution of paradise.

Columbus himself was profoundly influenced by Joachim and the discoverer's *Letters From the New World* (1493) clearly indicated that he thought he had discovered the terrestrial paradise of Adam and Eve somewhere in northern South America. He was also confident that he had discovered the fabled King Solomon's Mines whose riches would help rebuild the temple at Jerusalem, and that certainly within 150 years all mankind would be converted to Christianity. Thus, in a certain sense, Columbus himself assumed the role of historian and prophet and laid down the basic framework, however mystical, for the progressive historical tradition that has so dominated American writing. In his wake followed numerous Spanish historians, the most significant of whom was Geronimo de Mendieta, whose *Historia Eclesiastica Indiana* (1571) recounted the conquest of the New World strictly in terms of a Christian typology of progress, relating each step in the Conquest to incidents in the Bible. Mendieta even went so far as to portray Cortez as Moses smashing the heathen idols and the 12 Franciscans that he imported into Mexico as the reincarnations of the 12 Apostles (Phalen, 1956). Only Bartolome de las Casas in his numerous polemics on behalf of the Indians saw anything but progress resulting from the Spanish Conquest. His *Very Brief Account of the Destruction of the Indies* (1553), recounting the atrocities committed by the Spaniards against the Indians, was a critical, controversial work, eagerly translated by Protestant opponents of Spain. As such it forms the beginning of the "Black Legend" of Catholic and Spanish cultural inferiority in the New World.[2] It is also the spiritual ancestor of such contemporary Indian advocacy histories as Vine Deloria's *Custer Died For Your Sins* (1969) and Dee Brown's *Bury My Heart at Wounded Knee* (1971).

Biblical typology or cosmic drama as a framework for history was Medieval and Catholic or Hebraic in origin, but it was quickly adopted by Protestant theologians and historians. The Protestant version, however, closely followed the steps of the Seven Vials of Wrath in the Book of Revelation, celebrating the purity of the early Christian Church, seeing a decline into "Babylonian Captivity" with the ascent of the Popes, and the beginning of a coming millennium with the advent of the Reformation. Perhaps the most famous inspiration for Protestant historians was John Foxe's *Acts and Monuments* (1554) better known as Foxe's *Book of Martyrs*. Foxe recounted the tribulations of latter-day martyrs from John Huss onward, but his book, so full of trials and tribulations and physical horrors in which he took an unseemly relish, was in the end optimistic, even millennial. He saw England under Calvinism as the starting point for world redemption. The importance of these ancient works is, of course, that they established the fundamental myth or rhythm of American history which, until very recently, has been the story of inevitable triumph over adversity and progress toward a millennium in a world allowed by divine providence to start over again. No matter what its ideological or technical characteristics, American historiography has been a literature of Manifest Destiny. History, if not God, has been on our side. As the years went by history and God became synonymous.

No more than a cursory glance at very early American historiography reveals the theme of inevitable conquest over adversity and ultimate triumph. William Bradford's *Plymouth Plantation* (written 1630-1650, published 1855), Cotton Mather's *Magnalia Christi Americana* (1702), Edward Johnson's *Wonder Working Providence of Zion's Savior in New England* (1654) and the fragmentary survivals of Jonathan Edwards' projected historical work all ring the changes on this theme as does Captain John Smith's *The Generall Historie of Virginia, New-England and the Summer Isles* (1624). Bradford's work recounted in swelling prose the triumphs of the Pilgrims as they crossed the stormy ocean, endured the howling wilderness and prevailed over adversity to see a land of peace and plenty arise. Mather, the American Plutarch, wrote of "the Wonders of the Christian Religion, flying from the deprivations of Europe, to the American Strand . . . . " In so doing he celebrated the Christian triumphs of New England's larger-than-life founding fathers, some of whom were also his venerated ancestors. Johnson and Smith wrote the first significant versions of American frontier history with attendant epic overtones—the one celebrating the inland march of New England's Puritans, the other the difficult but promising conquest of Virginia's damp and bloody ground. Edwards with persuasive intensity interpreted all human history as culminating in the actual second coming of Christ to New England (Tuveson, 1968: 55-57, 100-101).

By and large, buttressed by centuries of Christian confidence and at the same time wishing to promote the New World and their own mighty deeds, early American historians wrote in the epic vein of Hakluyt or promotional pamphlet literature such as *Joyeful Newes Out of the Newe Found World.* From the beginning, "boosterism" has been innate in the American historical imagination. There is, of course, abundant evidence of darkness and depression in the sermons and closet notes of the early historians, as there certainly would be of later ones, but history, as Peter Gay (1968: 122 and passim) has observed, ·is public. It is also a vision in some sense of the long run of mankind and few historians have been willing, until recent times, to concede that humanity will not "endure and prevail." Mythologically perhaps it confronts the certainty of individual death with assurances of immortality for mankind.

Historians, the Revolution, and the Enlightenment

If history was eschatology for the early colonial writers, it underwent some refinement during the era of the American Revolution. Four significant histories of that event, or at least closely related to it, appeared by 1805. Among the most important was that of Governor Thomas Hutchinson of Massachusetts. A much-hated Tory political figure, Hutchinson produced a three volume *History of the Colony of Massachusetts Bay* (1764-1828) that carried the story of its turbulent times down to 1774, the eve of the Revolution. Hutchinson had many scores to settle, including an animus against the Puritans for their persecution of his ancestor Anne Hutchinson, but he wrote with a detachment that might even have commanded the notice of David Hume.

The most widely read historians of the Revolution however, were two men and a woman. William Gordon, a friend of John Adams, removed himself to England so that he could write objectively about the war. Unfortunately neither the English nor the Americans liked his book, *The History of the Rise, Progress And Establishment of the Independence of the United States of America* . . . (1788). David Ramsay, a South Carolinian, was much more successful with his *The History of the American Revolution* (1789), and some present day historians take pleasure in it despite the fact that, like Gordon's work, it was largely plagiarized from the *Annual Register*, a London-published running account of the recent war (Kraus, 1953: 62-73). The most ambitious history of the Revolution was Mercy Otis Warren's three volume *History of the . . . American Revolution . . .* published in 1805. Mistress Warren was a friend of Abigail Adams and derived a great deal of information from John Adams and other founding fathers. Her history, though highly patriotic, placed the war in the world context of the British Empire and then related it to the entire course of human history, thus making it a piece of patriotic typology (Kraus, 1953: 78-80). All four historians, however, the Tory Hutchinson, the copyists Gordon and Ramsay and the bluestocking Mercy Warren, attempted, or at least professed to have attempted, critical research in the sources. They strove in their own ways to achieve an objectivity that bespoke the impact of the Scientific Revolution on historiography. Still it would be many years before the American Revolution was properly served by historians.

The impact of the Enlightenment upon American historical writing is perhaps best illustrated by two other works not directly aimed at a Revolutionary War audience. The first, Thomas Jefferson's *Notes on Virginia* (1787), is an answer to aspersions cast on America by the Frenchmen Count Buffon and Abbé Raynal. Assuming the role of both geographer and historian, Jefferson fitted Virginia into a rationalistic Enlightenment version of the Great Chain of Being. He began with Virginia's geography—its boundaries, soil, topography, landscape, vegetation, climate, etc.—then worked his way up nature's ladder to the Indian, the Negro and finally the history of the white settlers' quest for free political institutions. Along the way Jefferson wrestled sincerely with the question of the Negro and the Indian, deciding regretfully that nature, according to the present evidence, had made them inferior to the white man. But, in general, nature and nature's creatures in America were in no way inferior to anything in Europe. On the contrary, by the canons of environmental determinism so prevalent in Enlightenment thinking, the unspoiled quality of nature in America had produced superior creatures and purer, better institutions. As history, Jefferson's *Notes on Virginia* occupied an uncertain position. Jefferson himself believed in a kind of continuous present in which no creature ever became extinct and yet he was forced continually into the past in his treatise on American space (Boorstin, 1948: 41-53). He also thought in terms of generations which, though not sacred as were the Puritan ancestors, nonetheless made the world as he found it beyond the limits of Monticello.

The other interesting work of the period, *A Brief Retrospect of the Eighteenth Century* (1803), was written in two volumes by Samuel Miller, a Presbyterian clergyman in New York City. Miller's work was encyclopedic but it had a point. He attempted to show that all of the achievements of the Scientific Revolution and the Enlightenment were not threats to orthodox religion in America but rather demonstrated the beneficence of God. Miller, a product of Scottish Enlightenment thought, attempted to show that God, in enlightening man, sharpening his reason, ingenuity and powers of moral philosophy, was distinctly on his side and never more so than in America. For Miller religion had no quarrel with science. He demonstrated this in the *Brief Retrospect*, the first intellectual history by an American. In so doing he charted the course that a powerful stream of American Protestant thought was to take for much of the nineteenth century (Hovenkamp, 1976).

Despite the impressive European Enlightenment works of Hume, Gibbon, Voltaire, Montesquieu and Condorcet, history as such hardly flourished in America during the Revolutionary Era and the early years of the Republic. On the other hand, history was not scorned. At one level it flourished in the patriotic mythmaking of Mercy Otis Warren and the indefatigable efforts of the huckster biographer, Parson Mason Weems (1800), who made Washington a god who "could not tell a lie" (see also, Wecter, 1941). On another level it was revered as a precious resource. No one was consulted by the founding fathers as much as Montesquieu. His *Spirit of the Laws* was a bible. In addition the men who were fashioning America ransacked the past—the works of Tacitus and Livy, Herodotus and Thucydides, even Molesworth's tragic history of the late Danish Republic—to find guidance in their own endeavors (Bailyn, 1967: 22-54). They made the Roman Republic a model and this extended even into a reverence for Virgil, Cicero and the architecture of Vitruvius. To the founding fathers history was a "usable past" or, in Voltaire's terms, "philosophy teaching by example," since men down through all ages were basically the same, part of a universal species whose true nature as individuals John Locke had so well understood. History reflected universal principles that remained unchanged or at most went in endless cycles paralleling Newtonian planetary motion (Persons, 1954). That was why the past was really usable and why busy men, building a nation, felt no urgent need to write new history except as propaganda. The age old histories along with the Bible contained all the truth that was necessary.

History, Patriotism and the Early Republic

Although Enlightenment views of history persisted through the Revolutionary Era, in countless ways Americans began to develop a new consciousness of time and a new sense of the impingement of history. In part this arose in response to local needs, if not pride, but in a more profound sense it arose out of larger developments in Western civilization itself. The decades following the Revolution saw the publication of numerous state histories and the formation of local historical societies. During the confusing formative period as the Republic came into being, state or colony histories became important devices for identifying the cultural or political unit to which one properly owed allegiance, be it Connecticut, Pennsylvania, New York, South Carolina—or the confederation of states soon to be called the United States. In the jostling among the new states for political power it seemed necessary to record clearly each colony's respective contribution to the successful revolution. Chronicles and compilations though most of them were, state histories served a social and political need. This was true even in the emerging frontier West. In 1784 John Filson of Cincinnati published a little book that was to have emotional impact far beyond what even he could have imagined. The book was entitled *Discovery, Settlement, and Present State of Kentucke*, and it had as an appendix a brief biography of Daniel Boone who became America's second (after Washington) great hero and the archetype of a continuing national myth. From Filson's Boone came Cooper's Leatherstocking and a whole sense of the romantic atavism of the frontier experience that was to culminate in Frederick Jackson Turner's historical vision of the frontier in American history and a thousand western epics in print and now on film.

The rising interest in native or local history began to create a literary market in America which in turn had a strange effect upon would-be men of letters in the early Republic. Washington Irving, for example, first gained fame in collaborating with James Kirke Paulding on a burlesque history, *Diedrich Knickerbocker's History of New York* (1809) which lampooned the quaint ways of the old Dutch aristocracy. Then Irving, lamenting the lack of history in America went to Europe. He became famous as a writer of tales virtually all of which, like Rip Van Winkle, involved time and history. Then he turned directly to the writing of history with his studies of the Alhambra, of the conquest of Granada, of Columbus, and at last with his American histories of John Jacob Astor's fur-hunting Astorians of the Rocky Mountains and *The Adventures of Captain Bonneville U.S.A.* (1837). The grandest historical subject of all, the Spanish conquest of the New World, he gave to a friend, William Hickling Prescott. Irving, early America's most famous writer, in a sense had to go to Europe to discover American history. The same largely applied to James Fenimore Cooper, who, in exile and trying to steep himself in ruined castles and decadent Venetian grandeur, nonetheless felt irresistably pulled back to the adventures of Leatherstocking, Uncas and old tales of Puritan and New York settlement. Not even the writing of *A History of the Navy of the United States of America* (1839) could wipe these visions of societal evolution away. Cooper as novelist, however, was fortunate. When he wrote the genre was in vogue. But slightly before his time, histories and chronicles were the only way narrative could be brought before a public heretofore nurtured on sermons, tracts, political pamphlets and moral uplift writing of the most directly relevant nature. Almost overnight, however, in the years after the War of 1812 the American past in any form became a vogue. Epic poems, novels, plays, histories and even document-collecting became fashionable. Jared Sparks began collecting the crucial diplomatic correspondence of the American Revolution partially to recover or preserve the past and partially to fuel an emerging sense of nationalism.

Romanticism and History

The renewed interest in time that began to overtake Americans was also the result of an earlier awakening to such matters in Europe. The critical eye of Enlightenment scholarship had been engaged in scrutinizing the past for outmoded "superstitions" for nearly half a century with the astonishing result that a new sense of history was reborn. As early as 1762 J. G. Winckelmann had unearthed the ruins of Herculaneum and Pompeii, while in the same year James Stuart and Nicholas Revett published their works on the architecture of the ancient world. A pagan vogue for the minute examination of the ancient world culminated in one sense in Edward Gibbon's great history *The Decline and Fall of the Roman Empire* (1776-88), in another sense with Napoleon's Egyptian campaign and the discovery of the Rosetta Stone, key to Egyptian history and in still another sense with the rise of German "higher" critical studies of the Bible and its authenticity, capped by David Friedrich Strauss' important *Das Leben Jesu* (1826).

In the sciences, time was fast becoming the dominant paradigm. Abraham Gottlob Werner and James Hutton argued over the aqueous or volcanic origins of the earth; William Smith in England and Thomas Say in America discovered the fossil dating method which enabled geologists to reconstruct a temporal sequence of ancient geological horizons; German *Natur*-philosophers became fascinated with the embryonic development of plants and their relationship to the history of species ("ontogeny recapitulates phylogeny"); Erasmus Darwin published his evolutionary *Zoonomia* while his grandson set out on the *Beagle* to trace the origin of species and Charles Lyell made geology a branch of history with his doctrine of uniformitarianism. In Europe at least the static world of Newton had become the changing, dynamic world of time and history.

In 1818, following in the footsteps of Washington Irving, a contingent of Boston scholars including George Ticknor, Edward Everett, and George Bancroft departed for Europe and Germany in particular. Others followed, including Theodore Parker, William Hickling Prescott and Francis Parkman. Out of these European experiences arose not only the American Romantic Movement but a fascination with one of Romanticism's central themes—history. Romantic America produced four notable historians: John Lothrop Motley, William Hickling Prescott, Francis Parkman and George Bancroft (Levin, 1959). They were all New Englanders and had been exposed to heavy doses of European Romanticism. All four were concerned with the evolution of civilizations and their works were grand epics and pageants.

Motley wrote on the rise of the Dutch Republic using acid portraiture and epic battle scenes to juxtapose the virtuous Protestant Dutch against the villainous Spaniards. William Hickling Prescott, virtually blinded in a college accident, took the development of the Spanish Empire as his subject. In 1838 he published *The History of the Reign of Ferdinand and Isabella the Catholic* in three volumes. His greatest works, however, were *The Conquest of Mexico* (1843) and *The Conquest of Peru* (1847). In these volumes he recounted the exciting story of conquest and commanded huge reading audiences in the United States. But, at the same time, his subject was civilization. The Spaniards he portrayed, not entirely without justification, as proto-Puritans whose will, self-discipline and efficiency contrasted with the pagan, sybaritic tendency of the Aztecs and the Incas. In grand operatic tableaux Prescott presented Cortez confronting Montezuma in gorgeous splendor, or before a cast of thousands with Cortez hurling the Aztec sacrificial idols from the Teocalli with seeming impunity. Such scenes clearly indicated that one civilization was replacing another. The time of the Aztecs had come.

Parkman, after scouting the West for himself in 1846, published *The Oregon Trail* which instantly made him famous and also ruined his health. As a result of his trip west, Parkman's eyes could never tolerate light. He could not see except dimly. His nerves permitted only short periods of concentration during a day, and his body was wracked with pain. Yet he too insisted on taking on the role of the historian. Working through most of the nineteenth century in absolutely heroic fashion, Parkman (1869-92) produced his monumental multi-volume history of the war between France and Britain for North America. Parkman was another master of narrative, preferring to conceal his message in descriptions of forests and lakes, portraits of towering archetypal figures like LaSalle or Montcalm and Wolfe, or in heroic action, though in his final volumes (esp., Parkman, 1887) he did make an attempt at writing social history.

Motley, Prescott and Parkman will perhaps forever be known as masterful Romantic narrators—men of letters who just happened to write history in extremely dramatic and lucid fashion. And yet they were much more. Each was an extensive and careful researcher, utilizing sources from archives all over Europe and the Americas in critical fashion. In this sense they were as "scientific" as any historians since their time. They also ever so subtly expoused the scientific currents of the day—superhuman causes for complex events they eschewed, and each saw man and society in evolution, with Parkman even raising the question of atavism which did not become fashionable until the late nineteenth century. However, like the Romantics, Motley, Prescott and Parkman preferred to conceal the stage machinery of scholarship and to proceed with their stories by means of symbols, images and significant, highly-charged (even melodramatic) actions. They were historians of uncommon men and uncommon events. Perhaps their elitist Boston backgrounds dictated their interests and subtle techniques.

George Bancroft, on the other hand, was a democrat—both philosophically and as a practicing politician (Levin, 1959: 5-6; Nye, 1944). Thoroughly familiar with the cultural revolutions of nineteenth century Europe and thankful for the free, levelling spirit of Jacksonian America, Bancroft detected a common spirit in the people that equipped each individual for democratic leadership. Consequently his ten-volume *History of the United States* was partisan—democratic and transcendental in spirit—"the best history of the United States from the Jacksonian point of view" declared Leopold von Ranke, and the "longest Fourth of July oration in American history" declared others. Bancroft's history, not always scrupulously researched, hardly pretended to be scientific. Rather, it was the outward or symbolic expression of the innate democratic spirit that Bancroft believed characterized the American people.[3] In this sense it was the long narrative counterpart to an essay by Emerson or Thoreau.

If democracy was Bancroft's theme, self-identity in a so-called democratic society was the theme of a now forgotten but important historian of mid-nineteenth century America, William Wells Brown. The first black novelist to publish in the United States, Brown was a fugitive slave from Lexington, Kentucky who escaped to freedom in 1847. Best known as the author of *Clotel, or the President's Daughter* . . . (1853), a novel about Thomas Jefferson's mulatto daughter, Brown, as a result of a tour of Europe, turned to history. In 1855 he published *St. Domingo: Its Revolution and Its Patriots*, then in 1863, *The Black Man: His Antecedents, His Genius, and His Achievements*. In 1874 he completed *The Rising Sun, or the Antecedents and the Advancement of the Colored Race*, his most extensive work. Brown's work is significant because it represented the way in which a minority, cast off from its traditions in the process of enslavement and transportation to America, sought in history to rediscover the roots of an identity. *The Black Man*, for example, was a compilation of 57 biographies of famous black historical figures including Benjamin Banneker, Nat Turner, Toussaint L'Ouverture, Crispus Attucks, Alexander Dumas, Denmark Vesey, and Frederick Douglass. Other black historians of the day added Hannibal and Hamilcar to their list in a world search for identity in an alien land.

The same technique of identity through history was employed by another group seeking liberation in American society at about the same time—women. Lydia Maria Child published *History of the Condition of Women in Various Ages and Nations* (2 vols., 1835) which saw the United States as the place where woman's dreams throughout the ages could potentially be fulfilled. Elizabeth Ellet celebrated the "creative spirited" woman in three works: *The Women of the American Revolution* (2 vols., 1848), *Pioneer Women of the West* (1852) and *Women Artists in All Ages and Countries* (1859).[4] In the books of these now all but forgotten writers whose works have previously seemed out of the "mainstream" of American historiography can be seen one of history's clearest utilities. Like George Bancroft, both blacks and intellectual women were also attempting to use the past to define America and chart its future possibilities for the groups they represented.

History Professionalized

While Americans at mid-century were writing epics in search of identity, European scholarship was growing progressively more scientific, philological and critical. In Germany the historical seminar developed along with the monograph and the Ph.D. Just as in Biblical studies, the accent in German historical seminars was upon origins of ideas, customs, institutions. This of course paralleled not only developments in science but it also echoed the German search for identity which began with Herder but which was accelerated during the era of Napoleonic occupation. In the 1860's young Americans trained in German seminars began to return to America imbued with the scientific spirit of inquiry and the "germ" theory of history which traced the institutions of freedom back to the tribes in Teutonic forests at the dawn of civilization. A group of these scholars led by Herbert Baxter Adams created the first American history seminar at the new Johns Hopkins University founded in 1876 entirely on the German model. The history seminar at Hopkins became justly famous as the cradle of such eminent American historians as Frederick Jackson Turner and Woodrow Wilson.

At the suggestion of Hopkins President Daniel Coit Gilman, Herbert Baxter Adams also took the lead in organizing the American Historical Association at Saratoga Springs, New York in 1881 (Goetzmann, 1968). The creation of the American Historical Association reflected the increasing professionalization of the learned professions in America. The National Academy of Science was organized in 1863. The American Social Science Association was founded in 1865; in 1876 the American

Chemical Society, and in 1883, the Modern Language Association. There were many others during the period and they all reflected an increasing organization and rationalization of American life from business and labor to transportation networks. They also reflected a desire to create conscious standards and principles to which all serious professionals could adhere.

Inevitably all this cast a shadow on the amateur historian like Parkman or Bancroft who created his own standards and principles. It relegated these historians to the status of crude but heroic pioneers; at age 83 Bancroft was invited to serve as president of the American Historical Association more out of sentiment and symbolism than in admiration for his work. Nonetheless a professional organization was necessary for historians in the United States because, thanks to the Land Grant College Act of 1862, universities were springing up all across the country and along with them departments of history that had to be staffed with competent, certified professionals. The American Historical Association and the network of professors it helped to develop saw to that and so rode on the crest of a long-term academic wave that lasted until the 1930's. The American Historical Association also sponsored the publication of reports, collections of source materials edited in model fashion, an *American Historical Review*, a Committee of Seven to establish guidelines for instruction in the public schools, and an annual meeting that rotated between Washington, New York and Chicago (Goetzmann, 1968).

Meanwhile the writing of "amateur" or non-academic history went on. James Schouler (1880-99) and Herman von Holst (1876-92) wrote widely applauded abolitionist histories of the Civil War. Their work was topped by the excellent eight volume treatise on the same subject by retired industrialist James Ford Rhodes (1893-1906). Senator Albert J. Beveridge (1916-19) wrote a monumental life of John Marshall; J. G. Nicolay and John Hay (1890) wrote a comparable life of Lincoln; and Theodore Roosevelt wrote histories and biographies about practically everything and everybody but the most important of his works was *The Winning of the West* (2 vols., 1889). His friend General Hiram M. Chittenden meanwhile wrote a definitive *History of the American Fur Trade of the Far West* (2 vols., 1902), while the novelist Edward Eggleston pioneered in social history with his *The Transit of European Civilization to North America* (1901). The New Yorker John Bach McMaster did Eggleston one better with his massive eight volume *History of the People of the United States* (1883-1913). McMaster, however, began as an amateur and ended as a professional. He taught for 37 years at the University of Pennsylvania and became a pillar of the American Historical Association (Goldman, 1945).

Out in California the antiquarian Hubert Howe Bancroft (1890) turned thoroughly professional, establishing in effect a history factory where under his supervision and under his name a team of researchers and writers turned out some 40 volumes on the history of California, every state and territory in the American West, the north Mexican states and the native races of the western hemisphere. Eastern reviewers were only with difficulty persuaded to notice them but they made an immense impact on western readers and California's search for identity. They represented the largest undertaking in "booster history" that America had yet seen (Caughey, 1945).

Though the whole vast range and variety of "amateur," "literary" histories continued to command large public audiences throughout the nineteenth century, by 1895 more than half of the academic historians had been trained in Germany in what came to be called "scientific history" (Higham, 1965: 92). Ironically enough, the men who made their living by writing books that sold were dubbed by the new academicians "amateurs" while the professoriat whose main task was teaching students and reproducing their own kind considered themselves "professionals." This split in historical ranks persists to the present time, much to the confusion of the general public. What the professoriat had achieved, however, was a whole new market for their printed works—a captive audience of students and historical societies, such as the Wisconsin State Historical Society, which they controlled. This was appealing to publishers in a day of ever-increasing business organization because it enabled them by counting student enrollments to forecast the market for certain types of books—notably texts—with much greater accuracy. It marked the beginning of a new era of mass-think and standard curricula in the public schools, junior colleges, state colleges and many universities. If scientific history became, as Higham (1965: 92) states, a "new orthodoxy" in theory, it was much more devastatingly so in the marketplace of hard practical economics.

The Varieties of Scientific History

Theoretically scientific history appears to have been a trifurcated effort. As it first came out of German seminars, it focused on methodology. The historian was not to seek the grand synthesis. He was not to chart the shape of time, nor was he to express any form of idealistic philosophy in his work. History may or may not have artistic symmetry—that was not the historian's concern. Rather his task was to locate sources— original documents—determine their validity and then their relationship to one another from as objective a point of view as possible. His task was to get the facts and these facts themselves, in true inductive fashion, would automatically suggest a pattern, however limited. Such studies produced the monograph, severely restricted in scope, more conscious of limits than implications. They also produced the scientific paper or article as a major vehicle of communication for the historian, and professional journals, largely subsidized ventures, which have proliferated in history from that day to this.

The stance of the historian was strictly objective. Unlike the romantic historian, he did not enter into the events themselves, but perforce stood aloof above men and movements in the past. So strong was this impulse to depersonalize history that focus on individuals gave way to the study of institutions—a concept borrowed from the emerging disciplines of economics and sociology. In what Gillispie (1960) has called in another context the cutting "edge of objectivity" the scientific historian was not concerned with why events happened but rather how they related to one another as a system. He focused on the "who, what, where, when and how" with as much critical precision, and sometimes pedantry, as he could muster. In short the scientific historian envied the physical scientist his laboratory, and in the seminar he created his own.

Perhaps the outstanding effort at scientific history in the sense outlined above was Justin Winsor's *Narrative and Critical History of the United States* (1884-89) a multivolume collaborative work consisting of a series of very erudite but disjointed essays loosely following the chronology of American history. In each essay or component of the work, the footnotes far overshadowed the running narrative and proved to be infinitely more interesting and lasting. Winsor's work remains a mine of fascinating undigested information. This bothered Winsor not a bit, for, as Higham (1965: 95) points out, he "confessed with positive pride that he had made history 'a thing of shreds and patches.'"

Less inclined to disjointed folly, in 1870 Henry Adams established a seminar at Harvard and undertook to teach Medieval history in the German method. As he (Adams, 1931; 302-303) put it, "He frankly acted on the rule that a teacher, who knew nothing of his subject, should not pretend to teach his scholars what he did not know, but should join them in trying to find the best way of learning it. The rather pretentious name of historical method was sometimes given to this process of instruction, but the name smacked of German pedagogy...." He added however, "as pedagogy, nothing could be more triumphant. The boys worked like rabbits, and dug holes all over the field of archaic society." Somewhat later, seeking a scientific base line for American history, Adams embarked on his *History of the United States During the Administrations of Jefferson and Madison* (1889-91). Definitely limited in scope, the study nonetheless ran to 9 volumes, and despite copious and extended use of documentary quotation and seemingly Olympian detachment the work proved to be a justification of the Adams family more than a balanced history of the period. Although the *History* was brilliantly written in places, Adams' own judgement of the work proved to be correct. It was a failure.

In a very real sense strict scientific history failed because the historian looking in from the outside failed to understand science. He truly believed for a time that science was pure induction, that the facts themselves suggested order, and that any phenomenon was worth studying. The function of hypothesis was not clear to the pioneer scientific historian. In fact he would have regarded it as a "philosophical" intrusion into the process of inquiry which was certain to destroy the desired objectivity. It would have taken him right back to the puerile Romantics.

The best scientific history was produced by men who did intrude with hypothesis. The prime example of this was, of course, the work of Frederick Jackson Turner (see Billington, 1973: chs. 4 and 5; Hofstadter, 1968: esp. 47-164). A man thoroughly trained in the exacting methods of the Hopkins seminar, Turner reacted strongly against the germ theory of history. His own dissertation researches in local Wisconsin history convinced him that environment, the crude exigencies of the wilderness and the frontier experience were the formative influences upon American behavior. Armed with all the apparatus from other social scientific disciplines—maps, census statistics, economic data, etc.—Turner tested this hypothesis to his satisfaction. The result was his address at the annual meeting of the American Historical Association in Chicago in 1893, "The Significance of the Frontier In American History" in which he proclaimed his hypothesis as hypothesis (see Turner, 1920). With Turner scientific history in America had come of age. Scientific research had produced a question of epic, even poetic grandeur that challenged the tradition, focused upon the American rather than the European scene, made local materials relevant for students, opened out onto numerous problems and questions that remain unsolved even today, and suggested a unique shape to the American character. Legions of historians have made careers answering questions that Turner raised in this one dramatic, suggestive address (see Billington, 1966).

Later Turner, becoming ever steeped in the skills of ancillary disciplines, advanced a second hypothesis. American history down to the Civil War could be interpreted primarily in terms of the dynamic interplay among geographic sections or regions of the country. This formed the thesis of his only real book, *Rise of the New West* (1906). His geographical hypothesis in this instance—far more complex and subtle than the frontier hypothesis—became almost an axiom in treating the history of the period. It has not been superseded even today. Several generations have carried it forward, including Turner's own contemporaries, Ulrich B. Phillips, a southern historian, and Charles Beard, also known for his economic interpretation of history. In a later period the Texan historian, Walter Prescott Webb, expanding on his own rural experience, refined the concept even further with his environmental study, *The Great Plains* (1931). The persistence of regional historical societies attests to the interest in the Turnerean geographic approach down to the present.

While Turner was developing his frontier hypothesis, still another school of scientific historians emerged with an equally intriguing hypothesis. In the 1890's Charles M. Andrews and Herbert Levi Osgood both revolted against the germ theory of history but in a way quite different from Turner. For Andrews, a Hopkins product, and Osgood, a Columbia Ph.D., the remote past in Teutonic forests had little relevance to what they had observed of Atlantic Coast civilization in the colonial era. Andrews' micro-study of a Connecticut River town suggested nothing of German customs or ancestry. Thus, along with Osgood, he concluded that historians should study the more immediate past and in particular he urged the mining of the resources of the British Public Records Office. Osgood himself moved to London to be in a position to do so. By 1907 he had published three volumes, entitled *The American Colonies in the Seventeenth Century* that launched what came to be known as the "imperial school" of American history. In the same year Osgood's student, George Louis Beer, added a volume entitled, *British Colonial Policy, 1754-1764*. This was the first of four volumes which treated British colonial policy since 1578 as a system. According to Beer the proper perspective on American history was through British eyes. Andrews, ever the perfectionist, published his work last of all, four volumes entitled, *The Colonial Period of American History* (1934-38). His work was far more comprehensive than those of Osgood and Beer in that he insisted that the whole New World system be included. For Andrews, Canada and the Caribbean colonies were interrelated with those of North America and crucial to British policy. So complete had been the researches of Osgood, Beer and Andrews, however, that rather than opening up new questions as Turner had done, they appeared to have supplied the last word (Higham, 1965: 162-165).

Still another aspect of scientific history derived from Charles Darwin and Herbert Spencer. As we have seen, modern history itself began with a sense of evolution and time quarried out of the continuous present theories of the Enlightenment. Nonetheless Darwin's theory of evolution provided a potential scientific buttress for evolutionary belief arrived at by other, less scientific means. Spencer's writings gave an overt direction to evolutionary development as mankind progressed inevitably to ever higher stages of civilization until it reached the stage of perfect equilibrium with the environment which Spencer called "equilibration." If nothing else Spencer's popular historical and socio-logical writings allowed scientific historians to feel that their researches were cumulative and that in their own field progress was inevitable (see Hofstadter, 1944: 31-50; Peel, 1971).

The problem with the Darwinian-progressive model was that few if any serious American historians followed it. As an intellectual concept it had to be dealt with but only John Fiske, the Harvard popularizer, and perhaps Captain Alfred Thayer Mahan, the naval historian who believed in survival of the fittest, could be seen directly paralleling Spencer's progressive outline (Hofstadter, 1944: 13-15, 19-22, 183-184). Indeed the most important disciple of Spencer was the founder of modern American anthropology, Lewis Henry Morgan. His *Ancient Society*, published in 1877, assumed that all men were the same everywhere but only in different stages of development that rose from "savagery" to "barbarism" to "civilization" according to technological attainments. Virtually the only significant group of historians who paralleled Spencer's progressive line were the Marxists who found Morgan's work intriguing and who espoused the same kind of deterministic view of history though starting from Hegel's dialectics (Herreshoff, 1967).

The two most prominent American historians to address themselves to the teleology of Spencerian evolutionary history and the implications of Darwin were Brooks and Henry Adams. Brooks Adams (1896) amalgamated Spencer, Morgan and Marx along with the laws of thermodynamics. Eschewing the teleology of Spencer and Marx, Brooks Adams in *The Law of Civilization and Decay* (1896) saw a cyclical or pulsating rhythm to history which was essentially directionless. He saw history as movement according to laws. Human society in movement oscillates "between barbarism and civilization or what amounts to the same thing, from a condition of physical dispersion to one of concentration." He classified societies according to the amount of measurable energy they possessed. Then Adams combined energy with mass (i.e. population) to determine the "velocity" of a civilization. Velocity in turn governed centralizaton or concentration of energy and resources and this was governed by the institutions of fear—religion, the military and the artistic establishment, soon to be replaced by the capitalist who promoted greed. Greed in turn promoted economic competition which, governed by the non-producing capitalist consumer, led to waste, decay, degradation and the replacement by another civilization, and so on endlessly through time. In *America's Economic Supremacy* (1900) Adams actually measured the rise of American supremacy and the corresponding degradation of Britain in tons of pig iron and pints of beer consumed per capita respectively.

Henry Adams, it is clear, never believed in a science of history.[5] His Harvard seminar experience with its cynicism (see p. 18) demonstrated this. Thus when, despite the fact that he detested pedantry and never attended the annual meetings of the American Historical Association, he was elected its president in 1894, he decided to send the members a letter calling their attention to the implications of science for their craft. "We cannot help asking ourselves" he wrote, "what would happen if some new Darwin were to demonstrate the laws of historical evolution" (B. Adams, 1919). Having implied that he was on the track of such a law he set sail for the South Seas on a pleasure cruise (Samuels, 1964). The best of what he had to say to Darwinistic historians was contained in "The Rule of Phase Applied to History" (1909) and "A Letter to American Teachers of History" (1910). In the former he posited a law of acceleration in history, building upon the Yale physical chemist Josiah Willard Gibbs' phase rule. Adams divided history into four phases delimited by the inverse square rule—the religious phase ending in 1600, the mechanical phase ending in 1900, the electrical phase the duration of which was the square root of 300 or 17½ years, and the ethereal phase, the square root of 17½ or four years, making human history terminate at about 1921. At that point all human history would end—especially as the historian Adams, who expected to be dead by then, would know it.

Thus using physical science as a model, Adams reduced scientific history to absurdity. In the "Letter to American Teachers of History," Adams further demonstrated the futility of scientific history. On the one hand, he observed that Darwinistic biology implied planetary progress; on the other, the law of entropy dictated that the universe was running down. The best that could be hoped for was equilibrium and equilibrium meant stasis or death—according to biologists quoted by Adams. In a way so clever and subtle that it seems to have escaped most historians, Adams proclaimed the utter irrelevancy of science to history. He himself turned from the dynamo to the Virgin and to worshipping the beauty that he found so serenely present in the cathedrals of Medieval France.

Progressive History

Still history could not or would not be quits with science and the philosophies emerging from it. The period from 1890 to 1915, sometimes called the Progressive Era, was also the great age of the Progressive historian who took his cue from the rapid flowering of American Pragmatism (see Hofstadter, 1968; White, 1949). Pragmatism, whose chief prophets were C. E. Peirce, William James, and John Dewey, began with the espousal of the "chance universe" implied by the chance mutations described by Darwin in *On The Origin of Species*. If the world was a world of chance, then there were no absolutely predictable scientific laws and human behavior was especially contingent. In a probabilistic universe the most problematic thing was man himself. Thus it behooved the historian who wished to be in step with the new science to avoid the long run prophetic teleologies of Spencer and concentrate upon short run problems bringing history to bear on their solution.

By the 1890's the country abounded in such problems. Monopolies and trusts dominated America. Railroads and grain elevator operators exploited the farmer and consumer alike. Banking rested in the hip pocket of J. P. Morgan. Even food was adulterated. On top of that depressions wracked the decade while muckrakers raked the underside of American life in popular journals. To many of these causes the professional historians responded. Their German training impressed them with the strong civil role that the professoriat enjoyed in Germany and they sought a similar role in an America that needed them (Higham, 1965: 11). In Wisconsin for example, Turner, Charles R. Van Hise, R. T. Ely and J. Allen Smith among others served as consultants to Governor Robert La Follette in one of the country's earliest "brain trusts" (Billington, 1973: chs. 11 and 12). There historian, economist and political scientist worked together to help solve some of the urgent problems of what rapidly became a very Progressive state. Involvement in political reform made the scholar's work relevant. In the historian's case it called forth a sense of the "usable past," as pure a pragmatic concept as any philosopher was able to imagine. Men like John R. Commons, Turner's friend, concerned with labor strife, turned to labor history in an effort to get to the bottom of the trouble (Higham, 1965: 178). Others turned to sectional analysis with regard to agricultural problems, marketing problems and freight rate differentials. Turner's theory of sections was especially useful here. Working with LaFollette in Wisconsin became a kind of Camelot to Turner, and when LaFollette left for Washington and the dairymen-vocationalists took over the running of the University, Camelot was sadly over and Turner left for Harvard.

In the East, E. R. A. Seligman and James Harvey Robinson went beyond pragmatism to Marxism in the attempted solution to social problems (Higham, 1965: 179). They both became convinced that any real answer to society's dilemmas must begin with a careful class analysis.

The classic in this genre was supplied by Charles A. Beard with his *Economic Interpretation of the Constitution* (1913). Beard, with a rigidly cultivated scientific objectivity, analysed by the "class affiliations" of the Constitution-makers and purportedly by induction came to the conclusion that each was motivated by greed, short-term motives and was a prisoner of his class. Beard thus epitomized the "amoral moralist" who knew how to use the past.[6] His classic study could be applied to any legislature, any public deliberative body. It was a searchlight in the darkness as powerful as that of any muckraker and because it was a history it was presumably more accurate and more lasting.

Beard became famous but there were other men employing similar techniques. Equally important in his time was the institutional economist Thorstein Veblen whose *Theory of the Leisure Class* (1899) was only the first of his many institutional analyses of the evils of American culture. This book traced the history of a leisure class who lived off the labors of others and demonstrated their power and superiority by consuming the world's goods as conspicuously if not as absurdly as possible. Veblen as writer invariably projected an ironic sense of comedy that was not to be duplicated until the days of Charlie Chaplin.

Out in Washington state a young literary historian, Vernon L. Parrington, who had once been the University of Oklahoma football coach, influenced by J. Allen Smith, began work on a masterpiece in the Progressive tradition that brought to light an American intellectual history. *Main Currents in American Thought* (Vols. I and II) finally came out in 1927 but it was the product of the earlier Progressive Era. In *Main Currents*, Parrington took a frankly political stand on behalf of Jeffersonian democracy and then applied a class test to the writers and intellectuals that America had produced. Rarely if ever did Parrington find a writer "deserting his class." If he did he was a real culture hero. Generally, however, Parrington's was a Manichean version of American thought designed to show that ideas, even literary creations, were class-determined and aligned in polar opposites. *Main Currents* was a monumental synthesis in the interests of reform (see Hofstadter, 1968: 349-434).

Hofstadter (1968: xvii) has aptly written of the Progressive historians, "If pragmatism . . . provided American liberalism with its philosophical nerve, Progressive historiography gave it memory and myth." He added that the Progressive historians "attempted to find a usable past related to the broadest needs of a nation fully launched upon its own industrialization, and to make history an active instrument of self-recognition and self-improvement." The failure of the Progressive historians stemmed from two things—their lack of a sense of the complexities of human behavior and their inveterate belief that if men could see society's wrongs they would right them. In this they harked back to the days of the Puritans whom they despised. The Progressive historians in their blind faith created a liberal hagiography for an audience more interested in expediency than morality.

Modernism and History

At about the same time as the rise of Progressive historiography many of the same figures, most notably James Harvey Robinson and Harry Elmer Barnes, were involved in The New History Movement (Higham, 1965: 111-120). The New History was at base economic and sociological, but it involved the historian deeply with all of the emerging social science disciplines to the point where history itself began to lose its identity. This was symptomatic of a time that prefigured "the death of history." While historians had been building university departments and becoming thoroughly professional, other breakthroughs in knowledge had occurred that threatened to move history out of its central role as organizer of human experience. Anthropology under Franz Boas came of age, providing alternative contemporary models for human conduct. Sociology became extremely relevant to current social problems as did economics. Science was amazed by Albert Einstein's relativity theory which altered man's concept of time itself. And Freudian psychology, beyond discovering another landscape of the mind, made everyman his own case historian. Literature was altered forever by research in Frazer's *Golden Bough* and other comparative mythologies as well as by the discovery of the stream of consciousness. In art, exotic anthropological models, such as primitive statues and African masks, provided new forms with great implications.

More important, with the shattering of time, traditional spatial perspectives were also altered, and cubism made the simultaneous experiencing of space possible. This was dramatically demonstrated in the Armory Show of 1913, the same year Beard's book on the Constitution appeared and John B. Watson announced the doctrine of behaviorism in psychology. All of this added up to a great western European cultural revolution now called "Modernism" which was a response to the crisis generated by the confrontation of a deep-seated tradition by new breakthroughs in knowledge and insight into human conduct.

As a result of Modernism, history lost its nerve as well as its subject matter in the fragmentation of time and consciousness. True, the Great War and the corrupt decade of the 1920's, not to mention the depression of the 1930's, were blows to the optimistic Progressives—blows to historians in particular who felt helpless and impractical. Their straightforward probings of human nature had failed to move men toward the good, the true and the beautiful. But the deeper cause for the collapse of history was a basically changed reality with which they were not yet equipped to deal. The 1920's saw carryovers from the Progressive Era such as Parrington's great work, and Charles and Mary Beard's *The Rise of American Civilization* (1927), but for the most part historians turned to iconoclasm as in James Truslow Adams' *The Founding of New England* (1921), diatribes on behalf of isolation such as those by Beard (1936a; 1936b; 1939; 1940; 1946), Harry Elmer Barnes (1930; 1973), and C. Hartley Grattan (1929; 1936; 1939), a return to colorful narrative in search of a lost tradition as in the work of Van Wyck Brooks (1944-52), Samuel Eliot Morison,[7] and Carl Sandburg (1926-39), or more searching expressions of despair echoed by Charles Beard and Carl Becker.

Becker delivered perhaps the most sweeping expression of the new relativism in his famous address, "Everyman His Own Historian" while Beard echoed the William James of "The Will to Believe" in 1871 in his "Written History an Act of Faith" (1934). Some notable historians abandoned ship as did Allan Nevins and his followers in 1939 when they founded the Society of American Historians dedicated to the proposition that history should be written to be read, not guarded as the private preserve of the professor and his captive student audience. The Society took as its hero Francis Parkman (Higham, 1965: 80-82).

And yet, though in disarray, if not despair, with history ranking very low in the priorities of new funding agencies such as the Social Science Research Council (Higham, 1965: 118), some historians persisted and laid the foundations for a post-World War II resurgence of history in a new identity. Morison, Kenneth Murdock, and Perry Miller at Harvard began to resurrect the Puritans. The former, especially in *The Builders of the Bay Colony* (1930), *The Puritan Pronaos* (1936) and *Three Centuries of Harvard* (1936), uncovered the lost humanity of the Puritan world. James G. Randall (1937), Charles Ramsdell (1937: 3ff), Howard K. Beale (1946), Avery O. Craven (1939, 1942), Allan Nevins (1947, 1950), and the young David Potter (1942) opened up the whole question of the Civil War, again making use of advances in psychology and a new sense of the contingency of human events. Diplomatic history flourished, especially under Samuel Flagg Bemis (e.g., 1923, 1926, 1935, 1943), who not only took the diplomacy of the American Revolution for his own special province in a spate of excellent books but also brought Latin America into the American diplomatic history ken. Beyond this he launched an impressive series in *American Secretaries of State and their Diplomacy* and later wrote definitive works on the foundations of American foreign policy (see Bemis, 1940). Able scholars such as Dexter Perkins (1941, 1955), Julius Pratt (1925, 1936), Justin Smith (1911, 1919), Isaac J. Cox (1918), Arthur B. Darling (1940), Charles Seymour (1921), and A. P. Whitaker (1934), along with Bemis, created virtually a whole new field of history. Concerned by the experience of the Great War, they translated this concern into understanding international relations for future reference.

Intellectual history, too, came of age in two extraordinary books that far surpassed the work of Parrington. Merle Curti of Wisconsin published *The Growth of American Thought* (1943) which he called "a social history of American thought." His subject was the growth of "knowledge, values, and the institutions of intellectual life." Never quite able to break away from the Progressive's affinity for institutions, Curti concentrated on the latter and largely avoided the dissection of philosophical ideas, but he performed a mighty service in describing the broad institutional base out of which arose American ideas. Ralph Henry Gabriel, who, along with Stanley T. Williams, an English professor at Yale, was one of the pioneers of the interdisciplinary American Studies Movement, wrote an even more subtle history of American ideas—*The Course of American Democratic Thought* (1940). Gabriel, much interested in religious ideas, sought for universal moral principles that ran through American life. These could serve to fortify the country against the demoralization of the depression and the menace of totalitarian Fascism and Communism which threatened to be the wave of the future when Gabriel published his book in the dark days of 1940.

Like the Progressives before him, Gabriel still searched for a "usable past." He did so, however, in a sophisticated fashion benefitting from the pre-war atmosphere at Yale created by Thurman Arnold, Bronislaw Malinowski and Jerome Frank. Using the anthropological culture concept as his matrix, Gabriel traced the adventures of three ideas through the history of American thought—natural law, individualism, and the mission of America. Selective rather than encyclopedic, Gabriel analysed symbolic and important figures in some depth. The ideas of these figures provided insight into the course of American democratic thought which was seen by Gabriel as an American state religion, not dictated but freely chosen and critically evaluated by the people. With Gabriel's quiet masterpiece, American historians had begun to know how to use and to relate to the new social sciences that threatened to overwhelm them. In 1951, largely under the auspices of historians and students of literature, the American Studies Association was formed, not to advance provincialism, but to continue the kind of cultural analysis that Gabriel and others of his generation had begun—in the days when history had almost, but not quite, lost its nerve.

The Post-War Search for Tradition

Victory over the forces of totalitarianism in World War II seemed to inspire a new sense of confidence in American historians. In the post-war years, buttressed by the prosperity in colleges crowded with returning veterans and then eventually the wartime "baby boom," academic historians and the public alike took a new interest in searching for and celebrating the American tradition. This was reflected in the proliferation and enlargement of departments of history and the spawning of numerous American Studies Programs, most notably at Yale, the University of Pennsylvania and Minnesota. It was also reflected in the launching of many large projects for the definitive publication of the papers of America's famous men beginning with the Jefferson and Franklin projects at Princeton and Yale respectively.

After Truman, outgoing presidents routinely established "presidential libraries" and massive public and private funding supported historical restorations such as Colonial Williamsburg and Mystic Seaport. The war itself produced at least one epic historical production, Admiral Samuel Eliot Morison's multi-volume *History of the United States Naval Operations in World War II* (1947-62), in the long run perhaps Morison's most impressive work. But then Morison, like the other historians of his time, fell to work celebrating the American tradition. His chief interest was the epic story of the European discovery of America which he described definitively in at least three volumes and a revision of his biography of Columbus. Morison also celebrated the feats of famous American sailors in biographies of John Paul Jones and Matthew Calbraith Perry.

At the same time in Richmond, Virginia, newspaper editor Douglas Southall Freeman worked steadily and successfully away at three impressive multi-volume projects—biographies of Virginia's heroes, Robert E. Lee and George Washington, and a detailed study of Lee's "lieutenants." Free-lance historian Bruce Catton helped launch a new, beautifully illustrated historical journal aimed at the public and called, significantly enough, *American Heritage*. This journal grew out of an earlier publication of the same name launched by the Society of American Historians who were dedicated to good popular history writing. It was a tremendous success. Catton himself reached large audiences with his multi-volume history of the northern side of the American Civil War, beginning with his impressive *Stillness at Appomatox* (1953; see also Catton, 1951, 1952).

Allan Nevins turned his formidable talents to the writing of volumes of American business history which, though as objective as he could make them, still tended to glorify American business. His history of the Standard Oil Company incorporated in two works, *John D. Rockefeller: The Heroic Age of American Enterprise* (1940) and *Study in Power: John D. Rockefeller, Industrialist and Philanthropist* (1953), sparked criticism from Progressive historians Ralph Hidy and Chester McArthur Destler. Likewise, Nevins' multi-volume history of the Ford Motor Company engaged him in debate with Matthew Josephson who was best known for his pre-war attacks on the American establishment, *The Robber Barons* (1935) and *The Politicos* (1938).

Critical voices were rare in post-war America, however. Rather the best work was still involved in charting the course of what Arthur Schlesinger Jr. (1949) called "The Vital Center." Schlesinger himself burst on the scene with a precocious work greatly influenced by Charles Beard, *The Age of Jackson* (1945). An immensely exciting work, *The Age of Jackson* was a Liberal, economically-oriented reassessment of Jackson that portrayed him as a public hero defending the people against the special interests. In a sense it read the New Deal into mid-nineteenth century America. This placed Schlesinger, a political activist, squarely in the Progressive historian tradition, and his masterful multi-volume history of *The Age of Roosevelt* (3 vols. 1957, '59, '60) was a major work of what Lionel Trilling was calling in a more general context "The Liberal Imagination." Countless historians worked this vein in post-war America. Among the best and brightest of them were Louis Hartz of Harvard, Eric Goldman of Princeton and Richard Hofstadter of Columbia.

Hartz, author of *The Liberal Tradition in America* (1955), saw no other American tradition than Liberalism, though he sometimes had to torture his definition of the word to make his point. The absence of feudal institutions in America, Hartz argued, ignoring slavery, enabled America to begin as a liberal nation and to continue in this political tradition throughout its history. Goldman, in his important book, *Rendezvous With Destiny* (1952), realized that liberal advance did not go unimpeded, but he pointed with some pride to a native reform tradition that always somehow seemed to get Americans back on the right track. Goldman's sentiments were echoed by Daniel Aaron in *Men of Good Hope* (1951) and later in *Writers on the Left* (1961).

The late 1940's and the 1950's were dominated by historians writing studies of the American reform tradition. Of all these Richard Hofstadter's work was perhaps the most impressive. His *The American Political Tradition* (1948) was a set of sometimes critical portraits that recharted the American mainstream in a way that identified "The Vital Center." His *The Age of Reform* (1955), carrying that story from Populism through the New Deal, was a landmark in American historiography. It not only suggested the extent to which Populist demands had been incorporated into legislation without the farmers even knowing that they had won, but it also introduced a new concept into American historiography, "the status revolution." Learning from literary criticism as well as sociology and anthropology, Hofstadter avoided a simplistic Beardian economic interpretation of political events and concentrated on the effects of belief and status competition. This dramatized a whole new school of historiography—the "symbol and myth school."

Mind Over Matters: The Symbol and Myth School

Hofstadter did not invent the method. Indeed Ralph Henry Gabriel had included in his pre-war book, *The Course of American Democratic Thought*, an important chapter on "Pre-Sumter Symbols of Nationalism." In addition the Texan pioneer of American Studies, Henry Nash Smith, had published in 1950 his important, *Virgin Land: The American West as Symbol and Myth*. Smith's book, by far the most successful to date in the genre, involved the use of literary analysis applied to a whole range of historical documents from political addresses to newspaper articles and dime novels. Smith succeeded in demonstrating that, more often than not, belief, more than reality, motivated actions in settling the American frontier. Specifically he pointed to the image of the West as a garden which impelled settlers to move with great expectations into the harsh, unpromising arid lands of the West described by John Wesley Powell (1878) in the nineteenth century and Walter P. Webb (1931) in the twentieth. Smith's book had two further aspects of significance. It underscored the idea that there did exist a common American myth or set of beliefs and therefore fitted into what was coming to be known as "the consensus school of American historiography." And, in adopting a literary method which avoided narrative and chronology, mixed genres, explored in belief a new reality, and strikingly juxtaposed figures and concepts, Smith produced a "modernist," experimental piece of American history.

Both Hofstadter and Smith have had many imitators. Such books as

Marvin Meyers' *The Jacksonian Persuasion* (1957), Leo Marx's *The Machine in the Garden* (1964) and John William Ward's *Andrew Jackson, Symbol for an Age* (1953) suggest the range of their influence. For more than two decades the "symbol and myth" approach was a mainstay of the interdisciplinary-minded, anthropologically-oriented American Studies scholar. Only in the mid-seventies has it come under fire from scholars who see it as a false short cut to extensive and serious analysis of culture. Its critics argue that, in a sense, the symbol and myth approach erroneously substitutes a part of reality for the whole. Synechdoche is its besetting sin (see Kuklick, 1972: 1435-1450).

History: Consensus and/or Paradox

Perhaps the major figure to emerge from the "consensus school" of historians was Daniel Boorstin of Chicago. Drawing his insights on America from his experience abroad, Boorstin saw America as an inventive, pragmatic nation that had survived because it avoided enslavement to any doctrinaire ideology except perhaps a mildly liberal Lockeanism. He made this point clearly in *The Genius of American Politics* (1953) and somewhat less overtly in *The Lost World of Thomas Jefferson* (1948). These works were overshadowed, however, by his monumental paean to pragmatic American consensus, *The Americans*. In these volumes, *The Colonial Experience* (1958), *The National Experience* (1965), and *The Democratic Experience* (1973), Boorstin concentrated on common men and common practical experience. He celebrated the "go-getters," "the boosters," the social inventors who managed to push America along by creating an endless series of satisfying community experiences that kept pace with advancing technology. Throughout the three volumes Boorstin rang the changes on Locke's theory of man and society in a state of nature. No one since the Founding Fathers had taken Locke quite so seriously and with such broad application. But beyond the fundamental influence of Locke, Boorstin saw no role for philosophies or ideologies in the meaningful experiences of Americans. He has, of course, been criticized for this and for essentially leaving confrontation as well as the tragic and the ironic out of the American story (Diggins, 1971: 153-180). Yet such was his ingenuity, so startling were his insights and imagination where concerned with commonplace America, that in some sense he has seemed the Ralph Waldo Emerson of American historiography.

A virtually unclassifiable historian of the post-war generation was

David Potter of Yale. Burdened with editing *The Yale Review*, Potter wrote little, but his book, *People of Plenty* (1954), made an impact on American thought almost comparable to that of Frederick Jackson Turner, whom he resembled in many ways. *People of Plenty* cast a shadow over the Progressive interpretation of the American experience that so dominated post-war America. Steeping himself in the social sciences, Potter offered his book as an example of interdisciplinary methodology, but also as a reinterpretation of the American past. It was not the frontier or Teutonic germs that had shaped America, but the fact of abundance. Americans, declared Potter, were literally people of plenty and this fact shaped all of our institutions and customs from the Madison Avenue marketplace to child-rearing habits. Abundance, wrote Potter, made democracy possible. The implications of his book were wide-ranging. In an era when Americans thought to export democracy to the world, Potter's work suggested that economic problems had better be solved first. Beyond this, with Turnerian end-of-the-frontier echoes, Potter's work raised the question as to what might happen to America when abundance ceased to be the prevailing condition. With Potter's work, the sunny optimism of Progressive historiography should rightly have come to an end.

Meanwhile in the 1950's and early 1960's other currents of thought and other visions were beginning to invade American historical thinking. A new despair had begun to arise in the midst of academic prosperity. In part this was generated by social scientists like Daniel Bell in *The End of Ideology* (1960), David Reisman in *The Lonely Crowd* (1950), and C. Wright Mills' slashing Marxist attacks in works like *The Power Elite* (1956). A certain kind of tragic vision had been introduced by the theologian-historian Reinhold Niebuhr whose most powerful books were *The Irony of American History* (1952), *The Children of Light and The Children of Darkness* (1944) and *Moral Man and Immoral Society* (1932). In the 1950's too, and echoing Niebuhr, European existentialism came to dominate many American intellectuals.

The pathos of paradox and situation, the essential contradictions of American life began to loom larger. Out of this climate two schools emerged. The first, in many ways, took its cue from Henry Adams and saw Americans not as people of plenty but as people of paradox. The clearest statement of this theme was made by R. W. B. Lewis in *The American Adam* (1955), which became a seminal book for many. Even earlier in placing American foreign policy in historical context, the political scientist Gabriel Almond, in *The American People and Foreign Policy* (1950), had seen the American character split between a shrewd Uncle Sam and a generous Statue of Liberty. The theme of paradox has been a powerful one in American historiography and refuses to die. Its most recent articulation has been Michael Kammen's imaginative *People of Paradox* (1972).

Existential History: Regions, Roots and Races

The great high point of existential historiography, however, was the monumental work of Perry Miller. Beginning as one of those pre-war historians who sought to locate and re-establish the American tradition, Miller first examined the Puritans. *Orthodoxy in Massachusetts* (1933) defined the particular political situation of New England's Non-separating Congregationalists and resurrected the Puritans as human beings. His magisterial *New England Mind* (2 vols. 1939, 1953), however, limned the whole landscape of Puritan thought in all its subtle intricacies, creating a world as fascinating if not fantastic as that being created at the same time by the Southern novelist William Faulkner. Miller's work, however, was divided into two volumes. The first, *The Seventeenth Century*, portrayed the emergence and development of Puritan thought. The second volume, *From Colony to Province*, charted the decline of Puritanism with a sense of tragic grandeur. Due to Miller, the intellectual history of colonial New England became virtually an industry within the historical profession. It would be impossible to trace accurately Miller's vast influence and unprofitable to list all of his disciples, but among the most prominent have been Alan Heimert in *Religion and the American Mind: From the Great Awakening to the Revolution* (1966); Edmund Morgan whose works include *The Puritan Dilemma* (1958), *The Visible Saints* (1963), *Roger Williams, The Church and The State* (1967) and a recent work on Virginia, *American Slavery, American Freedom, The Ordeal of Colonial Virginia* (1976); Darrett Rutman with *Winthrop's Boston* (1965) and Robert Middlekauff with *The Mathers: Three Generations of Puritan Intellectuals 1596-1728* (1971).

Miller's work has also evoked a reaction from a whole generation of post-Miller historians of New England. In the main they object to Miller's theme of declension but they also argue that the declension theme emerged because Miller focused so intently upon intellectuals and theology, per se (Dunn, 1972; 661-679). Taking their cue from the economic approach of Miller's successor, Bernard Bailyn, especially his *New England Merchants in the Seventeenth Century* (1955), and the work of Lucien Febre, Fernand Braudel and the French *Les Annales* school, a new generation of New England historians has seen continuity and the persistence of Puritan institutions and life styles well into the nineteenth century. The most notable of the post-Miller scholars have concentrated on family history, genealogy and town studies where one of Miller's disciples, Edmund Morgan, was a pioneer with *The Puritan Family* (1944). Other works in this vein include Michael Zuckerman's *Peaceable Kingdoms* (1970) and Kenneth Lockridge's *A New England Town: The First Hundred Years* (1970). Paul Boyer and Stephen Nissenbaum have even used post-Millerian techniques of social history to unravel definitively the mystery of the Salem Witchcraft Trials in *Salem Possessed* (1974).

Existential history did not begin and end in New England, however. Contemplating the situation of the defeated South, Wilbur J. Cash, a North Carolina newspaperman, wrote *The Mind of the South* in 1941. An indictment of the South, Cash's book at the same time was essentially a story of cultural tragedy. This theme was picked up by C. Vann Woodward, notably in *The Origins of the New South* (1951), *Tom Watson, Agrarian Rebel* (1938) and *The Burden of Southern History* (1960). Woodward with great sympathy saw the South as the only section of the United States that had experienced defeat and cultural occupation, which in turn gave Southerners a special perspective on American history. This held true for Woodward as a Southerner especially. He could see that the defeat of the South had two causes: Northern economic supremacy coupled with Southern complicity in greed, and the South's policy of institutionalized racism.

Woodward, however, did more than brood about the situation. In 1955, during the integration crises, he wrote *The Strange Career of Jim Crow*, which indicated that segregation in transportation facilities was not an ancient Southern custom, not rooted in the folkways and mores, but a comparatively recent development. The book strongly suggested that there was no validity to the Southern argument that federal laws could not legislate custom away—especially in the case of transportation facilities—because of the comparatively recent adoption of segregated transportation facilities. Woodward, who wielded great influence as spokesman for the enlightened South, combined the Progressive historian's desire to find a usable past with the existentialist sense of the irony and tragedy of history itself.

Southern historians, however, could look in turn at the story of the Negro and see further irony and tragedy in history. The first great voice to articulate this situation in modern fashion was the Marxist historian, W. E. B. DuBois, whose *The Souls of Black Folk* (1903) saw the Negro caught between a dominant white culture and his own black identity in a country to which he preferred, if allowed, to pledge allegiance. Surprisingly, it was not the black historians who picked up on DuBois's theme but white historians of black culture. Black historians tended to be progressive and optimistic and at times militant in their outlook rather than tragic and existential. Saunders Redding (1958, 1967), Benjamin Quarles (1948, 1953, 1961, 1962, 1969), Henry Bullock (1967), Daniel Thompson (1910, 1963), Earle Thorpe (1961, 1967, 1969, 1971), John Hope Franklin (1943, 1947, 1961, 1963, 1968), and John Blassingame (1972, 1973), to name the most prominent of recent black historians, all have seemed Progressive in their recounting of the black experience.

White historians, on the other hand, have seemed closer to DuBois or the black novelist, Ralph Ellison, whose *Invisible Man* (1952) was the great American existential novel of the 1950's. Kenneth Stampp in his *The Peculiar Institution* (1956) tried to rewrite Ulrich Phillip's pioneer work but saw nothing ironic in thinking of the Negro as a "white man in a black skin." Stanley Elkins in *Slavery* (1959) likened the black slave's experience to life in Nazi concentration camps and, drawing heavily upon T. W. Adorno's *Authoritarian Personality* (1950), pictured the black as being "Samboized" by the ordeal. In slavery not only the Negro's African culture disappeared but his ego was pulverized and re-shaped again. For Elkins the tragedy was that in ante-bellum America, unlike Latin America with its Church, there were no institutions to exercise moral suasion over white tormentors. Critics of Elkins have believed that he painted too glowing a picture of Latin American institutions and that he carried the concentration camp analogy too far. Black reactors to Elkin's work found the "Sambo" portrait insulting and counter-productive to their search for a black identity.

Perhaps the best, most searching historical account of the origins and rise of racism in America has been Winthrop Jordan's *White Over Black* (1968). The most interesting, sympathetic, yet not patronizing description of ante-bellum black culture has been Eugene Genovese's *Roll Jordan Roll* (1974). David Brion Davis at Yale has attacked the problem of American slavery from a world perspective in his two volumes to date, *The Problem of Slavery in Western Culture* (1966) and *The Problem of Slavery in the Age of Revolution, 1770-1823* (1975) while Carl Degler at Stanford has attempted a comparison of slavery between the cultures in the hemisphere in *Neither Black nor White: Slavery and Race Relations in Brazil and the United States* (1971). George Frederickson in *The Black Image in the White Mind* (1971) and Thomas Gossett in *Race: The History of an Idea in America* (1965) have also added significantly to the rapidly growing literature on the subject (see Stanton, 1960).

The greatest controversy has been generated by Robert Fogel and Stanley Engerman's *Time on the Cross* (1974), a cliometric study of the slave and slave conditions in the South. Employing massive research teams and computers, Fogel and Engerman used statistics and intricate sampling formulae to prove that slavery was profitable and hence, not likely to die out; that slaves did have a culture of their own and a family life; that the slave was relatively better off than the northern worker of the same period; and that slaves were upwardly mobile. At first Fogel and Engerman's work was enthusiastically received and the profession stood in ignorance and awe of their new research technique as well as their findings (Woodward, 1974). But soon rebuttal (David, *et al.*, 1975; Gutman, 1975) followed as historians questioned their research, sampling techniques, and conclusions. A dramatic, heavily-attended symposium (Walton, ed., 1975) took place at Rochester, New York in 1974 which ended in the denunciation of their work though not its conclusive refutation. History had intersected with present politics (Haskell, 1975: 33-39).

A Saga Re-examined: The New Western History

While numerous historians have been scrutinizing the South from modern perspectives still another set of scholars has begun to reassess the role of the West in the life of the nation. This group forms what might loosely be termed the "post-Turner school." For many western historians a dialogue with Turner and his ardent disciple, Ray Allen Billington, continues to be the main focus of their work. In 1954 Stanley Elkins and Eric McKittrick reopened the Turner question with their collection *A Meaning for Turner's Frontier* in which they included an essay comparing the frontier situation with that of a World War II instantly-created town. They found in the town's experience many analogies to Turner's description of the frontier which, to them, made his thesis plausible. Other defenses of Turner were supplied by Billington in *America's Frontier Heritage* (1966) and Merle Curti's (1959) computerized study of Trempealeau County in Wisconsin.

The arch foe of the Turner thesis was George Wilson Pierson of Yale whose essays critical of Turner, written over many years, finally resulted in a substitute hypothesis—the theme of mobility. This he incorporated into *The Moving American* (1972).

Meanwhile several other approaches to the western experience suggested themselves to post-Turnerians. One, generated by Earl Pomeroy in *The Territories and the United States* (1947) focused upon the political ties between the West and the East using territorial politics as the immediate subject matter. Building upon Pomeroy's theme, Howard R. Lamar wrote *Dakota Territory* (1956) and *The Far Southwest* (1966), both of which argued for the political determination of cultural units. This flew directly in the face of the environmental determinism of

Turner and Walter Webb. In *The Far Southwest*, for instance, Lamar analysed a region that was geographically homogeneous but yet formed the setting for four quite different cultural patterns in Utah, Arizona, Colorado and New Mexico. These cultural patterns were determined, Lamar argued, by the kinds of economic and political systems brought *to* the region, not *generated out* of the region. The role of the federal government in developing or impeding the development of the West has also formed the subject for books by William Turrentine Jackson (1952), Robert Utley (1963, 1967, 1974), Richard Bartlett (1962), and William Goetzmann (1959).

In Goetzmann's work, which was strongly influenced by the American Studies Movement, a transcendance of economic and political determinants was attempted in a larger vision of the impact of American culture on the West. His two books, *Army Exploration in the American West* (1959) and *Exploration and Empire: The Explorer and the Scientist in the Winning of the American West* (1966) examined the role of art, photography, science, belief, myth and the military as well as politics and economics in forming an overall view of the West in the American mind. Goetzmann argued that explorers, scientists and artists who went West were "programmed" to interpret what they saw in terms largely fashioned in Eastern cultural centers. The early impresions thus formed largely governed the later course of Western development in a self-fulfilling prophecy. Goetzmann thus combined aspects of the symbol and myth school with detailed institutional history as well as a broadened view of the history of science in his attempted revision of Western history.

Four notable recent works following similar lines are: Roderick Nash, *Wilderness in the American Mind* (1967), G. Edward White, *The Eastern Establishment and the Western Experience* (1968), Kevin Starr, *Americans and the California Dream* (1973) and Richard Slotkin's *The Frontier Myth of Regeneration Through Violence* (1973). A variation on the role of belief in fashioning Western behavior is presented by Michael Lesy in his striking *Wisconsin Death Trip* (1973) which uses photography as its primary medium supplemented by newspaper accounts and state insane asylum records to present a view of Jackson County, Wisconsin far different from and much bleaker than that revealed in Curti's study of Trempealeau County. Lesy's book essentially added the dimension of psycho-history to Western history.

Still other Western historians studied the rise of cities and towns. Richard Wade's *The Urban Frontier* (1959) cogently argued that key cities supplied the values and habits of large areas in the West. Robert Dykstra refined this view in his perceptive study *The Cattle Towns* (1968). Gerald Nash in his *The American West in the Twentieth Century* (1973) saw the West as entirely dominated by towns and cities in an "oasis" culture, while Raynor Banham in *Los Angeles, a City of Four Ecologies* (1971) discussed the rise of the sprawling western metropolis and its ever-expanding sphere of influence in terms of the interplay between urban and natural landscapes.

Concurrently with ongoing studies of white settlements, another group of historians has been studying the Indian and American Indian policy. The works of F. P. Prucha (1962), Robert Utley (1963, 1967, 1974), and Wilbur Jacobs (1950, 1966, 1972) are noteworthy in this field as are Alvin Josephy's *The Patriot Chiefs* (1961) and *The Indian Heritage of America* (1968). Peter Farb in *Mankind's Rise to Civilization* (1968), has offered the interesting idea that Indians perished before the white man's onslaughts because their culture was too advanced and too refined and hence too inflexible. Other more popular works on the Indian which come under the heading of "advocacy history" are Vine Deloria's *Custer Died For Your Sins* (1969), Dee Brown's *Bury My Heart At Wounded Knee* (1971) and Leslie Fiedler's *The Return of the Vanishing American* (1968). Perhaps the most fruitful new approach to Indian history is that of Richard Metcalf (1974). By showing how white sources can be combined with anthropological information to reconstruct Indian political history Metcalf has opened up a new field for Western historians. In many ways all of these recent works suggest that the field of Western history is rapidly attaining a high degree of sophistication and complexity and that the West is now "old" and "jaded" enough perhaps to offer itself as a subject for tragedy and as an example to other developmentally emerging sections of the world.

Radical History

Like virtually everything else in America, history did not pass serenely through the decade of the 1960's. Indeed it learned much from it. Concerned about the war in Vietnam and America's global policies, a new school of radical diplomatic historians emerged, led by William Appleman Williams (1959, 1967), Walter Lefebre (1963, 1967), and Barton J. Bernstein (1966, 1968). Intersecting with their work and distinctly Leninist in its outlook was the work of Gabriel Kolko, especially *The Politics of War: The World and United States Foreign Policy* (1968). The outlook embodied in many of these works was perhaps unwittingly echoed or keyed by Senator J. William Fulbright's widely disseminated, *The Arrogance of Power* (1966), which contrasted sharply with Walt Whitman Rostow's *The Diffusion of Power* (1972). In this period old-fashioned multi-archival diplomatic history seemed to be rapidly giving way to histories, justifications and interpretations of American policy that somehow reflected a prevalent post-war view that what America did or planned to do was all that mattered.

Domestic policy also formed the backdrop and *raison d'être* for the new radical historians who called for a new approach to and reassessment of the American past. The most prominent of the radical historians were Eugene Genovese in *The Political Economy of Slavery* (1967), Herbert Aptheker, perennially interested in slave revolts, Staughton Lynd in *Intellectual Origins of American Radicalism* (1968) and *Class Conflict, Slavery and the United States Constitution* (1967), Christopher Lasch in *The New American Radicalism* (1965) and David Herreshoff, *American Disciples of Marx* (1967).

The consistent point driven home relentlessly by the radical historians was the need to examine American history not with an eye to consensus but to confrontation. They assailed consensus historians as myth-makers who willingly or not glorified America and averted their eyes from its contradictions, crimes and absurdities. Moreover, they accused traditional historians of being "elitist" in that they focused on prominent men and unusual events rather than studying the common man and woman. Jessie Lemisch (1968) sounded this note most clearly when he called for history to be written "from the bottom up." And as a final corollary the radical historians insisted that the historian not pretend to be neutral. Fairness, they characteristically asserted, demanded that history be value-oriented, that the historian use his work to right the wrongs of the past and present. Thus the radical historians more clearly than any other group of American historians appeared to be living in and for the present. The writing of history was not "science" but self-expression—a present-oriented species of activism that formed one very logical consequence of Peckham's view of history.

1976: History Alive and Well

If Peckham was right and history can be only the reflection of present sentiments using vestiges of the past as a kind of language, then Clio's—or Time's—American adventures as recounted in this essay represent not a reconstruction of what actually happened but rather a Bicentennial view of the importance or function of past historiography today. Moreover it is clear that J. H. Plumb's announcement of "the death of history" is premature. Since, as this essay demonstrates, the writing of history grows out of a concern for present events at all times; since it is a form of self-expression about those current events using special, very powerful convincing devices, it would appear that the present, with its multiplicity of causes, concerns, and problems, coupled with the occasion of the Bicentennial, is perhaps demanding more history and more *kinds* of history than at any previous time.

In a recent essay calling for a re-charting of the mainstream of American experience Robert Sklar (1975) seemed to suggest that indeed there was no mainstream but rather that there were many streams and rivulets which have marked the course of American experience. "Herstory" or woman's history has assumed a commanding importance as has the history of the blacks, the Mexican-Americans, the Oriental-Americans and the First Americans. All forms of ethnic history and minority history necessitating studies in ethnology, have risen to central importance. And now that the extended family and the nuclear family have all but vanished, they are commanding great attention from the historian. So too has the history of children and the inarticulate assumed a new importance in a society that is census and welfare conscious (Calhoun, 1973; Coles, 1963, 1967, 1970, 1971a, 1971b, 1972). This has led in very recent times to the rapid advance of cliometrics or computer based research borowed from opinion poll sampling techniques. History seems to be moving away from the idiosyncratic and the particular to the general and the study of the masses who, in the words of Braudel, "move very slowly."

A concern for the masses and the inarticulate has also led to a heightened interest on the part of historians in the evidence of material culture. Historical archeology is a fast-rising vogue that goes beyond mere antiquarian interest. A fascination with material culture has led in turn to architectural history and ecological history, and a new importance attaches to the history of science and its effect on culture. Here the most influential book has been Thomas Kuhn's *The Structure of Scientific Revolutions* (1962, rev. 1970). And surely the most intriguing of the behavioral sciences for the historian is psychology. A new school of psycho-history (see Crunden, 1973) with its own journal *The History of Childhood Quarterly* has appeared within the last five years. Drawing sustenance from the theories of people as widely diverse as Sigmund Freud, Carl Jung, Harry S. Sullivan, J. B. Watson, Geza Roheim and Erik Erikson, psychohistory nonetheless still appears to have two major defects. It is only as convincing as the psychological theory upon which it rests, and available in-depth information is far too scanty to be very persuasive to the discerning reader. It will hardly do to assert, as has one recent historian (Rogin, 1975), that, because Andrew Jackson's mother left him ashore to work on a Revolutionary War prison ship and subsequently died, all of Jackson's actions can be explained by an acute case of "mother deprivation."

Nor will the current rage for Marxist theory among a determined band of historians be broadly convincing despite detente. Even less promising, though perhaps revealing of the time, is a cross-fertilization between Marxism and psycho-theory that has begun to appear in some books (Rogin, 1975: 86). Clearly some historians (see White, 1973) at the present time appear to be impatient with complexity and longing for models or abstractions—a "metahistory" that will make the task of understanding mass man or woman much simpler. They are at one with Henry Adams in those confusing days before the Great War when, "sorely perplexed" and disoriented by science and changing times, he called for "the aid of another Newton."

And yet with all its confusions and complexities, reflective of the present time, history appears to possess greater power in the popular mind than historians think it has. In a very real sense, since the days when Thomas Jefferson wrote "posterity shall judge," virtually every American figure has somehow felt himself accountable to the historians of a future generation. Recent presidents have been acutely conscious of their possible places in history—even to the extent of disastrously recording their every moment by means of recording machines and their human counterparts, (e.g., Goldman, 1969; Schlesinger, 1965; Sorensen, 1963, 1965, 1969). Thus, in the minds of our public figures, history, as in the days of ancient Rome, becomes a popular tribunal. A court beyond the last resort, posterity, no matter what the ontological basis of history may come to be, will inexorably judge.

Notes

1. The best overall treatment of American historiography is Higham (1965). The present author is much indebted to this work. Other studies include Kraus (1953), Wish (1962), Cunliffe and Winks (1969), Skotheim (1966, 1969), Duberman (1969), Van Tassel (1960), Wish (1960), Loewenberg (1972), Handlin, et al. (1954), Basler, et al. (1960).

2. See Hanke (1959: 74–96). Page 77 reproduces a page from the English translation of Las Casas' book, dated 1583.

3. For a characteristic expression of his philosophy, see Bancroft (1954).

4. The best treatment of these writers is Conrad (1976).

5. Jordy (1952) gives Adams the label "scientific historian" but then demonstrates that Adams did not believe in scientific history.

6. See White (1949: 27–31, 32–46). White (1949: 76–93), however, applies the term to Veblen.

7. Morison (1942) is a good example. After the war Morison also sailed across the Atlantic in a replica of Columbus's ship.

References

Adams, B. 1896, 1910. The Law of Civilization and Decay (New York: Macmillan).

———, ed. 1919. The Degradation of the Democratic Dogma (New York: Macmillan).

Adams, H. 1931. The Education of Henry Adams (New York: Modern Library): 302-303. Orig. ed. privately printed, 1907; first public printing, 1918.

Bailyn, B. 1967. The Ideological Origins of the American Revolution (Cambridge, Mass.: Harvard University Press).

Bancroft, G. 1954. "The Office of the People in Art, Government and Religion," in J. L. Blau, ed., Social Theories of Jacksonian Democracy (New York: Liberal Arts Press): 263-273.

Bancroft, H. H. 1890. Literary Industries (San Francisco: H. H. Bancroft Co).

Barnes, H. E. 1930. World Politics in Modern Civilization (New York: Alfred A. Knopf).

———. 1973. The Chickens of the Interventionist Liberals Have Come Home to Roost: The Bitter Fruits of Globalony (New York: Revisionist Press).

Bartlett, R. 1962. Great Surveys of the American West (Norman, Okla.: University of Oklahoma Press).

Basler, R. B., D. H. Mugridge, and B. McCrum. 1960. A Guide to the Study of the United States of America (Washington, D.C.: U. S. Government Printing Office).

Beale, H. K. 1946. "Causes of the Civil War," Social Science Research Council Bulletin No. 54.

Beard, C. 1936a. The Devil Theory of War: An Inquiry into the Nature of History and the Possibility of Keeping out of War (New York: Vanguard).

———. 1936b. The Discussion of Human Affairs (New York: Macmillan).

———. 1939. Giddy Minds and Foreign Quarrels: An Estimate of American Foreign Policy (New York: Macmillan).

———. 1940. The Old Deal and the New (New York: Macmillan).

———. 1946. American Foreign Policy in the Making, 1932-1940: A Study in Responsibilities (New Haven: Yale University Press).

Bemis, S. F. 1923. Jay's Treaty (New York: Macmillan).

———. 1926. Pinckney's Treaty (Baltimore: Johns Hopkins University Press).

———. 1935. The Diplomacy of the American Revolution (New York: Appleton-Century).

———. 1940. John Quincy Adams and the Foundations of American Foreign Policy (New York: Alfred A. Knopf).

———. 1943. Latin American Policy of the United States (New York: Harcourt Brace).

Bernstein, B. J., ed. 1966. The Truman Administration (New York: Harper and Row).

———, ed. 1968. Towards a New Past: Dissenting Essays in American History (New York: Pantheon).

——— and A. J. Matusow, eds. 1972. Twentieth Century America (New York: Harcourt, Brace, Jovanovich).

Beveridge, A. J. 1916-19. Life of John Marshall, 4 Vols. (Boston: Houghton Mifflin).

Billington, R. A. 1966. America's Frontier Heritage (New York: Holt, Rinehart and Winston).

———. 1973. Frederick Jackson Turner, Historian, Scholar, Teacher (New York: Oxford University Press): esp. chs. 4 and 5.

Blassingame, J. 1972. The Slave Community: Plantation Life in the Antebellum South (New York: Oxford University Press).

———. 1973. Black New Orleans 1860-1880 (Chicago: University of Chicago Press).

Boorstin, D. 1948. The Lost World of Thomas Jefferson (Boston: Henry Holt).

Brooks, V. 1944-52. Makers and Finders, 5 Vols. (New York: E. P. Dutton).

Bullock, H. A. 1967. A History of Negro Education in the South from 1619 to the Present (Cambridge, Mass.: Harvard University Press).

Calhoun, D. 1973. The Intelligence of a People (Princeton, N. J.: Princeton University Press).

Caughey, J. W. 1945. Hubert Howe Bancroft: Historian of Western America (Berkeley: University of California Press).

Catton, B. 1951. Mr. Lincoln's Army (Garden City, N. Y.: Doubleday).

———. 1952. Glory Road (Garden City, N. Y.: Doubleday).

———. 1953. Stillness at Appomatox (Garden City, N. Y.: Doubleday).

Coles, R. 1963. The Desegregation of the Southern Schools (Boston: Atlantic Monthly Press).

———. 1967. Children of Crisis (Boston: Atlantic Monthly Press).

———. 1970. Uprooted Children (Pittsburgh: University of Pittsburgh Press).

———. 1971a. The Middle Americans (Boston: Atlantic Monthly Press).

———. 1971b. Migrants, Sharecroppers, Mountaineers (Boston: Atlantic Monthly Press).

———. 1972. Farewell to the South (Boston: Atlantic Monthly Press).

Columbus, C. 1493. Letters from the New World (Barcelona: Pedro Posa).

Conrad, S. P. 1976. Perish the Thought: The Intellectual Woman in Romantic America (New York: Oxford University Press).

Cox, I. J. 1918. The West Florida Controversy, 1798-1913 (Baltimore: Johns Hopkins University Press).

Craven, A. O. 1939. The Repressible Conflict (Baton Rouge, La.: Louisiana State University Press).

———. 1942. The Coming of the Civil War (New York: Charles Scribner's Sons).

Crunden, R. M. 1973. "Freud, Erikson, and the Historian: A Bibliographic Survey," Canadian Review of American Studies, 4 (Spring): 48-63.

Cunliffe, M. and R. Winks. 1969. Pastmasters (New York: Harper and Row).

Curti, M. 1959. The Making of an American Community: A Case Study of Democracy in a Frontier Community (Stanford: Stanford University Press).

Darling, A. B. 1940. Our Rising Empire, 1763-1803 (New Haven: Yale University Press).

David, P. A., H. G. Gutman, R. Dutch, P. Temin, G. Wright. 1975. Reckoning with Slavery: Critical Essays in the Quantitative History of American Negro Slavery (New York: Oxford University Press). Introduction by K. Stampp.

Diggins, J. P. 1971. "The Perils of Naturalism: Some Reflections on Daniel

J. Boorstin's Approach to American History," *American Quarterly*, 23 (May): 153-180.

Duberman, M. 1969. *The Uncompleted Past* (New York: Random House).

Dunn, R. 1972. "The Social History of Early New England," *American Quarterly*, 24 (December): 661-679.

Franklin, J. H. 1943. *The Free Negro in North Carolina 1790-1860* (Chapel Hill, N. C.: University of North Carolina Press).

———. 1947. *From Slavery to Freedom: A History of American Negroes* (New York: Alfred A. Knopf).

———. 1961. *Reconstruction: After the Civil War* (Chicago: University of Chicago Press).

———. 1963. *The Emancipation Proclamation* (Garden City, N. Y.: Doubleday).

———. 1968. *Color and Race* (Boston: Houghton Mifflin).

Gay, P. 1968. *A Loss of Mastery: Puritan Historians in Colonial America* (New York: Alfred A. Knopf).

Gillespie, C. C. 1960. *The Edge of Objectivity: An Essay on the History of Scientific Ideas* (Princeton, N. J.: Princeton University Press).

Goetzmann, W. H. 1959. *Army Exploration in the American West, 1803-1863* (New Haven: Yale University Press).

———. 1968. "Foreward," *General Index to the Papers and Annual Reports of the American Historical Association* (Washington, D. C.: Carrollton Press).

Goldman, E. F. 1945. *John Bach McMaster: American Historian* (Philadelphia: University of Pennsylvania Press).

———. 1969. *The Tragedy of Lyndon Johnson* (New York: Alfred A. Knopf).

Grattan, C. H. 1929. *Why We Fought* (New York: Vanguard).

———. 1936. *Preface to Chaos: War in the Making* (New York: Dodge).

———. 1939. *The Deadly Parallel* (New York: Stackpole).

Gutman, H. G. 1975. *Slavery and the Numbers Game: A Critique of "Time on the Cross"* (Urbana: University of Illinois Press).

Handlin, O., A. M. Schlesinger, S. E. Morison, F. Merk, A. M. Schlesinger, Jr., P. H. Buck. 1954. *Harvard Guide to American History* (Cambridge, Mass: Belknap Press). O. Handlin, ed., 2nd edition, 1967; F. Friedel, ed., 3rd edition, 1974.

Hanke, L. 1959. *Aristotle and the American Indian* (Bloomington, Ind.: University of Indiana Press).

Haskell, T. L. 1975. "The True and Tragical History of Time on the Cross," *New York Review of Books* (October 2): 33-39. Review of David, *et al.* (1975), Gutman (1975), and Walton (1975).

Herreshoff, D. 1967. *American Disciples of Marx* (Detroit: Wayne State University Press).

Higham, J. 1965. "The Historical Profession," "Theory," "American History," in J. Higham, L. Krieger, and F. Gilbert, *History* (Englewood Cliffs, N. J.: Prentice-Hall).

Hofstadter, R. 1944. *Social Darwinism in American Thought* (Boston: Beacon Press).

———. 1968. The Progessive Historians, Turner, Parrington, Beard (New York: Alfred A. Knopf).

Hovenkamp, H. 1976. "Science and Religion in America: 1800-1860," unpublished PhD dissertation (University of Texas at Austin).

Jackson, W. T. 1952. Wagon Roads West (Berkeley: University of California Press).

Jacobs, W. 1950. Diplomacy and Indian Gifts (Stanford: Stanford University Press).

———. 1966. Wilderness politics and Indian Gifts (Lincoln, Neb.: University of Nebraska Press).

———. 1972. Dispossessing the American Indian (New York: Scribners).

Jordy, W. 1952. Henry Adams, Scientific Historian (New Haven: Yale University Press).

Kraus, M. 1953. The Writing of American History (Norman, Okla.: University of Oklahoma Press).

Kuklick, B. 1972. "Myth and Symbol in American Studies," American Quarterly, 24 (October): 1435-1450.

LeFeber, W. 1963. The New Empire: An Interpretation of American Expansion, 1860-1898 (Ithaca: Cornell University Press).

———. 1967. America, Russia and the Cold War, 1945-1966 (New York: Wiley).

Lemisch, J. 1968. "The American Revolution Seen From the Bottom Up," in B. J. Bernstein, ed., Toward a New Past: Dissenting Essays in American History (New York: Pantheon): 3-29.

Levin, D. 1959. History as Romantic Art (Stanford: Stanford University Press).

Loewenberg, B. J. 1972. American History in American Thought: Christopher Columbus to Henry Adams (New York: Simon and Schuster).

Metcalf, R. 1974. "Who Should Rule at Home: Native American Politics and Indian-White Relations," Journal of American History, 61 (December): 651-665.

Morison, S. E. 1942. Admiral of the Ocean Sea, 2 Vols. (Boston: Little, Brown).

Nevins, A. 1947. Ordeal of the Union, 2 Vols. (New York: Charles Scribner's Sons).

———. 1950. The Emergence of Lincoln, 2 Vols. (New York: Charles Scribners' Sons).

Nicolay, J. G. and J. Hay. 1890. Abraham Lincoln: A History, 10 Vols. (New York: Century).

Nye, R. 1944. George Bancroft, Brahmin Rebel (New York: Alfred A. Knopf).

Parkman, F. 1869-1892. France and England in North America (Boston: Houghton Mifflin).

———. 1887. The Old Regime in Canada (Boston: Houghton Mifflin).

Peckham, M. 1970. "Aestheticism to Modernism: Fulfillment or Revolution?" in The Triumph of Romanticism (Columbia, S. C.: University of South Carolina Press).

Peel, J. D. Y. 1971. Herbert Spencer: The Evolution of a Sociologist (New York: Basic Books).

Perkins, D. 1941. Hands Off: A History of the Monroe Doctrine (Boston: Little, Brown).

———. 1955. The American Approach to Foreign Policy (Cambridge, Mass.: Harvard University Press).

Persons, S. 1954. "The Cyclical Theory of History in Eighteenth Century America," American Quarterly, 6 (Summer): 147-163.

Phalen, J. 1956. The Millenial Kingdom of the Franciscans in the New World: A Study of the Writings of Gerónimo de Mendieta 1525-1604 (Berkeley: University of California Press).

Plumb, J. H. 1970. The Death of the Past (Boston: Houghton Mifflin).

Potter, D. 1942. Lincoln and his Party in the Seccession Crisis (New Haven: Yale University Press).

Powell, J. W. 1878. Report upon the Lands of the Arid Regions of the United States (Washington, D. C.: U. S. Government Printing Office).

Pratt, J. 1925. Expansionists of 1812 (New York: Macmillan).

———. 1936. Expansionists of 1898 (Baltimore: Johns Hopkins University Press).

Prucha, F. P. 1962. American Indian Policy in the Formative Years (Cambridge, Mass.: Belknap Press).

Quarles, B. 1948. Frederick Douglass (Washington, D. C.: Associated Publishers).

———. 1953. The Negro in the Civil War (Boston: Little, Brown).

———. 1961. The Negro in the American Revolution (Chapel Hill, N. C.: University of North Carolina Press).

———. 1962. Lincoln and the Negro (New York: Oxford University Press).

———. 1969. Black Abolitionists (New York: Oxford University Press).

Ramsdell, C. W. 1937. "Changing Interpretations of the Civil War," Journal of Southern History, 3 (Feb.-Nov.): 3ff.

Randall, J. G. 1937. Civil War and Reconstruction (Boston: D. C. Heath).

Redding, J. S. 1958. The Lonesome Road: The Story of the Negro's Part in America (New York: Doubleday).

———. 1967. The Negro (Washington, D. C.: Potomac Books).

Rhodes, J. F. 1893-1906. History of the United States from the Compromise of 1850, 7 Vols. (New York: Macmillan).

Rogin, M. P. 1975. Fathers and Children: Andrew Jackson and the Subjugation of the American Indian (New York: Alfred A. Knopf).

Samuels, E. 1947, 1958, 1964. Henry Adams, 3 Vols. (Cambridge, Mass.: Belknap Press).

Sandburg, C. 1926-1939. Abraham Lincoln, 6 Vols. (New York: Harcourt, Brace).

Schlesinger, A. M., Jr. 1949. The Vital Center (Boston: Houghton Mifflin).

———. 1965. A Thousand Days: John F. Kennedy in the White House (Boston: Houghton Mifflin).

Schouler, J. 1880-1899. History of the United States under the Constitution, 6 Vols. (New York: Dodd, Mead).

Seymour, C. 1921. Woodrow Wilson and the World War: A Chronicle of Our Own Times (New Haven: Yale University Press).

Sklar, R. 1975. "The Problem of an American Studies 'Philosophy': A Bibliography of New Directions," American Quarterly, 27 (August): 245-262.

Skotheim, R. 1966. American Intellectual Histories and Historians (Princeton, N. J.: Princeton University Press).

———, ed. 1969. The Historian and the Climate of Opinion (Reading, Mass.: Addison Wesley).

Smith, J. H. 1911. The Annexation of Texas (New York: Baker and Taylor).

———. 1919. The War with Mexico (New York: Macmillan).

Sorensen, T. C. 1963. Decision-Making in the White House (New York: Columbia University Press).

———. 1965. Kennedy (New York: Harper and Row).

———. 1969. The Kennedy Legacy (New York: Macmillan).

Stanton, W. 1960. The Leopard's Spots: Scientific Attitudes towards Race in America, 1815-59 (Chicago: University of Chicago Press).

Thompson, D. H. 1910. The Highlanders of the South (New York: Eaton and Mains).

———. 1963. The Negro Leadership Class (Englewood Cliffs, N. J.: Prentice-Hall).

Thorpe, E. E. 1961. The Mind of the Negro: An Intellectual History of Afro-Americans (Baton Rouge: Ortlieb Press).

———. 1967. Eros and Freedom in Southern Life and Thought (Durham, N. C.: Seeman Printery).

———. 1969. The Central Theme of Black History (Durham, N. C.: Seeman Printery).

———. 1971. Black Historians: A Critique (New York: Morrow).

———. 1972. The Old South: A Psychohistory (Durham, N.C.: Seeman Printery).

Turner, F. J. 1920. The Frontier in American History (New York: Henry Holt).

Tuveson, E. L. 1968. Redeemer Nation (Chicago: University of Chicago Press).

Utley, R. M. 1963. The Last Days of the Sioux Nation (New Haven: Yale University Press).

———. 1967. Frontiersmen in Blue: The U. S. Army and the Indians 1848-1905 (New York: Macmillan).

———. 1974. Frontier Regulars: The United States Army and the Indian 1866-1891 (New York: Macmillan).

Van Tassel, D. D. 1960. Recording America's Past (Chicago: University of Chicago Press).

Von Holst, H. 1876-1892. The Constitutional and Political History of the United States, 8 Vols. (Chicago: Callaghan).

Walton, G. M., ed. 1975. "A Symposium on Time on the Cross," Explorations in Economic History, 12 (Fall): 333-457.

Webb, W. P. 1931. The Great Plains (New York: Ginn and Co.)

Wecter, D. 1941. The Hero in America: A Chronicle of Hero Worship (New York: Charles Scribner's Sons).

Weems, M. 1800. A History of the Life and Death, Virtues and Exploits of General George Washington with Curious Anecdotes equally honorable to himself and exemplary to his young Country Men (Philadelphia: M. Carey). Recent edition published in 1918 by J. B. Lippincott.

Whitaker, A. P. 1934. The Mississippi Question, 1795-1803: A Study in Trade, Politics, and Diplomacy (New York: Appleton-Century).

White, H. 1973. Metahistory: The Historical Imagination in Nineteenth Century Europe (Baltimore: Johns Hopkins University Press).

White, M. 1949. Social Thought in America: The Revolt Against Formalism (New York: Beacon Press).

Williams, W. A. 1959. The Tragedy of American Diplomacy (Cleveland: World).

———. 1967. The Roots of the Modern American Empire (New York: Random House).

Winks, R., ed. 1968. The Historian as Detective: Essays on Evidence (New York: Harper and Row).

Wish, H. 1960. The American Historian (New York: Oxford University Press).

———., ed. 1962. American Historians (New York: Oxford University Press).

Woodward, C. V. 1974. Review of R. Fogel and S. Engerman, Time on the Cross, New York Review of Books, 21 (May 2).

Economics:

Its Direct and Indirect
Impact in America, 1776-1976

JOSEPH J. SPENGLER

Duke University

The content and status of economic science in the United States were long influenced by the importance attached to "useful knowledge" (Reinhold, 1975) and the degree to which Americans found British economics either acceptable or in need of adaptation to American conditions. Political economy, while not yet considered a branch of "useful knowledge," had been highly regarded by the founding fathers, essentially exponents of laissez-faire and critics of concentration of power who appreciated commercial knowledge (e.g., commerce, geography, agriculture, money and banking). Alexander Hamilton built his defence of manufactures upon Adam Smith; James Madison, like Franklin, was a forerunner of Malthus; J. B. Say was also to become influential (Spengler, 1940: 3-59, esp. 10, 22-24). American writers on economics accepted the "ideology of wealth," that "a deep and abiding interest in the things of the market place" was "morally desirable, or at least morally acceptable" (Rotwein, 1973).

American writers were slow to contribute significantly to the growth of "economics" as a science and to make it a dominant element in the American "Mind" and a force in the development of America and its economy (see Dorfman, 1946-1959). Undoubtedly, American economic life already was viewed as too complex and dynamic to be caught within the nets of the economist qua economist (e.g. see Tarascio, 1975); whence "economics" fell short of being Newtonian in its impact upon American thought and civilization. Indeed, the content of social science often resembled the content of court decisions in that, not being easily subject as was natural science to empirical testing, it could be kept alive by repetition and self-serving disciples until effectively challenged by propagators (e.g., late nineteenth-century institutionalists and German-trained economists) of a new point of view (perhaps aided by a favorable climate of opinion), or by a group of bright young scholars capable of deducing corollaries of a theory (e.g., the explicators of J. M. Keynes' *General Theory*) and bringing its policy implications within the orbit of skilful publicists and opinion-shapers (see Dorfman, 1946-1959; Ellis, 1948; and Haley, 1965).

In the colonies and later in the United States economic matters commanded the attention also of ethical, political, philosophical, legal, and jurisprudential writers. For there as elsewhere the essential universality of man's pursuit of self-interest aroused concern lest this pursuit run too counter to so-called common interests and hence require to be made appropriately subject to ethical rules reflecting the interests of the community. Only as the price system began to be perceived as a self-correcting system that tended to curb anti-social pursuit of self-interest did these market-regulating disciplines lose influence to economics as such. (In comparison, British economics had taken on a scientific character by the seventeenth century. Letwin, 1963).

Interest in economic phenomena was manifest in the English-speaking settlements from their establishment. For "with the political and religious purposes of the early Americans were mingled hopes of individual economic improvement, and aspirations that the whole pattern of economic life might be arranged in conformity with moral ideals." (Johnson, 1932, preface) While this economic thought, fragmentary and spiritually akin to medieval economic thought, failed to make economic behavior subordinate to ethical tests, it did lend support to economically oriented ideals and it influenced Benjamin Franklin and his contemporaries. (Dorfman, 1946-1959: I; Johnson, 1932; Parrington, 1930). This thought also continued the medieval belief—a belief of much older vintage—in the vastness of the bounty of God or Nature that needed but to be mixed with man's industry in order for his needs to be satisfied, a bounty whose sufficiency, though questioned, was not challenged until in the nineteenth century.

While it may be assumed that Americans were utility maximizers, or at least what H. A. Simon calls "satisficers," it is not entirely clear how the content of this utility changed over time, nor the degree to which such change affected the character of competition. Even if in the tradition of Adam Smith and some of his contemporaries, we assume with Arndt (1972) that "people in a society act from two motives: (a) desire for real income and (b) desire for status," we may still infer that in America competition long continued to be little adulterated or constrained by "desire for status" and that therefore competition was more intense in America than in less flexible European economies. Only in the long run, as Keynes (1963: 365) suggested, would the "desire for superiority" become ascendant over the desire for absolute goods. The South may have been a partial exception insofar as status carried more weight and somewhat cushioned competition and what Hezekiah Niles (in Chevalier, 1961: x) in 1815 called the American's "almost universal ambition to get forward." That a society so animated associated success with fitness was demonstrated by the post-1860 vogue of Herbert Spencer's philosophy and "Social Darwinism" (Hofstadter, 1944: ch. 2), a philosophy no longer in vogue now that many a Congressman believes welfare and equity to depend largely upon his legislative actions, much as Rostand's rooster believed the sun's rising depended upon his crowing.

Most of our discussion is focused upon the post-Civil War period because not until later in the nineteenth century did American contributions to economic analysis become sufficiently outstanding to command wide attention, enhance understanding of American society notably and contribute to its modification. These contributions do not support J. M. Keynes' (1936: 382) exaggerated view of the role of ideas as such; for many forces, only some ideational and many of short time dimension, brought about change, often unwanted in the end— change easier to identify after 1875 than before the Civil War.

Sociologists and economists long differed respecting the degree to which the allocation of goods and services should be governed by competition and the price system. Before the Civil War sociology was held in higher repute in the South than in the North, presumably because the sense of belonging to a definitely ordered society was much stronger in the South (Sydnor, 1940: 19). In general, Southern economists, while differing in respect of some essentially political issues, supported laissez-faire, free trade, and private property (Leiman, 1966; Dorfman, 1946-1959: chs. 20-22). In contrast some Southern sociological writers denied that society could be built upon a system of liberty and laissez-faire; only a benevolent or socialist economy such as the Southern slave economy could avoid the evils associated with laissez-faire (Fitzhugh, 1854, 1857; Hughes, 1854; Wish, 1943; Bernard, 1937: 154-174, 1938: 1-12; Bernard and Bernard, 1943: ch. 16; Hawkins, 1936; and Miles, 1974: 273-274).

Soon after the Civil War, confidence in laissez-faire, strong in the North before the Civil War, was reenforced ideationally and ideologically by the philosophy of Herbert Spencer and the derivative doctrine of "Social Darwinism" and given standing by Theodore Roosevelt's support (Burton, 1965: 103-118). This philosophy later was countered by a philosophy directed against laissez-faire as well as against Social Darwinism—a philosophy to whose formulation sociologists (with the exception mainly of W. G. Sumner) were the major contributors. This counter-philosophy had the ideational and ideological support of a number of economists and publicists, together with the political support of movements aimed at concomitants of industrialization, "trustification," and so on (e.g. see Page, 1969; Hofstadter, 1944; and Spengler, 1950).

Many leading sociologists (e.g., Ward, Small, Giddings, Cooley, Ross, and in some respects, Sumner) were given to "broad social theorizing" and "system-making," in "the general belief that theoretical sociology would somehow play a major constructive role in the progressive development of our society." "They were all," as Page (1969: 249-251) notes, "impressed by the anti-class elements of American democracy and by the social virtues of that 'classless' segment of society—the middle class". . . . "They desired . . . the superordination of *community* over all intracommunal groups." They distrusted "the 'Lords of Creation' at the one extreme and the class-pointed proletarian leaders at the other." After World War I, however, "broad systematizing, historical speculation . . . gave way to detailed empirical research in problem areas somewhat narrower in scope" and hence to compartmentalized sociological theory and research, thus following in the path of economics. These somewhat parallel trends did not, however, eliminate conflict between economic and sociological conceptions (e.g., those of Giddings, Cooley, and Ward) of optimal economic organization but they did greatly increase the range of inquiry within which each science could significantly complement the other (see Leontief, 1948; and Spengler, 1940b).

Background

During the first of the three periods, 1776-1865, 1865-1920, and 1920-1976 the conterminous geographic base of the country was extended to its present perimeters, an infrastructure was gotten under way, and the slave system was abolished. Externalities were not conspicuous. Laissez-faire was in the saddle and the economic role of the state was restricted on constitutional, philosophical, and ideological grounds as well as by the belief that governmental support of the development of infrastructure (especially transport) should be largely confined to state and local levels where the benefits were mainly incident. Accordingly, public employment was limited (e.g., federal employment rose from 4,837 in 1816 to 36,672 in 1861 while population was growing from about 8.7 million to about 32 million) and non-military redistributive expenditures (e.g., poor relief, welfare, "subsidies," etc.) were minimal and essentially the responsibility of local governments (Goodrich, 1960). Except for being subject to duties and taxes, economic activities were virtually unregulated at the federal level. As yet very few individuals derived any income from teaching "economics" or writing about economic subjects. Even in England between 1765 and 1850, of 25 important economists only one found in his practice as an economist a major source of his income (Stigler, 1965: 38).

The period 1865-1920 witnessed the maturation of the American economy, an increase in the fraction of the population in cities 25,000 and over from 15.1 percent in 1870 to 35.7 percent in 1920, together with an increase in trade union membership from about 300,000 to about 5,048,000 (while the population was increasing only about 200 percent). It also saw the emergence of new problems (e.g., monopoly, employer-employee conflict, socialism, laggard growth in the South), continuing concern with monetary issues, and the organization and professionalization of economists, together with gradual growth of their influence in public affairs. While the regulative role of the state increased (e.g., Interstate Commerce Act, Sherman Act, Federal Reserve Act), it remained limited in scope. Federal employment increased about 900 percent, from 36,672 in 1861 to 396,494 in 1913, over five times as fast as the population. Meanwhile, federal expenditure exclusive of interest on the public debt increased about 1,000 percent. The wholesale price index fell from 151 in 1816 to 89 in 1861. Wholesale prices, about one-seventh higher in 1913 than in 1861, rose about 90 percent between 1913 and 1918. Between 1890 and 1913 total federal and state expenditure on welfare did not rise above 3 percent of Gross National Product even though individual states began to assume some responsibility for forms of social welfare (e.g., workmen's compensation; pensions for the blind, orphans, etc., retirement programs, etc). (Monetary figures are in current dollars; from U.S. Bureau of the Census, 1960.)

Favorable and unfavorable economic conditions (prosperity, depression, war, a 1,200 percent increase in college enrollment) made 1920-1976 an Age of Opportunity for economists. Between 1922 and 1971 the ratio of welfare expenditures to Gross National Product (GNP) rose from around 3 percent to about 17 percent and the ratio of all government expenditure to Gross National Product nearly trebled; meanwhile, state, local, and federal (civilian) employment increased about 400 percent. In Britain (Worswick, 1972), the economic and political status of economists improved greatly, though not as markedly as in the United States, where teaching posts, together with employment in public agencies, multiplied as did opportunities in the private sector, to which after 1900 schools of business administration served as bridges for persons with economic training, thus conferring prestige upon business and thereby diverting able persons to business (Copeland, 1958; Gordon and Howell, 1959). Public and foundation money for economic research grew unprecedentedly as did the number of publication outlets for research. With this growth and concomitant expansion of the membership of the American Economic Association, founded in 1886, from 572 in 1895 to 6,936 in 1950, 14,127 in 1965, and 18,766 in 1974 the concerns of economists multiplied and the scope for economic fashions increased (Stigler, 1965; Bronfenbrenner, 1966; Black, 1963).

Seventeen-Seventy-Six to Eighteen-Sixty-Five

It is, of course, a matter of more than temporal coincidence that Adam Smith's *Inquiry into the Nature and Causes of the Wealth of Nations* and the American Declaration of Independence appeared in the same year. For both works expressed a spirit of revolt against the concentration and abuse of political power, and Smith (1937) himself looked forward to the realization of his principles of economic freedom in America, particularly if capital shortage and comparative advantage should motivate America to pursue a policy of internal and external freedom of trade (Fay, 1934; Hamilton, Madison and Jay, 1937). While the founding fathers were familiar with the works of Adam Smith—*Wealth of Nations* was used as a textbook by Bishop James Madison, president of William and Mary College, and first teacher of political economy in America (O'Conner, 1944)—and later those of J. B. Say, their major concern was not with economics and politics as such but with the centuries-old problem of taming power and guarding the freedom of the individual (Spengler, 1940a). Of a different background than Alexis de Tocqueville (1836), the founding fathers worried less about tyranny of the majority. Their approach was not doctrinaire but pragmatic, in particular that of Benjamin Franklin, most representative of the French "Enlightenment," and that of Thomas Jefferson who was well acquainted with both Enlightenment ideas and those of David Hume. Jefferson's views varied from agrarian through laissez-faire to sometimes protectionist (Grampp, 1945, 1946, 1947; Luttrell, 1975).

The cultural and ideational background of most Americans was not conducive to widespread interest in economics, especially in its explicitly theoretical aspects. Problems rather than theories commanded their attention. For, as de Tocqueville (1836) observed, there is not "a country in the world where, in proportion to the population, there are so few uninstructed, and at the same time so few learned individuals." Even the rich who enjoyed leisure had no inclination to study, having had their tastes shaped in their youth when, being without wealth and "absorbed in business," they lacked the time to develop "a taste for study." "There is no class, then, in America in which the taste for intellectual pleasure is transmitted with hereditary fortune and leisure, and by which the labours of the intellect are held in honour. Accordingly there is an equal want of the desire and the power of application to these objects." Forty-four years later the educational state of the population was not much more favorable to the study of economics; census data (1960: ch. H, 207, 210-211) show only about two-thirds of those aged 5 to 17 years were enrolled in school, and of these only about one percent were in secondary school; only 2.72 percent of those 18 to 21 years old were enrolled in institutions of higher education. In 1880 high school graduates approximated only 2.5 percent of the population 17 years old and college graduates only about one-third of one percent of those 18 to 21 years old. The ratio of secondary to primary students rose, however, from about one percent in 1870 to about 5.5 percent in 1910; as Dorfman (1946-1959: chs. 19, 25) suggests, this upward trend is traceable in part to a growing need in business for training available in secondary school.

The American social milieu was unfavorable to legislative intervention[1] and favorable to competition and the pursuit of self-interest and remained so—more so than the still variedly feudal and corporate European milieu. Men were considered potentially equal, but with the laurels going to the better performers. The country had been settled and continued to be "settled mainly by enterprising immigrants seeking economic opportunities and economic freedom," by men who, aided by "revolutionary improvements in technology, a free labor supply, and free access to the markets and raw materials of the world," would bring an Age of Enterprise into being within little more than a century after the Declaration (Cochran and Miller, 1942: 2, 354).

The physical milieu of America, its vast areas remaining to be settled, the entrepreneurial capacity of many of its citizens, the multitude of opportunities on the horizon, and so on—these conditions differentiated America from France, the British Isles, and later Germany, countries whence came the foreign economic ideas known to Americans interested in economics. Because these conditions differed from corresponding conditions in Britain and France and because Americans were interested in practical economic counsel rather than in theory as such, various American economists familiar with Maltho-Ricardian economics responded unfavorably to those of its tenets which seemed to be at variance with American conditions even if in keeping with physical constraints apparently present in Britain and Europe. This anti-Maltho-Ricardian view continued to find expression in writings of nineteenth-century American economists (e.g., Raymond, Henry Carey, A. H. Everett, S. N. Patten) concerned with American conditions (Teilhac, 1936; Dorfman, 1946-1959; Spengler, 1933; Spiegel, 1960). Even when economics had become more sophisticated, American empirical thought occasionally reflected the country's natural bounty. Most illustrative is the work of Simon Nelson Patten (1852-1922) who, as a student in Germany, was struck by the contrast between it and America. His work reflected "his distinction between the pain-deficit and pleasure-surplus stages in human progress, his insistence that there is no natural limitation on progress but that productive power is subject to the law of increasing rather than decreasing returns, his recognition that improvements in consumption may contribute to further progress quite as much as improvements in production, . . . his distrust of competition as a regulator of economic relations and confidence in cooperation and other forms of socialization" and in "aggressive interference of government with the free play of economic forces" (Seager, 1924: xvii). Patten, as Tugwell (1923: 175) later observed, rejected the "English view of nature as a hostile force." "It was the contrast between his native fields and the culture built upon their bounty and the frugal middle-class life of the small German industrial city that gave him the key to what seemed to him the way of economic salvation. He saw frugality there for the first time, saw a little being made to go a long way, saw actual skimping being carried on successfully." Whence he concluded that "the possibilities of progress" lay in "the adaptation of wants to nature's determination" much as the Germans had done.

While a policy of economic liberalism, or individual economic autonomy, was beginning to flourish in England and France in the later eighteenth century, the forces making for its continuing growth in the United States must have been reenforced by the range of opportunity evident—and this despite the fact that protectionist policies, usually present in developing countries, were advocated on nationalist grounds, and in the belief that manufacturing would thereby be encouraged. Grampp's (1965) careful review of the Constitutional Convention, Federalist policy and ideology, and Republican policy indicates laissez-faire and the spirit of classical liberalism to have been dominant (Dorfman, 1946-1959).

Writing at the close of the period dealt with by Grampp, de Tocqueville (1836) described the competitive spirit reigning in America. There men are "on a greater equality in point of fortune and intellect . . . than in any other country of the world, or, in any age of which history has preserved the remembrance." Each American merchant and trader, having to compete with his countrymen, could compete successfully with those of foreign lands; his superiority was attributable not to lower input costs or "physical advantages" but to the Americans' "moral and intellectual attributes," attributes comparable to the "new system of tactics" introduced "into the art of war" by the French during the "campaigns of the Revolution." The Americans were neither handicapped by extreme division of labor nor by "the axioms of their profession" or by the "prejudices of their present station." "Perpetual change" kept the "minds of the citizens in a perpetual state of feverish agitation which admirably invigorates their exertions." This spirit of enterprise, adventure, and innovation entered into the American's "political laws, his religious doctrines, his theories of social economy, and his domestic doctrines." De Tocqueville thus anticipated that capacity for competition which even today sustains our tradition of laissez-faire in comparison with Europe's tradition of planning and the acceptance of government controls (Sundquist, 1975; Spengler, 1962), an American view probably running back to Governor Bradford's (1899: 157-164) unfortunate experience with collectivism at Plymouth Plantation immediately after its settlement.

The Americans, De Tocqueville expected, would "become, like the English, the factors of a great portion of the world." "When I contemplate the ardour with which the Anglo-Americans prosecute commercial enterprise, the advantages which befriend them, and the success of their undertakings, I cannot refrain from believing that they will one day become the first maritime power of the globe." Unlike the rather widely accepted view "that as America grew older she would take on the characteristic form of the great European nations," De Tocqueville wrote: "The time cannot be foreseen at which a permanent inequality of conditions will be established in the New World." He did not foresee that within 135 years the idea of equality would become ex cathedra and sovereign, transcendant over freedom and probably over efficiency in the absence of an institutionalized tradeoff between equality and efficiency (Nisbet, 1974; Okun, 1975). Nor did he anticipate the transmutation of the old argument that God created the poor to make wealthy givers of alms happy into the legal argument that the incompetent and unproductive indigent had a "property" right in governmental largess (Funston, 1975; Boudon, 1974: 28n.)

Two characteristics dominate the content of economic literature of pre-1861 vintage. First, the tools and the modes of argument usually were not rigorous, for the training of most authors (e.g., lawyers, clerics, publicists, politicians) was not rigorous and their discussion was directed at broad audiences and issues (e.g., promotion of manufactures, development of transport and ports, monetary instability and currency problems, the formation of corporate and other forms of business association, what to do about slavery (Miller, 1927). Although it was generally believed that population and the economy would continue to grow and settlement to spread, perhaps too rapidly, opinion respecting the future of slavery varied.[2] While simple projections of population and settlement were attempted, use of mathematics in economic analysis was uncommon, though several works were published, such as Ellet's (1839) outstanding *Essay on the Laws of Trade*, Galloway's (1853) *Ergonomy*, and Vethake's (1938) *Principles of Political Economy*. Statistical matter was used to describe economic progress, to support arguments, and to evaluate propositions (Seaman, 1846; Seybert, 1819; Pitkin, 1835; deBow, 1852).

Second, economic works often were intended to support sets of policies (e.g., agrarian works; nationalist protectionist works such as those of Matthew and Charles Carey; Thomas Cooper's defense of freedom and trade from a Southern point of view; works of the so-called clerical school of political economy, continuator of British classical political economy). Influential until into the 1880's, the clerical economists prepared the way for the later ascendancy of English neoclassical "economics" and made this country less congenial than it might otherwise have been to the historical school and the later institutional school. As opponents of radicalism and protectionism and spokesmen for laissez-faire, monetary conservatism, and a competitive economy, the clerical economists expressed views more to the taste of mercantile and banking interests than to those of manufacturers; they strengthened the case for dependence on the discipline of the market, thus preventing the erection of barriers in the way of potential entrepreneurs.

Eighteen-Sixty-Five to Nineteen-Twenty

Between the 1870's and the 1890's economics became a science and a profession, meanwhile ceasing to be an adjunct to a philosophy that treated simple "natural laws" as final truths (cf. Clark, 1936: 2). But progress was slow. As late as 1880 there were not many more than ten fulltime professional economists (Coats, 1961; Spengler, 1968), and their prestige (even when recognized abroad) as well as influence remained small.

Early in this period, with the Southern plantocracy destroyed by the Civil War, the business man was in the saddle and De Tocqueville's observation (made in 1836) of the lawyer's role remained valid: "the lawyers as a body, form the most powerful, if not the only counterpoise to the democratic element." Bar and bench dressed up ideas of laissez-faire "in constitutional grab" and translated the "laissez-faire views of academic and popular theorists and businessmen" into constitutional doctrine, thus making the courts "the ultimate censors of virtually all forms of social and economic legislation" (see Fine, 1964; chs. 2-5; Spengler, 1969: 7-9). Despite the need for expertise to deal with popular demands for the regulation of railroads, economists were slow to win recognition. As Wyman (1911) described it, "the general feeling around 1885" was that "it was better to leave all alone . . . to leave people work out their own salvation." "So far as any direct influence upon our courts is concerned," wrote a lawyer (Humble, 1908: 379, 384) as late as 1908, the economists' "textbooks might as well be written in Chinese." This is not entirely surprising for, as J. M. Clark (1936: 8) could still say in 1935: "The unfortunate fact seems to be that the consensus of economists has no absolute authority, and no right to claim it," in part perhaps because they failed to foresee how regulation might prove less favorable to competition than alternative arrangements (e.g., see Phillips, 1975).

At least three forces initially contributed to improvement in the professional status of economics and the emergence of need for the economist's expertise. (a) Confidence in unqualified laissez-faire and its supporting ideology became less strong, though faith remained in the realization of harmony (as assumed, e.g., by Henry Carey and his followers, F. Bastiat, etc.) and in man's ability to achieve harmony through appropriate changes in the distribution of power and the organization of the economy. Indeed, a vision of a competitive system was emerging, of a system which, while not free of defects, already performed quite well and would improve. In time an indigenous marginalism developed, but not one with emphasis upon optimization as such since this ran counter to the views of emerging institutionalists and empiricists.

(b) The marginalist revolution, a replacement for such indigenous marginalism as lurked in the literature, together with a growing spirit of reform, sharpened both economic theory (Goodwin, 1972; Stigler, 1965: 571-586) and criticism of laissez-faire, brought into question by fear that the combination movement in transport and industry would put buyers at increasing disadvantage. This spirit of reform also found growing political support, at least until 1914-1918, as well as the support of some economists on ideological or ideational grounds (Hofstadter, 1944, 1955; Fine, 1964).

"A profound reorientation of the utmost importance" (Clarke, 1936a) accompanied the foundation of the American Economic Association in 1885. For this association was dominated by younger economists under German influence. They were critical of the "regnant extreme individualism of the eighteen-eighties" and sought a voice in economic policy for economists (Dorfman, 1949; also Coats, 1960, 1964). Economists like H. C. Adams (1887), A. T. Hadley (1885), and R. T. Ely (1900) showed the new attitude toward laissez-faire and the degree of competition, partly as a result of their finding (perhaps inspired by D. Lardner's work) that the presence of relatively heavy fixed costs gave rise to "natural monopoly" and discriminatory pricing and hence made regulation essential. It remained for J. M. Clark (1923) to inquire into the extent of overhead costs and their analytical and regulatory significance. Here we have a striking instance of the impact of technology on costing and pricing. Also contributive to loss of faith in laissez-faire was the attention directed to "unearned" increments by Henry George in his popular *Poverty and Progress* (1879), a concept to which the Fabians later sought to give greater scope.

(c) American economists began to win international recognition, initially as a result of competent works on special subjects, according to the English economist, Cliff Leslie. In 1880 he described American economic statistics as superior to English statistics and referred specifically to the work of David A. Wells, Francis A. Walker, theorist and empiricist, William G. Sumner, C. F. Dunbar, and Simon Newcomb (mathematician who developed an equation of exchange and a map of the flow of currency) (Clark, 1936a: 2). Later J. B. Clark's work, especially on distribution (Jalladean, 1975) and statics and dynamics, in Homan's (1928) estimation, "earned for him the reputation of being one of the five or six great Anglo-Saxon theorists" (see also Hollander, 1927). The work of Thorstein Veblen, student of industrial organization and the trade cycle, critic of neoclassical economics, and anticipator inter-alia of the role of human capital, immaterial capital, and science, was a major intellectual source of the institutional approach to economic study, an approach supported also by J. R. Commons and in some measure by J. M. Clark (Dorfman, 1934; Arrow, 1975; Clark, 1936, 1957). This approach, though complementary to both neoclassical and "Keynesian" economics, initially diverted attention unduly from exchange and price (cf. Arrow, 1975 and Davenport, 1913). Later Schumpeter (1951) included three American economists (F. W. Taussig, W. C. Mitchell, and Irving Fisher whose "name will stand in history principally as the name of this country's greatest scientific economist") among 10 great economists—economists who had completed much of their work by 1920.

The period under consideration witnessed at least 9 or 10 favorable developments in economics in the United States. These reflected response to (a) the multiplication and occasional specialization of economists now become professional, and to (b) concern emerging with urbanization, the development of a labor movement, anxiety about industrial combination, and anticapitalistic literature. Social Darwinism emerged only to be reduced to tolerable proportions. Consumption and family economics, destined for attention in the 1920's and sophisticated treatment in the 1970's (e.g. see Schulz, 1975), was popularized by S. N. Patten and in 1912 described by W. C. Mitchell (1950) as in need of greater study (Friedman, 1952: 237-282; Stigler, 1965: 203-233). J. R. Commons's work anticipated the later conflict-resolution theory of K. E. Boulding, Thomas Schelling, and others. Frank Knight (1921) introduced the concept of uncertainty into distributive theory (cf.

Arrow, 1974: 1-10). Irving Fisher developed his equation of exchange, illuminated money, income, and utility theory, and helped introduce mathematical methods into economic analysis even as did H. L. Moore, especially in his work on economic cycles and statistical demand theory. The concept of perfect competition was carefully formulated by Frank Knight, continuing in the steps of J. B. Clark. W. C. Mitchell had his work on business cycles well under way before World War I, though not until in the 1920's and 1930's was his final work completed. T. N. Carver inquired into the theories of productivity and economic development. Soon after this period's close J. M. Clark (1926, 1939) completed the first edition of a study that reflected the regulatory philosophy and assessed some of the monetary and competition-sustaining legislation emerging in this period (cf. Harter, 1962). Expansion of the economic apparatus of the state in and after the 1890's, partly in response to war, made for the employment of economists and increase in their prestige and this in turn may have softened their opposition to extension of the economic role of the state.

Nineteen-Twenty to Nineteen-Seventy-Five

Despite the profession's having come of age and attained quite high status as a result of its intellectual and related achievements between the 1880's and 1920, satisfaction with the state and prospect of economics was not unqualified. Veblen feared that obsolete preconceptions would distort economic analysis and that insufficiency of unifying principle would persist in the face of growing need for it, a need suggested also by the increasing degree of specialization (Adzrooni, 1943: 3-15). Paul Homan (1928) referred to "the present impasse," the "diversity of thought" and method, differences in postulates, and uncertainty respecting the course of comparative emphasis upon "doctrines," "*facts* scientifically ascertained, or a *technique*."

Seven years later with the country facing a crisis as grave as the "slavery question," J. M. Clark (1936a: 8-9, 11) expressed doubt whether systematic "free scientific inquiry" had "a perpetual undisturbed lease on life," should private industry no longer find support in its producing plentifully and efficiently. Theoretical uncertainties had replaced certainties, and even when economists achieved consensus, it was without "absolute authority," and progress was slow at best. Yet the object of regulation had become the whole of industry and not a mere sector adapted to regulation. Whence Clark (1961: 54) favored a more evolutionary, flexible, trial-and-error approach as exemplified in his own work lest otherwise economists become "prisoners of their own techniques and tools of analysis," a fear to which Leontief (1974: 833) recently gave expression in his Nobel Prize lecture.

Professional and public dissatisfaction with economics as a science and with the role actually being played by the economist remained great in the 1970's. Sometimes forgotten, of course, is the fact that incompatibility between actual institutions and the matrix of conditions required to support a proposition empirically, especially one in macrotheory, often is the source of its seeming invalidity. Overlooked, for example, are Federal Reserve Board policies of New Deal vintage, labor legislation born of "popular economics," which is, as Bronfenbrenner (1975) notes, "still widely current among free-floating intellectuals if not among professional economists," and post-World-War II antiunemployment legislation, a slodgy amalgam of which, even if not reenforced by deficit-financed wars and "great societies," guarantees continuous inflation (Bronfenbrenner, 1970). Underlying continuation of these developments is a legal philosophy favorable to rising entitlements and property rights in governmental largess (Funston, 1975).

Despite periodic expression of concern at the course of economic thinking and the economic and political instability to which economy and polity here and abroad have been subjected by war, depression, and inflation, the period 1920-1975, if not a Golden Age (Spengler, 1974), has been without precedent in the extent and richness of its analytical and empirical contributions. The period has proved so analytically fruitful because of the momentum in the analytical economics of the preceding period and the challenges issuing out of the period's checkered history and continuing mistakes in economic and political policy. Also indirectly contributive have been improvements in data and our knowledge of the flow of money and resources as well as advances in quantitative techniques, model construction, computerization, simulation, and so on.

Considerable impetus was given to empirical inquiry from the start of this period. The Brookings Institution began its distinguished inquiries. Herbert Hoover as Secretary of Commerce and later as President brought about a number of reports, among them reports on waste and standardization, on *Recent Economic Changes in the United States* (1929), and on *Recent Social Trends* (1933). In the 1930's the Temporary National Economic Committee and The National Resources Planning Board brought out many reports bearing upon the structure and functioning of the American economy and upon natural-resource and other limits to continuous demographic and economic growth. After World War II attention was again drawn to emerging shortages of critical and strategic resources by the Paley report, reports of the U. S.

Department of Interior, and by the newly established Resources for the Future, Inc. Unfortunately, these reports were neglected, in part because the time horizon of politicians and businessmen is very short and economists remained seduced by the belief that Technological Progress was a universal solvent.

Although in time macroeconomic theory and concerns came to dominate economic thinking, initially as a solvent of unemployment and eventually as an agent of modernization, monetary and exchange stabilization problems similar to those emerging at the close of the Napoleonic Wars arose at the close of World War I, along with the disequilibrating Reparations Issue, treated realistically by Harold Moulton and the Brookings Institution but in a kind of vacuum[3] by theorists oblivious to the quasi-rigidity of most peace-time economies. In the wake of these problems came others associated with the Great Depression set in motion by contractile Federal Reserve Board policies. Then came some 30 years of problems associated with wars, post-war adventurism, the emergence of the Soviet power bloc, the destruction of European-American world hegemony, and the ascendancy of "great societies."

Inquiry into the capacity of nations to produce, having been suggested by Veblen and later by Brookings Institution studies of the capacity of nations to pay war reparations, was extended to the United States by the Brookings Institution. Moulton (1935a) found that even in prosperous 1929 the country's "productive facilities" "were utilized only to about 80 percent of capacity" and that in 1932 output was about 45 percent below capacity. This failure was traced to failure to reduce prices as costs fell—a failure giving rise to maldistributed profits and (especially) wage gains which accrued only to particular groups. For more than 50 years, and especially since 1918, "through the devices of corporate consolidation, pools, trusts, cartels, trade associations, and code authorities" [e.g., N.R.A.] and often "with the active assistance of governments," "the tendency to centralize economic advantage, to protect existing business enterprises by protecting the price structure" had been strong and growing (see also Moulton, 1935b: 5-46).

The Brookings Institution's findings lacked an effective group of disciples to disseminate them and put them in a more theoretical setting, a group comparable to "the legendary Cambridge Circus" of young economists who helped Keynes move initially from the *Treatise* to the *General Theory* and ultimately to sharpen and propagate its message. Accordingly, the Brookings microeconomic approach was superseded by the Keynesian macroeconomic approach which, as Patinkin (1975: 268) observed, "defined the framework of . . . research in macroeconomics for decades to come."

Interest in economic growth, always notable in American works, received renewed stimulus from studies of unemployment, trade-cycle, and income problems in the 1920's and early 1930's (Burns, 1934; Kuznets, 1930; Horowitz, 1975). This interest became more analytical and model-oriented in the 1940's and almost swamped interest in some areas of inquiry as growthmania became a religion (see Kuznets, 1949). Achievement of full employment and modernization of the underdeveloped world had become the ruling illusory objectives,[4] objectives to be achieved through monetary and fiscal policies, in disregard of trade-union, corporate, government, and other constraints upon competition and of the continuous inflation that results when so-called "policy" is focused upon the "present" and the "short run" to the neglect of the "long run" (cf. Dehem, 1974). Lost sight of as well was the "institutional structure in which the economy operates" and the role of the "firm" as a "political instrument" adept at getting the "rules" tilted "substantially to its advantage" (Goldberg, 1974; Coase, 1974).

Especially notable of the analytical achievements of economists in the period under review have been the growth of regional and location theory under the leadership of Walter Isard along with the life cycle approach and the identification and isolation of utility and its augmentation if not its optimization as the main source of behavior—two approaches facilitated by great improvement in the quantification and measurement of economic phenomena[5]. A life cycle approach—an approach somewhat complementary to the cohort approach and applicable to behavior, engagement in which at one time affects and/or is affected by behavior at another time—had been used already by Irving Fisher (1907, 1930; and Tobin, 1967: ch. 9); it both illuminates behavior over time when responses are interrelated and facilitates augmentation of utility over time within family, business, and other temporally bounded contexts. Study of behavior in terms of utility reveals how it is dominated by utility considerations (see, e.g., Schultz, 1975).

The Cobb-Douglas function, an outgrowth of three or more decades of marginal productivity analysis, was finally developed in the late 1920's, making possible quantification of the study of productivity (Clark, 1928; Cobb and Douglas, 1928; Douglas, 1934), measurement of substitution at the producer and/or the consumer level, and estimation of elasticity of factor supply; it thus contributed to flexibility of the economy and augmentation of the utility derivable from an economy's stock or flow of resources. Furthermore, the Cobb-Douglas function, by facilitation measurement of marginal productivity, also facilitated identification of the source of unexplained output (e.g., that imputable to education or to inputs of "science"). It thus contributed to the analytical study of economic growth after the 1930's.

The subject of competition and the functioning of the price system, having been popularized by the work of Frank Knight as well as by that of Edward Chamberlin and Joan Robinson and their followers in the early 1930's, came back into its own on the eve of World War II, when J. M. Clark (1940) tried to give a practical turn to its analysis and again after the war when he as well as others sought an escape from what Clark (1961) called "the negative conclusions stemming from the Chamberlin-Robinson group of theories" (also see Stigler, 1965: ch. 8). Some economists, for example Fetter (1937), even feared the emergence of a corporate state and totalitarian monopoly as competition declined.

Welfare, nearly always a fundamental concern of the economist, has become the object of increasingly sophisticated analysis since World War II. This analysis has assumed two forms. (a) As a result of the initial work of Paul Samuelson and J. R. Hicks the so-called pure theory of welfare has been enlarged and sharpened. (b) Partly as a result of improvement in welfare theory but mainly as a result of increasing skill in the measurement of the costs and benefits of particular policies, actions, etc., it has become possible to determine net pay-off in many instances as well as to assess externalities and discover the marked degree to which government intervention is either cost-increasing and utility-reducing or generative of sheer waste of inputs. Distributive aspects of welfare have, of course, presented greater difficulties and extended concern with "welfare" issues into the realms of philosophy and politics exemplified in the work of Rawls (1971) and Nozick (1974), thus destroying formerly recognized economic boundaries.

Of increasing concern in many areas of inquiry have been mechanisms (including those carrying information) that bear upon degree of centralization of economic decision-making (Hurwicz, 1974; Radner, 1974), or connect decision-makers of diverse size, or are imbedded in input-output table or other models (Almon, 1974), or underlie multiplier and accelerator relations, or equilibrate what appear to be cumulative movements (Swan, 1962: 421-426). Associated with these inquiries have been inquiries into decision-making (e.g., Gore and Tyson, 1964; Halperin, 1975) within organizations and systems, into the nature of the feedback apparatus operative therein along with the divisiveness issuing out of struggles for power within systems. Ironically, with the softening of the capitalist order under the exploitative political order it supports, "the Mafia organization," it is said (Bunn and Tosca, 1974: 20) "may be the best example of working capitalism we have in America." Meanwhile, not only specific approaches of economists, but the epistemological basis of modern economic theory is being questioned (Mini, 1974).

Conclusion

Having traced the development of economic science over the past two centuries, we may return to the three questions raised. (1) No American has dominated economics as did Alfred Marshall between the 1880's and the 1920's, or as did J. S. Mill between the 1840's and the rise of Marshall, or as did J. M. Keynes (see Hicks, 1947: 1-4) between the mid-1930's and the 1960's. The day of individual domination is over, however; even Keynes's "general theory" had a natural history to which many contributed, initially to its formulation as well as to preparation for its acceptance and later to its clarification, exposition, and propagation (e.g., see Patinkin, 1975). Only techniques (e.g., Leontief's input-output table) may be closely identified with their creators. Economic theory has not been subject to critical experiment as has natural science theory or to paradigmatic development à la Kuhn; essentially collective products, bricks in the edifice of economic theory seem to evolve as do many components of man's culture. Since the 1920's, however, American economists have contributed notably to the world pool of economic knowledge, especially to its quantification, so essential to the formulation and assessment of policy.

Inquiry within the realm of economics as of other social sciences has been subject to two sources of influence, exogenous events and conditions, and conditions endogenous to the body of economic theory. In the course of the nineteenth century the development of economic theory was governed largely by endogenous factors, e.g., reflective thinking (Eagley, 1968). However, with the growth of information in what is becoming an Age of Grantmanship and the development of instruments (e.g., computers and supplementary apparatus) for the accumulation and processing of information, especially since World War II, exogenous forces and empiricists are becoming increasingly influential, but with two results, underestimation of the potential flexibility of an economy and the swamping of reflective and synthesizing thought by infatuation with the factual and the particular.

Search for computational ease and the postulation of fixity in various relationships tends to lead forecasters to underestimate the capacity of economies to adjust to change (e.g., Behravesh, 1975; Worswick, 1972). Judgment and reflective thinking may be clouded, even as Henry Adams (1920: 126) feared, by addition of new information to the already elephantine body of current information (Etzioni, 1975)—information of which much is useless or misleading and conducive to intellectual stasis and concern with the immediate and the devising of short-run policies likely to prove costly in pressure-group-ridden democracies, though on occasion the negative pay-off may be slow in materializing. Illustrative is "wage inflation," "an immediately pressing problem" "closely connected with Keynesian economics," "a problem of Keynesian economics," now "a much less cheerful subject" than in 1936, as Hicks (1974: 60, 84-85) notes (cf. Okun, 1975).

(2) The growth of economics in the sense of an apparatus of thought has contributed particularly to our ability to anticipate and assess effects consequent upon changes in socioeconomic parameters as well as to our capacity to isolate and measure externalities and negative economic effects (e.g., unemployment, inflation, malallocation of resources, maldistribution of the national product, consumer exploitation, and so on) of interference with the monetary system and the competitive processes, mainly by federal and state governments and secondarily by organized special-interest groups and quasi-monopolies. This apparatus is also contributing, as a result both of institutional approaches to the study of economies and of a growing awareness of the role of institutional parameters, to inquiry into the optimization of institutional structures in terms of regnant welfare objectives and options.

(3) Given the pandering of economically undertrained legislators (in control of an increasingly Robin-Hood-like apparatus of state) to the self-serving demands of special interest groups (e.g., trade unions) and the shortsighted demands of ill-informed voters, economists cannot contribute greatly to the nature of life in the United States. Even had economists had more influence, the nature of life would have been dominated in the main by uncircumscribed technological change, together with the commercialization of American society, its conversion into a "republic of appetites" and "overchoice," the widening of the gap between producers, distributors, and employees, on the one hand, and consumers on the other, and the generation of hostility to private enterprise.

With the changes under way and in prospect, however, the scope for salutary contributions to policy on the part of economists is likely to increase markedly, in part because the body economic like the body politic is becoming more disease ridden. Were the economy allowed to function largely in keeping with the rules of a completely competitive economy free of uncompensated externalities, output would be superior in quantity, quality, and equity of distribution to what it is at present. Moreover, economists as economists could make a much greater contribution than today when some of those who aspire to the flesh pots of Camelot if not to the inner chambers of power, or who become associated with politically oriented state agencies, abandon their custodianship of the long run under the illusion that they can forecast and manipulate the politically paramount short run (Dehem, 1974; Viner, 1958: 113-120; Behravesh, 1975). Perhaps were all elective personnel chosen by lot, say one-half each year out of a universe of persons with at least bachelor's degrees from accredited institutions, few legislators would have time and opportunity to become effective errand boys for special interests and the role of the economist in government could become more effective. Politics then could no longer swamp economics as it does today, relevant expertise could become effective, and economists, confronted by economically subversive political demands (e.g., printing-press finance of war and a "great society"), could resign with salutary effect (see Weisband and Franck, 1975). Under present conditions, however, economic expertise, even when present, cannot,[6] as a rule, guide policy although consensus dominates economic thinking to the very cutting edge of the science, for manipulators of concentrations of economic power, together with their political servitors, will deny effectiveness to possessors of expertise. Witness the failure of administrations from Truman's to Ford's to prevent continuous erosion of the purchasing power of the dollar.

As has been observed, however, economic expertise often is wanting. (a) The economist tends to neglect the constraints imposed by institutional parameters, often because he supposes current societal and economic structures will persist despite man's shrinking resource base and the increasing concentration of economic and political power in the hands of trade unions, conglomerates, bureaucracies, and a very powerful though economically undertutored legal profession, with the result that Hobbes's Leviathan may appear preferable. (b) Because of emphasis upon the short-run, long-run consequences of actions (e.g., disregard of impending resource shortages) are overlooked and little attention is devoted to the corrosive impact of commercialization on tastes, stable values, and happiness. For, as R. A. Easterlin (1974: 90-125) points out, "economic growth does not raise a society to some ultimate state of plenty. Rather, the growth process engenders evergrowing wants that lead it ever onward." (c) As Georgescu-Roegen points out, received economics, based on classical mechanics, disregards "the Entropy Law," most economic of all natural laws, and hence fails to deal rationally and ethically with the shrinking dowry of nature at man's disposal and "to recognize our limitations in relation to space, to time, and to matter and energy." As a result the interests of future generations in this dowry are sacrificed to the concerns and greed of present and near-present generations and the duration of the human species is shortened (Georgescu-Roegen, 1971, 1975: 369-378; Friedland, 1975: 437-450).

Notes

1. The Trenton, N. J. *Federalist* carried this item April 23, 1810, about the Congress: "This imbecile ignorant body of men still linger out their worse than useless sitting. Six dollars a day are a great temptation of any body of men whose time elsewhere employed would not produce one." I owe this to Professor Frank T. deVyver.

2. George Tucker predicted that population growth would reduce the relative price of free labor, making slavery unprofitable and resulting in its discontinuance. See Snavely (1964); also Fogel and Engerman (1974). Defenders of the slave system found in it a barrier to the population pressure that was likely to develop outside the South. (See Spengler, 1936b: 360–389.) Both Benjamin Franklin and James Madison had anticipated Malthus's principle of population. (See Spengler, 1935; Spengler, 1936a: 715.) Francis Walker believed as had Franklin that immigration might depress American fertility.

3. A European observer of the political and analytical conflict respecting reparations remarked "that the horrors of peace were worse than the horrors of war." Cited by Lutz (1930: 29). See also Keynes' preface to the French translation of his *Economic Consequences of the Peace*, Vol. 2 of his *Collected Writings* (1971) and Fetter (1968).

4. Originally, J. M. Keynes believed, as much growth as a people desired would result, given full employment and money of stable value; but he contended that a policy of wage reduction would not suffice to bring about full employment as economists had assumed. (See Patinkin, 1975: 257, 262, 268.)

5. H. A. Simon has restated the theory of choice and replaced "the goal of *maximizing* with the goal of *satisficing*, of finding a course of action that is 'good enough,' " thus allowing for the boundedness of the rationality of both the consumer and entrepreneur by bringing the "choice problem" within "the powers of human computation." (See Simon, 1957: 196-206 and chs. 14–15.) On the economist's neglect of man's illusions, telescoped view of consequences of today's actions, and mode of habit formation, see Scitovsky (1974: 223–235).

6. That they do not do so has been noted by Abelson (1975). See also Federal Reserve Board Chairman Arthur F. Burns as cited in report of hearing of Senate Banking Committee, *U. S. News & World Report*, May 19, 1975, p. 50. On wage-price policy actualities in 1945–1971 see Goodwin (1975).

References

Abelson, P. H. 1975. "Science Advice for the Executive Branch," Science, 187 (Jan., 1975): 119.

Adams, H. 1920. The Degradation of Democratic Dogma (New York: Macmillan).

Adams, H. C. 1887. The Relation of the State to Industrial Action, Publications of the American Economic Association, 1 (January): 471-549.

Adzrooni, L., ed. 1943. Essays in Our Changing Order (New York, Viking): 3-15.

Almon, C., *et al.* 1974. 1985: Interindustry Forecasts of the American Economy (Lexington, Mass.: Lexington Books).

American Economic Association and Royal Economic Society. 1965. Surveys of Economic Theory, 3 vols. (London: Macmillan).

Arndt, H. W. 1972. "Prestige Economics," Economic Record, 48 (December): 584-592.

Arrow, K. J. 1974. "Limited Knowledge and Economic Analysis," American Economic Review, 65 (March): 1-10.

———. 1975. "Thorstein Veblen as an Economic Theorist," The American Economist, 19 (Spring): 5-10.

Behravesh, N. 1975. "Forecasting the Economy with Mathematical Models: Is It Worth the Effort?" Business Review of Federal Reserve Bank of Philadelphia, (July-August): 15-25.

Bernard, J. and L. L. Bernard. 1943. Origins of American Sociology (New York: Crowell): ch. 16.

Bernard, L. L. 1937. "Henry Hughes, First American Sociologist," Social Forces, 15 (October): 154-174.

———. 1938. "The Historic Pattern of Sociology in the South," Social Forces, 16 (October): 1-12.

Black, R. D. C. 1963. Economic Fashions (Belfast: The Queen's University).

Boudon, R. 1974. Education, Opportunity, and Social Inequality, Changing Prospects in Western Society (New York: Wiley).

Bradford, W. 1899. History of Plymouth Plantation (Boston: Wright, Potter).

Bronfenbrenner, M. 1966. "Trends, Cycles, and Fads in Economic Writing," American Economic Review, 56 (May): 540-552.

———. 1970. "A Reconsideration of 'Nixonomics' and 'Stagflation,'" Speech published by the Research Department of the Bank of Korea (September 28, 1970).

———. 1975. "Some Reactionary Suggestions on the Labor Front," South Atlantic Quarterly, 70 (Spring): 237-243.

Bunn, R. G. and A. J. Tosca. 1974. "Mafia: Parallels with Legitimate Business," University of Michigan Business Review, 26 (November): 20.

Burns, A. F. 1934. Production Trends in the United States Since 1870 (New York: National Bureau of Economic Research).

Burton, D. H. 1965. "Theodore Roosevelt's Social Darwinism and Views on Imperialism," Journal of the History of Ideas, 26 (March): 103-118.

Chevalier, M. 1961. Society, Manners and Politics in the United States (Garden City: Doubleday). First published in 1836.

Clark, J. M. 1923. Studies in the Economics of Overhead Costs (Chicago: University of Chicago Press).

———. 1926, 1939. Social Control of Business (Chicago: University of Chicago Press).

———.1928. "Inductive Evidence on Marginal Productivity," American Economic Review/Supplement, 18 (March): 449-467.

———. 1936a. "Past Accomplishments and Present Prospects of American Economics," American Economic Review, 26 (March): 1-11.

———. 1936b. Preface to Social Economics (New York: Farrar and Rinehart).

———. 1940. "Toward a Concept of Workable Competition," American Economic Review, 30 (June): 241-256.

———. 1957. Economic Institutions and Human Welfare (New York: Knopf).

———. 1961. Competition as a Dynamic Process (Washington, D. C.: Brookings Institution).

Coase, R. H. 1974. "The Choice of the Institutional Framework: A Comment" Journal of Law and Economics, 17 (October): 493-96.

Coats, A. W. 1960. "The First Two Decades of the American Economic Association," American Economic Review, 50 (September): 555-574.

———. 1961. "The American Political Economy Club," American Economic Review, 51 (September): 624ff.

———. 1964. "The American Economic Association, 1904-1929," American Economic Review, 54 (June): 261-285.

Cobb, C. W. and P. H. Douglas. 1928. "A Theory of Production," American Economic Review/Supplement, 18 (March): 139-165.

Cochran, T. and W. Miller. 1942. The Age of Enterprise (New York: Macmillan).

Copeland, M. T. 1958. And Mark an Era. The Story of Harvard Business School (Boston: Little Brown).

Davenport, H. J. 1913. The Economics of Enterprise (New York: Macmillan).

De Bow, J. B. D. 1852. The Industrial Resources of the Southern and Western States, 3 vols. (New Orleans, De Bow's Review).

Dehem, R. 1974. "Living Beyond the Short Run," Canadian Journal of Economics, 7 (November): 453-457.

de Tocqueville, A. 1836. Democracy in America (London: Saunders and Otley). Henry Reeve, trans.

Dorfman, J. 1934. Thorstein Veblen and His America (New York: Viking Press).

———. 1946-1959. The Economic Mind in American Civilization (New York: Viking).

———. 1955. "The Role of the German Historical School in American Economic Thought," American Economic Review/Supplement, 45 (May): 17-28.

Dorfman, J., et al. 1963. Institutional Economics (Berkeley: University of California Press): chs. 1-3.

Douglas, P. H. 1934. Theory of Wages (New York: Macmillan).

Easterlin, R. A. 1974. "Does Economic Growth Improve the Human Lot?" in P. A. David and M. W. Reder, eds., Nations and Households in Economic Growth (New York: Academic Press): 90-125.

Ellet, C. 1839. An Essay on the Laws of Trade (Richmond: P. D. Bernard).

Ellis, H. S., ed. 1948. A Survey of Contemporary Economics, I (Philadelphia: Blakiston).

Ely, R. T. 1900. Monopolies and Trusts (London: Macmillan).

Etzioni, A. 1975. "Effects of Small Computers on Scientists," Science, 189 (July 11), editorial page.

Fay, C. R. 1934. "Adam Smith, America and the Doctrinal Defeat of the Mercantile System," Quarterly Journal of Economics, 48 (February): 204-216.

Fetter, F. A. 1937. "Planning for Totalitarian Monopoly," Journal of Political Economy, 45 (February): 95-110.

———. 1968. "The Transfer Problem," in C. R. Whittlescy and J. S. G. Wilson, eds., Essays in Money and Banking (Oxford: Oxford University Press): 63-84.

Fine, S. 1964. Laissez Faire and the Welfare State (Ann Arbor: University of Michigan Press).

Fisher, I. 1907. The Rate of Interest (New York: Macmillan Co.)

———. 1930. The Theory of Interest (New York: Macmillan Co.)

Fitzhugh, G. 1854. Sociology for the South, or the Failure of Free Society (Richmond: Morris).

———. 1857. Cannibals All! or, Slaves without Masters (Richmond: Morris).

Fogel, R. W. and S. L. Engerman. 1974. Time on the Cross: The Economics of American Negro Slavery (Boston: Little, Brown).

Friedland, E., et al. 1975. "Oil and the Decline of Western Power," Political Science Quarterly, 90 (Fall): 437-450.

Friedman, M. 1952. "The Economic Theorist" in A. F. Burns, ed., Wesley Clair Mitchell. The Economic Scientist (New York: National Bureau of Economic Research): 237-282.

Funston, R. 1975. "The Double Standard of Constitutional Protection," Political Science Quarterly, 90 (Summer): 261-287.

Galloway, S. 1853. Ergonomy, or Industrial Science (Athens, Georgia: A. M. Scudder).

Georgescu-Roegen, N. 1971. The Entropy Law and the Economic Process (Cambridge: Harvard University Press): introduction.

———. 1975. "Energy and Economic Myths," Southern Economic Journal, 41 (January): 347-381.

Goldberg, V. P. 1974. "Institutional Change and the Quasi-Invisible Hand," Journal of Law and Economics, 17 (October): 461-492.

Goodrich, C. 1960. Government Promotion of American Canals and Railroads (New York: Columbia University Press).

Goodwin, C. D. W. 1972. "Marginalism Moves to the New World," History of Political Economy, 4 (Fall): 351-370.

———. 1975. Exhortations and Controls (Washington, D. C.: Brookings Institution).

Gordon, R. A. and J. E. Howell. 1959. Higher Education for Business (New York: Columbia University Press): chs. 2, 8-10.

Gore, W. J. and J. W. Tyson, eds. 1964. The Making of Decisions (Glencoe: Free Press).

Grampp, W. D. 1945. "John Taylor: Economist of Southern Agrarianism," Southern Economic Journal, 11 (January): 255-268.

―――. 1946. "A Re-examination of Jeffersonian Economics," Southern Economic Journal, 12 (January): 263-282.

―――. 1947. "The Political Economy of Poor Richard," Journal of Political Economy, 55 (April): 132-141.

―――. 1965. Economic Liberalism, I (New York: Random House): Part 3.

Hadley, A. T. 1885. Railroad Transportation (New York: G. P. Putnam and Sons).

Haley, B. F., ed. 1952. A Survey of Contemporary Economics, II (Homewood, Ill.: Irwin).

Halperin, M. H. 1975. Bureaucratic Politics and Foreign Policy (Washington, D. C.: Brookings Institution).

Hamilton, A., J. Madison, and J. Jay. 1937. The Federalist (New York: Tudor Publishing Co.).

Harter, L. G., Jr. 1962. John R. Commons. His Assault on Laissez Faire (Corvallis: Oregon State University Press).

Hawkins, R. L. 1936. Auguste Comte and the United States 1816–1853 (Cambridge: Harvard University Press).

Hicks, J. 1974. The Crisis in Keynesian Economics (New York: Basic Books).

Hofstadter, R. 1944. Social Darwinism in American Thought 1860-1915 (Philadelphia: University of Pennsylvania Press).

―――. 1955. The Age of Reform: From Bryan to F.D.R. (New York: Knopf).

Hollander, J. H., et al., eds. 1927. Economic Essays Contributed in Honor of John Bates Clark (New York: Macmillan).

Homan, P. T. 1928. Contemporary Economic Thought (New York: Harper).

Horowitz, D. 1975. "Textbook Models of American Economic Growth, 1837-1911," History of Political Economy, 7 (Summer): 227-251.

Hughes, H. 1854. Treatise on Sociology, Theoretical and Practical (Philadelphia: Lippincott, Grambo).

Humble, W. H. 1908. "Economics from a Legal Standpoint," American Law Review, 42 (May-June): 379-386.

Intriligator, M. D. and D. A. Kendrick, eds. 1974. Frontiers of Quantitative Economics (Amsterdam: North-Holland).

Jalladean, J. 1975. "The Methodological Conversion of John Bates Clark," History of Political Economy, 7 (Summer): 209-226.

Johnson, E. A. J. 1932. American Economic Thought in the Seventeenth Century (London: P. S. King): preface.

Keynes, J. M. 1936. The General Theory of Employment, Interest and Money (New York: Harcourt, Brace and Co.).

―――. 1963. "Economic Possibilities for our Grandchildren," Essays in Persuasion (New York: Norton): 358-373. First published in 1931.

―――. 1971. Collected Writings (London: Macmillan).

Knight, F. 1921. Risk, Uncertainty and Profit (Boston: Houghton Mifflin).

Kuznets, S. S. 1930. Secular Movements in Production and Prices (Boston: Houghton Mifflin).

―――, ed. 1949. Problems in the Study of Economic Growth (New York: National Bureau of Economic Research).

Leiman, M. M. 1966. Jacob N. Cardozo's Economic Thought in the Antebellum South (New York: Columbia University Press).

Leontief, W. 1974. "Structure of the World Economy," American Economic Review, 64 (December): 823-34.

Letwin, W. 1963. The Origins of Scientific Economics (London: Methuen).

Luttrell, C. B. 1975. "Thomas Jefferson on Money and Banking: Disciple of David Hume and Forerunner of Some Modern Monetary Views," History of Political Economy, 7 (Summer): 156-173.

Lutz, H. L. 1930. "Inter-Allid Debts, Reparations, and National Policy," Journal of Political Economy, 38 (Feb.): 29.

Miles, E. A. 1974. "The Young American Nation and the Classical World," Journal of the History of Ideas, 35 (April-June): 259-74.

Miller, H. E. 1927. Banking Theories in the United States Before 1860 (Cambridge: Harvard University Press).

Mini, P. V. 1974. Philosophy and Economics (Gainesville, University Presses of Florida).

Mitchell, W. C. 1950. The Backward Art of Spending Money (New York: Kelley): ch. 1. First published in 1937.

Moulton, H. G. 1935. "The Trouble with Capitalism Is the Capitalists," Fortune, 12 (November): 5-46.

Nisbet, R. 1974. "The Pursuit of Equality," The Public Interest, 35 (Spring): 103-120.

Nozick, R. 1974. Anarchy, State, and Utopia (New York: Basic Books).

O'Conner, M. J. L. 1944. Origins of Academic Economics in the United States (New York: Columbia University Press).

Okun, A. M. 1975. "What's Wrong with the U. S. Economy?" Quarterly Review of Economics and Business, 15 (Summer): 21-34.

Page, C. H. 1969. Class and American Sociology: From Ward to Ross (New York: Schocken). First published in 1940.

Parrington, V. L. 1930. Main Currents in American Thought, I (New York: Harcourt, Brace).

Patinkin, D. 1975. "John Maynard Keynes: From the Tract to the General Theory," Economic Journal, 85 (June): 249-271.

Phillips, A., ed. 1975. Promoting Competition in Regulated Markets (Washington, D. C.: Brookings Institution).

Pitkin, T. 1835. A Statistical View of the Commerce of the United States of America (New Haven: Durrie & Peck).

Rawls, J. 1971. A Theory of Justice (Cambridge: Harvard University Press).

Reinhold, M. 1975. "The Quest for 'Useful Knowledge' in Eighteenth-Century America," Proceedings of the American Philosophical Society, 119 (April 16): 108-132.

Rotwein, E. 1973. "The Ideology of Wealth and the Liberal Economic Heritage: The Neglected View," Social Research, 40 (Summer): 269-292.

Schultz, T. W., ed. 1975. Economics of the Family: Marriage, Children and Human Capital (Chicago: University of Chicago Press).

Schumpeter, J. A. 1951. Ten Great Economists from Marx to Keynes (New York: Oxford).

Scitovsky, T. 1974. "Are Men Rational or Economists Wrong?" in P. A. David and M. W. Reder, eds., Nations and Households in Economic Growth (New York: Academic Press): 223-235.

Seager, H. R. 1924. "Introduction" in R. G. Tugwell, ed., Simon Nelson Patten's Essays in Economic Theory (New York: Alfred A. Knopf).

Seaman, E. 1846. Essays on the Progress of Nations (New York: Baker and Scribner).

Simon, H. A. 1957. Models of Man (New York: Wiley).

Smith, A. 1937. Wealth of Nations (New York: Modern Library).

Snavely, T. R. 1964. George Tucker as Political Economist (Charlottesville: University of Virginia Press).

Spengler, J. J. 1933. "Population Doctrines in the United States," Journal of Political Economy, 41 (August): 433-467.

———. 1935. "Malthusianism in Eighteenth Century America," American Economic Review, 25 (December): 691-707.

———. 1936a. "Addendum," American Economic Review, 26 (December): 715.

———. 1936b. "Population Theory in the Ante-Bellum South," Journal of Southern History, 2 (August): 360-389.

———. 1940a. "The Political Economy of Jefferson, Madison, and Adams," in D. K. Jackson, ed., American Studies in Honor of William Kenneth Boyd (Durham: Duke University Press): 3-59.

———. 1940b. "Sociological Presuppositions in Economic Theory," Southern Economic Journal, 7 (October): 131-157.

———. 1950. "Evolutionism in American Economics, 1800-1946," in Stow Persons, ed., Evolutionary Thought in America (New Haven: Yale University Press): 202-266.

———. 1962. "Competition and Monopoly in Economic Development," in John P. Miller, ed., Competition, Cartels and Their Regulation (Amsterdam: North-Holland): 7-58.

———. 1968. "Economics: Its History, Themes, Approaches," Journal of Economic Issues, 11 (March): 5-30.

———. 1969. "Evolution of Public Utility Industry Regulation: Economists and Other Determinants," South African Journal of Economics, 37 (March): 3-31.

———. 1974. "Was 1922-1972 a Golden Age in the History of Economics?" Journal of Economic Issues, 8 (September): 525-553.

Spiegel, H. W. 1960. The Rise of American Economic Thought (Philadelphia: Chilton).

Stigler, G. J. 1965. Essays in the History of Economics (Chicago: University of Chicago Press).

Sundquist, J. 1975. Dispersing Population: What America Can Learn from Europe (Washington, D. C.: Brookings Institution).

Swan, T. W. 1962. "Circular Causation," Economic Record, 28 (December): 421-426.

Sydnor, C. S. 1940. "The Southerner and the Laws," Journal of Southern History, 6: 3-23.

Tarascio, V. 1975. "Intellectual History and the Social Sciences," Social Science Quarterly, 56 (June): 37-54.

Teilhac, E. 1936. Pioneers of American Economic Thought in the Nineteenth Century (New York: Macmillan).

Tobin, J. 1967. "Life Cycle Saving and Balanced Growth," in Ten Economic Studies in the Tradition of Irving Fisher (New York: Wiley): ch. 9.

Tugwell, R. G. 1923. "Notes on the Life and Work of Simon Nelson Patten," Journal of Political Economy, 31 (April): 153-208.

U. S. Bureau of the Census. 1960. Historical Statistics of the United States, Colonial Times to 1957 (Washington, D. C.: U. S. Government Printing Office).

U. S. News & World Report. May 19, 1975: 50.

Vethake, H. 1838. The Principles of Political Economy (Philadelphia: P. H. Nicklin & T. Johnson).

Viner, J. 1958. The Long View and the Short (Glencoe: Free Press).

Weisband, E. and T. M. Franck. 1975. Resignation in Protest (New York: Grossman/Viking).

Wish, H. 1943. George Fitzhugh, Propagandist of the Old South (Baton Rouge: Louisiana State University Press).

Worswick, G. D. N. 1972. "Is Progress in Economic Science Possible?" Economic Journal, 82 (March): 73-86.

Wyman, B. 1911. "State Control of Public Utilities," Harvard Law Review, 24 (June): 624-634.

Young, A. 1927. Economic Problems New and Old (Boston: Houghton Mifflin): ch. 12.

Sociology in America:

The Experience of Two Centuries

ROBIN M. WILLIAMS, JR.

Cornell University

Intellectual fields are not organisms; they do not literally grow or mature or die. They do not really have ancestors or progeny, at least not in any very neat or determinate way. The search for disciplinary ancestors seems a particularly untidy venture—potentially even more capricious than genealogical efforts to identify illustrious rather than unworthy lines of descent in the endlessly backward-spreading web of births and marriages.

Scholarly or scientific "fields," "disciplines," or "specialities"—what are the referents to which such terms apply? As historical phenomena, fields of study "emerge" when someone succeeds in eliciting a socially validating and confirming response to the naming and description of a set of intellectual aspirations and activities. When Comte put forward the term "sociology" he so labeled a diverse congeries of ideas, facts, intentions, plans, interests, and hopes. Some of the components of the new field were as ancient as recorded human thought. But some other elements of sociology as it gradually took on a public identity were, indeed, new. The newness was both in the particular content of concepts and empirical assertions and in new combinations of ideas. What were the sources of the ideas that formed the basis for the first sociology in Europe? As a first conventional approximation we may point to the philosophical and historical precursors—especially Bacon, Montesquieu, Vico, Saint-Simon, the Scottish moral philosophers and jurists, Adam Smith, Buckle, deTocqueville. After the work of Comte and Spencer, then, there was a public identity and a programmatic vision of a new social science, providing a focus for the interests and aspirations that were to become "sociology."

But of course, still other precursors and founders easily can be found, and often are invoked. Note the common references to proto-sociology among the ancient Greek philosophers and historians—especially the Sophists and the great Thucydides. Also, most histories of sociology pay their respects to Ibn Khaldun, the one brilliant Arab contributor during the European late medieval times. On the other hand, if we are interested in the origins of modern sociological method-ology, we are likely to look back to the British pioneers in social sur-veys and "political arithmetic" and to the Continental mathematical and statistical precursors from Quetelet on.

Quantitative social research grew out of Baconian ideas, the rise of calculable business (commerce, life insurance), the idea of govern-mental policy based on information, mercantilism, and growing inter-ests in health and population. The early political arithmeticians, starting with John Graunt (1620-1674), made substantial methodological con-tributions, e.g., Edmund Halley's life tables (1693), or Gregory King's elaborate classification of social strata (1696). Indeed, social demog-raphy became a thriving branch of study during the eighteenth century, culminating in Malthus' *Essay on Population* in 1798.

Increasingly systematic efforts to explain social phenomena in natural-istic terms (and, especially, to explain social consequences by social causes) began to appear in the late seventeenth century; these con-tinued along with development of accumulations of data and improved means of analysis during the eighteenth century.

The most general intellectual prerequisites for the development of sociology were the same as for the other social sciences—essentially "desacralization" of society, naturalism, and faith in reason and the lawfulness of social phenomena (Martindale, 1960: 35). The various fields developed at different times and at different rates, depending to a large extent upon extrinsic social and cultural conditions; no "neat sequence" was followed, and borrowings and reciprocal influences were continuous (Martindale, 1960: 43). For sociology in the United States a special impetus was created by the nineteenth-century fusion of "...a passion for social reform and an adoration of science" (Bernard and Bernard, 1927: 845).

By the desacralization of the social order we mean the development of the view that human social arrangements were not simply the ex-pression of a fore-ordained divine or natural order, that civil society did not have to be identical with or subsumed under some particular political form, and that social order and disorder could not be ex-plained as somehow inherent in the nature of human individuals (Eisen-stadt, 1968: 23-24). Historical studies of the development of sociology in Europe and in America seem to agree that an essential intellectual background was the combination of skepticism or secularism with a belief in social causation. The specific lines of influence are numerous. One important sequence runs from Pierre Bayle in the seventeenth century through Montesquieu (who, clearly, sought natural laws of society), Turgot, and Condorcet to Saint-Simon and Comte and then to Durkheim; another sequence runs through the Scottish moralists and legal theorists—Ferguson, Millar, Kames—to Adam Smith (Mitchell, 1968, 1970). When we add Herbert Spencer and Henry Sumner Maine, we are led immediately to the American founders, Giddings, Ward, and Sumner.

Frequently, the French Enlightenment has been cited as the primary source of ideas essential for the development of sociology. Rather neglected, in comparison, has been the British background[1] (cf. Schneider, 1967, 1969), e.g., Mandeville, Hume, Ferguson, and Adam Smith. No doubt the American rationalists and deists in the generation of 1776 did help to prepare a cultural setting favorable to the later nineteenth-century social science; certainly the faith in reason, in natural order and in potential human progress was important among educated Americans in the century from 1776 to 1876. Yet the influence of English-language writers, especially those who derived in substantial measure from the Scottish moralists, appears important, and probably needs renewed research (Schneider, 1967). For example, Adam Ferguson—cited by Karl Marx as foremost in developing the conception of division of labor in society—was widely read among eighteenth century Americans (Lehmann, 1968: 370). Drawing upon the historical approach of Montesquieu and the critical methods of Hume, his developed system of what was then called moral philosophy included a comprehensive and astute protosociology, much of which is relevant today. No less a sociologist than Ludwig Gumplowicz (1892:67) regarded him as "the first sociologist". Ferguson's discussions of the inherently social nature of humans, the importance of language, and the indispensibility for personal development of participation in a community foreshadow the emphases of the first American sociologists a century later.

The notion that sociology could only develop in unstable societies undergoing rapid change is plausible but does not accord well with the historical record. Neither social instability nor collective conflict was marked in mid-eighteenth century France, England or Scotland. Rather it was new attitudes toward religion and the Church that helped to turn attention in a new way toward civil society. These intellectual currents stimulated attempts to explain social events and institutions in a naturalistic, historical and comparative manner; such essentially sociological perspectives are evident in the generation of scholars who wrote at the time of the American Revolution. The development of such perspectives, in both France and Britain, was encouraged by efforts to bring about reforms in taxation and in governmental administration in a spirit of rational appraisal (Mitchell, 1970: 131ff.). The more positive attitude toward curiosity about human societies was further stimulated and developed in the nineteenth century by enhanced awareness of the massive changes that were leading to an urban-industrial Great Society. Awareness of change and of sociocultural diversity helped create an *interest*, which could use the *ideas* inherited from the earlier historical and philosophical developments. Neither the social changes nor the ideas alone were sufficient to account for the emergence of a continuing field of study. The structural changes in society constituted a favorable context, but the proximate origins of sociology resided in " . . . certain beliefs and ideas, of conflicts of thought, and . . . of consequent changes in attitudes on the part of a small number of educated men" (Mitchell, 1970: 130).

None of the first sociologists in Europe or America, of course, could have been a sociologist at the start. Great diversity of ideas and purposes was an expectable characteristic of an emerging field (cf. Abrams, 1968: 3 on the origins of the first national sociological society in London in 1903).

Like the other social sciences, American sociology was continuously in close touch with and strongly influenced by European predecessors and contemporaries. Although only a few (Znaniecki, Sorokin, MacIver, Wirth, Lazarsfeld) of the 66 presidents of the American Sociological Association were not American-born, most of the early leaders studied in Europe, and nearly all major contributors have been strongly influenced by European sociology, as well as by ideas derived from the broader cultural heritage. After the first programmatic sketches by Comte, Marx and Spencer, the basic ideas they set forth carried forward into the late nineteenth century, when American sociology first clearly emerged. Then between 1890 and 1920 the major beliefs and aspirations of the new field were rather fully elaborated—the work of a single generation of major figures (Lengermann, 1974:11). Indeed, within a period of 20 years American sociology contributed its first major set of native works, e.g., Giddings' *Principles of Sociology* (1896), Cooley's *Human Nature and the Social Order*, Ward's *Pure Sociology*, Ross' *Social Psychology* (1908).

Influences of Life in America upon Sociology

After 1776, the American experiences in a New World were quickly seen as The American Experiment, i.e., the trying-out of democratic government on an unprecedented scale in a society of unprecedented mobility and rapid transformations—vast intercontinental migration, rapid expansion, industrialization, cultural diversity and assimilation.

The first sociological thought after 1776 was embedded—like the nascent political science, anthropology and economics of the times—in the political thought of the Founding: an undifferentiated amalgam of normative prescriptions and empirical diagnoses. The writings of the Revolutionary generation were above all based on the premises of the Enlightenment, combined with the British heritage of law and programmatic social policies.[2] As the nineteenth century unfolded there was a continuous interplay between ideas received from the European background and the intellectual and social conditions in America.[3]

One direct line of intellectual succession from 1776 is from Adam Smith's *The Wealth of Nations* and *Theory of Moral Sentiments* to Albion W. Small. Small wrote the very first textbook in sociology (in collaboration with George E. Vincent in 1894), taught the second college course ever given, was chairman of the first graduate department of sociology in the world (University of Chicago, 1892), and founded the *American Journal of Sociology*. In *Adam Smith and Modern Sociology* (1907), Small traced sociology back to Smith's theory of sympathy and interpreted *The Wealth of Nations* as a basic sociological study of economic process (cf. Martindale, 1960; 189-191).

As we initially suggested, ideas do not "descend" like genes, they migrate and wander. Thus, doctrines of social conflict developed out of observations of political affairs eventually influenced early economists, whose notions are picked up by an English clergyman, Malthus, who is concerned about population growth, and his ideas are taken by a biologist, Darwin, who develops a theory of evolution, which in turn becomes a seductive analogy for class struggles and inequality in human society for Sumner and many others.[4] Different individuals in early American sociology looked to *different* "fathers"—Ward to Comte and Spencer; Small to Schmoller, Adolf Wagner, Adam Smith, Ratzenhofer, and Simmel; Sumner to Malthus, Spencer, Lippert, Gumplowicz, and Ratzenhofer; and so on.

To properly analyze the influence of American society upon American sociology would require a major research effort, organized along the lines of Merton's complex paradigm for the sociology of knowledge (Merton, 1957: 460-488): What putative effects are in question; where are the alleged social influences located; how are existential bases and outcomes related; why does all this occur? Among items to be further investigated would be: social origins of sociologists (class, ethnicity, region, religion, mobility patterns, etc.); group structures (universities, government, voluntary association, invisible colleges); communication flows (who read what; who communicated what to whom); sources of support and acceptance or of unreceptivity, resistance and attack.

We may conceive of the problem for purposes of the present necessarily brief and cursory treatment in this way: sociology in America represents a continuously emerging product of a complex interplay among (1) received ideas, (2) social values and concerns, (3) structural opportunities and constraints, and (4) organizational and institutional factors.

We already have discussed the general background of basic ideas. Many of the ideas that formed the world-view of the early sociologists attracted interest because of the connections they were perceived to have with broader social values and concerns. Some examples are in order.

SOCIAL VALUES AND CONCERNS

Sociology as a distinct intellectual undertaking emerged during that amazingly short period during which the nation went from an economy of small family enterprises to a system of giant corporations—roughly between the Bargain of 1876 and the founding of the American Sociological Society in 1905. The period was one of a vast inpouring of immigrants, of great rural-urban migration, urban growth, industrialization, concentration of wealth and economic power, great distress among farmers and workers, political ferment (e.g., the Populist movement). Sociology was one of many efforts to understand these unprecedented and rapid changes. Keen interest in such changes and in the political issues related to them is apparent in the works of Giddings, Sumner, Ward, Cooley, Ross, and Veblen. As Hinkle and Hinkle (1950 : 1) make the point: "Emerging in a social setting of rapid urbanization and industrialization after the Civil War, the field concerned itself with social problems. In studying these problems early sociologists employed the assumptions of natural law, progress, meliorism, and individualism."

The beginnings of sociology in this country are commonly held to be found " . . . in a series of movements and organizations that combined a spirit of reform and a zeal for scientific study drawn from European philosophical and scientific currents" (Odum, 1951: 57). Histories of the field commonly indicate that it has shared strongly in the individualism, pragmatic ameliorism, empiricism, and value-diversity often noted as features of the wider intellectual scene. Perhaps generally underestimated, however, is the extent to which sociological individualism has been *fraternal and community-oriented* rather than atomistic and self-oriented. Individual effort and individual motivation and development as conceived by the pioneer sociologists strongly emphasized interindividual relations and influences—consciousness of kind, primary groups, the looking-glass self, significant symbols, the generalized other, and many other cognate and similar concepts. This sense of basic interdependence is perhaps not wholly surprising when we note that the first generations of sociologists came primarily from rural areas and small towns—many from the Midwest—from less affluent rather than wealthy families, and in many cases from ministerial backgrounds (cf. Glenn and Weiner, 1969). But such origins alone are very far from explaining the community-relational emphasis. Part of its sources lie in the essential awareness induced by sociological theory and by direct observations of social life. In any case, we suggest that considerable modification must be made in the description by Hinkle and Hinkle (1954: vii): "Perhaps the outstandingly persistent feature of American sociology is its *voluntaristic nominalism* . . . the assumption that the structure of all social groups is the consequence of the aggregate of its separate, component individuals and that social phenomena ultimately derive from the motivations of these knowing, feeling, and willing individuals." It should not be forgotten that the much-discussed Protestant individualism was part of a total belief system that emphasized both humanitarianism and active reform of the "world."

Nor can even the "psychologistic individualism" that early became prominent in American sociology be attributed to borrowing from European scholars: the borrowed ideas quickly were transformed. Thus, what had initially been conceptions used to interpret mass or collective behavior—e.g., Tarde's notions of suggestion and imitation—became person-centered in the United States when used by Ross, Baldwin, Cooley, and G. H. Mead. The influence of the pragmatism of James and Dewey upon the development of a person-centered sociology and social psychology was direct and strong. An empirical person-centered approach fitted beautifully the nineteenth-century intellectual climate. Not strange, therefore, was the fact that development of a sociological social psychology was one of the most productive sectors of American sociology from the 1890's into the 1930's.

Ethical and political concerns clearly entered strongly into incentives for the early development of sociology. As Odum notes, economists and industrialists sought in sociology to redefine and supplement traditional modes of economic thought, e.g., John R. Commons and Richard T. Ely sought to establish an American Institute of Christian Sociology (Odum, 1950:59).

A continually received heritage was thus continually being reworked in relation to an emerging body of American ideas and in relation to the observations and experiences of American sociologists with the society around them.[5] This complex interplay was occurring in a fluid and expanding system of higher education. American sociology, accordingly, was an integral part of the development of a broader American intellectual scene (cf. Parrington, 1930:III).

To the extent that ideological struggles have been important in

American life since the 1890's, sociology necessarily has had to be concerned, both to analyze ideologies and their connections with social processes and to define its own posture as a field vis-à-vis the various ideologies. In the broadest sense, the main opposing political ideologies in the United States have shared a common set of value-axioms—the radicals arguing that the status quo violates those values, the conservatives claiming that the present society is the best hope for realizing the major values. Under those conditions, there is a premium upon "facts" that can be used to support one view or the other.[6] Much of the demand for sociological studies no doubt has stemmed from the desire to find data to reinforce one's own position and to discredit the views of opponents.

The empirical, rather than philosophical, bent of the field was reinforced by knowledge of the British social survey movement. And there was the direct influence of the British Social Science Association upon the American Social Science Association that helped to establish a conception of social science as an aid in coping with growing "problems" of an urbanizing, industrializing society. This view developed in the setting of rapid change, ethnic diversity, social conflict, religious-humanitarianism aspirations, political democracy and pragmatic utopianism. A dynamic and basically hopeful society was a hospitable setting for melioristic social science, which rapidly come to see American society as its "supreme living social laboratory" (Odum, 1950: 55).

The notion that social science in general and sociology in particular should be both science and secular theology—explaining social behavior and also telling us what society ought to be—was prominent in the earliest sociological promulgations and has been a persistent thread in later developments. The demand for evaluations continues today—sometimes to the detriment of explanatory science.

In numerous instances from 1876 to 1976 the influence of social issues and accompanying tensions and conflicts upon American sociology has been direct, immediate, and substantial. Such issues were important in the initial decision to found a national professional society separate from other social science disciplines and from social work. The tension between "scientific" and "activist" interests later helped to bring about the formation in the 1950's of the Society for the Study of Social Problems. Still later the turmoil of the 1960's produced the Caucus of Black Sociologists and led to the establishment within the American Sociological Association of staff positions to deal with professional problems relating to women and to racial and ethnic minorities. Movements for black liberation resulted in increased attention to the highly important contributions made to the discipline by black sociologists, from W.E.B. DuBois at the turn of the century to the present. Throughout the history of the profession, black sociologists have seen in sociology " . . . the intellectual tools for the redefinition of race relations and, in turn a positive element for social change" (Blackwell and Janowitz, 1974: xiv). Similar views have been held by many other elements within the field.

STRUCTURAL OPPORTUNITIES AND CONSTRAINTS

Sumner gave the first course in sociology in the United States—so far as known, the first anywhere—in 1875. It was 15 years later that the second was introduced by Small at Colby College; in 1893 the first department was formed at the University of Chicago; in 1895 Small established the *American Journal of Sociology*; and in 1905, the American Sociological Society was formed by sociologists dissatisfied with their place in existing social science associations. The field thus moved from first public appearance to full institutionalization in 30 years.

This very rapid development was facilitated by the existence of considerable freedom of inquiry within the loosely organized, decentralized universities. Mass education helped to provide resources and audiences. Strong interests in social reform provided much of the popular acceptance needed by the new field. University organization made the establishment of a new field less difficult than in Great Britain or Europe (cf. Reiss, 1968)—an important point to which we return later.

American society provided in high degree the conditions that are essential for the growth of a new social science. There was a high degree of differentiation of the political order from the civil society, of Church from State, and of the economy from the environing societal community. Cultural diversity and obvious social change made it plausible to think that different ways of life might be feasible within the same political association (cf. Eisenstadt, 1968). The development of sociology as a science obviously depended upon freedom of inquiry and freedom of expression (Inkeles, 1964:116-117). Although at various times and places within the United States there have been serious interferences, the degree of permissiveness has far exceeded that of any totalitarian or autocratic society. Finally, the field found essential opportunities in the context of " . . . mass public education, a loosely organized, decentralized university system, and large resources for the financial support of research . . . " (Reiss, 1968:17).

Symbolic of both permissiveness and the legitimacy accorded to the hopeful new social sciences is the fact that Congress established a charter of incorporation of the American Social Science Association in 1899—shortly after incorporation of the Daughters of the American Revolution (1896), and shortly before chartering Rockefeller's General

Education Board (1903). The Association thus was established at the beginning of the period which brought the institutionalization of foundations as a major form of philanthropy—and an important resource for struggling research sociologists in later years.

ORGANIZATION AND INSTITUTIONALIZATION

The rapid development of sociology in the United States in comparison with the slow and episodic course in Europe is all the more striking in view of the early emergence of both powerful theories and vigorous empirical research in Germany, in France and in Britain. But it is clear that both in Germany and in Great Britain, the *lack of institutionalization of sociology as a discipline* led to the failure to develop cumulative scientific work. In France, a similar fate was only partly averted by the work of LePlay, in one direction, and that of Durkheim, the most important figure in the transition to modern sociology. But these men left disciples, not organized disciplines. In the United States, sociology was late in entering the academic arena. But, when it did appear, it rapidly became institutionalized—even though it often was greeted by great hostility and protracted resistance. Its far-from-promising beginnings soon were overcome as an outgrowth of its acceptance in some of the major universities—through the research of graduate students, the interest it aroused among undergraduates, and the growth of a professional cadre to spread the new discipline (Reiss, 1968:6-10).

The cumulative development of the field occurred even though the sharp separation of disciplines in American universities led very early to the removal of sociology from the close connection with law, philosophy, and history that existed in European universities. At the same time, the separate organization of schools of medicine, law, nursing, and social work militated against integration of sociology with professional and paraprofessional training. And the need to establish credentials as a science led many sociologists to reciprocate the rejection they experienced from the humanities and arts (cf. Reiss, 1968:4). Yet a permanent organization within the universities was achieved and was indispensible.

Academic institutionalization was decisive not just because it "legitimized" the field and provided dependable, if modest, financial support but because of the further consequences: e.g., continuity in recruiting research personnel and in improving research methods, relative freedom from pressure to produce quick panaceas for social betterment, access to large numbers of students, a home for journal publishing, a base of operation for wide-ranging professional activities.

Entrance into academic social structure occurred in two radically different ways. Most dramatic—and successful—was the *de novo* establishment of a full-fledged department in a new setting of expanding resources, as in the prototype of the University of Chicago. More usual was the beginning of sociological courses and research by individuals within departments—departments of economics, social studies, political science, social ethics and social welfare, and so on. Thus rural sociology typically began as a poorly-defined subspeciality in departments of agricultural economics.

A new field of study is likely to meet with maximum resistance if it seeks to displace an existing set of ideas, practices and practitioners; somewhat less resistance may be anticipated if the new field simply aims to investigate "new and previously unexamined phenomena" or to use "new research technologies"—aims that "thus do not challenge prevailing views" (Cole and Zuckerman, 1975:141). Avoidance of cognitive challenge to vested ways of thought, therefore, may facilitate tolerance of an upstart discipline. Similar considerations apply to the way in which the nascent field enters the social structure of intellectual activities, especially in the universities.

Sociology initially survived and developed in America partly because much of its work dealt with matters that had been rejected or ignored by established disciplines: the family, crime and delinquency, rural and urban communities, ethnic groupings, social stratification, recreation, "social problems"—or "grand theories" of social evolution and the like. It seems safe to assume that few of the established aristocrats of academe in the 1890's and early 1900's would have seen any fundamental *cognitive* challenge in such rag-picking on the periphery of the intellectual market-place. Yet sociology obviously could become a claimant for scarce resources as well as a threat to monopolies of academic prestige. Necessarily, as with all new fields, it began as promise and program rather than demonstrated performance. And, the very name —a "barbaric neologism"—suggested ideological threat ("socialism") and vulgar practical concerns. Perhaps not surprising, then, that ". . . sociology found little sanction among the early humanists and arts faculties, whose advice to the great body of students was such as to ostracise the new subject" (Odum, 1950:17).

Sociologists responded by vigorously cultivating their own garden. In the relative freedom of the newer midwestern settings, as at the University of Chicago, the lessons of rejection and ossification were not forgotten. As Faris notes, Albion Small and his associates saw ". . . the inhibiting consequences of doctrines, schools of thought, and authoritative leaders . . . " and they "encouraged open, modest searching in the spirit of an inductive science" (Faris, 1970:128). The emphasis went to the direct empirical study of social life and to the development of research methods suited to that task.

Contributions to Sociology by Scholars in the United States

An inevitably controversial listing of some 62 major advances in social science since 1900 shows that sociologists participated in 14 of the cases, of which only two did not include American workers (Deutsch, Platt, Senghaus, 1971). Among the distinctive American contributions is cited the development of functional theory to a new level of comprehensiveness and influence. Among many sociologists throughout the world, the formulations of Parsons and Merton are necessary referent points for any critical development of theory. Indeed, Rocher (1975: 153) is not exaggerating when he judges that: "Outside Parsonian theory, only Marxism offers the sociologist such an all-embracing theoretical system and tool of analysis."

In the intellectual world perhaps more than in many other sectors of society, a few individuals can initiate large effects, if freedom of inquiry and favorable channels of communication exist. Thus, the rapid development of sociology of science during the last 15 years can be traced in substantial measure to the internationally influential work of Merton (Coser, 1975).

The difficulty of distinguishing sociological from other social science contributions is apparent in several instances listed by Deutsch, Platt and Senghaus. In the social science of *circa* 1890-1930, the interdisciplinary mix is well-illustrated by the difficulty of distentangling economics and sociology in the works of such persons as Sumner, Commons, or Veblen. In Veblen's work, many of the most central theses concerned institutional factors in economic processes (Spengler, 1972)—e.g., pecuniary culture, conspicuous consumption, scientific curiosity, an "instinct of workmanship," "the state of the industrial arts," and the like. Veblen shared with Ward and Giddings the acceptance of an evolutionary model of social change, even as he rejected optimistic evaluations of the growth of commercial and industrial society. His iconoclastic work still stands as a contribution from the United States to the larger body of international sociological thought.

Within modern sociology there has been no dearth of other icon-breakers or of critical disagreements concerning basic assumptions and perspectives. For example, a prominent theme since the early 1960's among self-described "critical sociologists" has been the alleged deficiencies of structural-functional schemes in accounting for social change and social conflict. Such criticisms often have set Marxian or neo-Marxian interpretations over against Parsonian formulations.

But more recent critics have seen a deeper cleavage among fundamental paradigms—most importantly " . . . a continuing dialectic between the dominant theme of structural determinism and the submerged theme of voluntaristic individualism" (Bash, 1974:484). Thus Atkinson consigns to the same category—a deterministic sociology of structural constraints—the works of Marx, Parsons, Marcuse, Dahrendorf, Rex, Durkheim, and to a lesser extent Weber. This perhaps rather breathtaking rearrangement rests on the premise that all the theorists named see human social behavior as primarily determined by an exterior, constraining social system, rather than primarily by the active interpretations and evaluations of autonomous persons. No doubt the extent of contrast is easily overdrawn, for as Atkinson himself shows, all the major theorists of recent times have recognized and dealt with *all* the main elements of the so-called dialectic (cf. Bottomore, 1975).

The contrast between voluntaristic and social deterministic emphases overlaps to an important extent with the differences between "cohesion" (or, "consensus") perspectives and "conflict" perspectives. And, again, recent critics tend to see the differences as less important than their similarities. The similarities include a view of society as a system of statuses into which individuals are socialized (a system having great capabilities for constraining individual variations); an emphasis on power as a structural characteristic, and on institutions, roles, norms, authority, and legitimacy. The main differences lie in the use by "conflict theorists" of *class* as a key concept; a system of social class is seen as a central structure because it is thought to generate massive differences in interests, values, beliefs—and power. But even these differences diminish or disappear in analyses which assert that systematic "mystification" created by dominant classes serves to produce consensus, or when conflicts are linked to all authority relations (Dahrendorf) rather than to class per se (Atkinson, 1971; 126-43).

How should we characterize American sociology in the terms of a determinism-voluntarism debate? Certainly it is clear that the dominant tendency of American sociology since the early decades of this century has been to seek out social determinants of conduct. Attention has been focused upon the constraining and defining power of culture and social structure over the individual's behavior, and much analysis has been preoccupied with detecting the hidden or latent collective consequences of aggregated social actions—in depressions, wars, evasion of institutional rules, and social costs or externalities in actions of sub-units of the society.

But alongside this emphasis upon the structural constraints and incentives that affect the behavior of individuals, there has been a continuing counter-emphasis. In particular, a strong current of microsociological and sociopsychological research and theory has characterized the field from the 1890's to the present. In the early period, the study of the fine-grained interactions that constitute the background and to some extent the necessary basis for macro-structures has one major source in the remarkably modern analyses by Georg Simmel—of play, of sociability, of deception and secrecy, of interpersonal conflict. Simmel's powerful insights have been carried into sociology in the United States initially through the Chicago School and more recently by L. A. Coser, Merton, and E. Goffman. A second line of development begins with Cooley and E. A. Ross and converges with James, Dewey, Baldwin, and G. H. Mead. This sociological social psychology antedated a similar development in psychology. It contributed to the basic concepts of primary group, self-conception, role, socialization, significant symbolization, learning of language, and many other seminal ideas.

Descriptive sociology appeared as early as the account of Lawrence, Kansas, in Small and Vincent's 1894 textbook, and was represented by the detailed community studies of the early 1900's (e.g., J. M. Williams, N. L. Sims). The study of the detailed social ecology of communities was initiated by Charles J. Galpin, a rural sociologist, in the highly influential work, *The Social Anatomy of a Rural Community*, which mapped "natural areas" as defined by patterns of use of services—trade, schools, churches, entertainment, and so on. The ideas of natural areas and of ecological processes were productively developed by Robert E. Park and his colleagues and successors in Chicago. The accumulation of descriptive studies of diverse kinds was a dominant characteristic during the period from the end of World War I into the late 1930's. There was a preference for ahistorical and atheoretical work, and a positive suspicion of theory as "speculative." Urban and rural field studies and detailed monographs were the prototypes of respected professional activity. Macrosociology was often suspect (cf. Rocher, 1975:-12-15).

Much of the painstaking empirical work was highly dated and localized and left no residue of analytical generalizations or theoretical reformulations. Yet the attitude of commitment to first-hand investigation, the respect for facts, the willingness to do tedious tasks in the interest of science, the slow development of research techniques and practical skills—all these characteristics later were important in the relatively distinctive American integration of detailed empirical study with systematic concepts and theoretical schemes. Striking examples of this melding of European and American styles of sociology appeared in the use of sophisticated survey methods to generate theoretically-relevant data—exemplified in the 1940's by the work of Stouffer, Lazarsfeld, Guttman, Cottrell, Merton, and numerous others. Thus Merton took the data of surveys and showed what theoretically illuminating results could be achieved by treating *rates of individual behavior as outcomes of structurally relevant choices among institutionally defined and constrained alternatives* (cf. Stinchcombe, 1975:12). What this approach implies is that "stimuli, "utilities," and "reward-value" (or reinforcement) are culturally defined, that opportunities are socially structured (neither random nor individually capricious), that aggregated individual choices have structural consequences, that "motives" are socially situated and socially generated.

Another contribution to sociology from the American experience was the development of effective modes of organization that combined college and university teaching and field research. The forms were varied, ranging from the rural sociologists in land-grant colleges and agricultural experiment stations to the research centers and institutes attached to large urban universities. The same decentralization and flexibility that had originally opened doors to a fledgling science provided scope for productive organization of research of greatly increased scale and technical sophistication.

The many substantive contributions which resulted defy listing or summarization but a few will be mentioned in the following section.

The Effects of Sociological Work upon the Understanding of American Society

To attribute precise effects from the work of a quite heterogeneous field of study to "our understanding of American society" would be presumptuous at best, and irresponsible at worst. In the absence of detailed empirical analysis of what particular ideas and findings have been communicated to specified recipients, any appraisals of impact are likely to be idiosyncratic. Present company is not an exception. On that highly tentative basis, we believe that American sociology has substantially affected the understanding of the society that can be gained from the scholarly literature. An enormous advance is represented by the accumulation of critically selected and codified generalizations in the various descriptive subfields—political, education, military (Bowers, 1968), health and medical (Suchman, 1968), economic, stratification, social demography, racial and ethnic (cf. Williams, 1972, 1975b), complex organizations, crime and delinquency (Bordua and Reiss, 1968), family, and so on. The contributions include also synoptic interpretations of the total society (e.g., Lipset, 1963; Williams, 1970; Zeitlin, 1970) and comparative studies (e.g., Marsh, 1967; Hollander 1969; Schermerhorn, 1970).

If we follow the Durkheimian injunction to seek the cause of a social fact in another social fact, it is not unreasonable to take our first look at "facts" of the same general type. Thus if we want to explain a change in military tactics of the U.S. we may wish initially to look for changes in the tactics of past or potential adversaries; or, we may hypothesize that increased centralization of government is one response to increased centralization of economic power. If then we start with a knowledge-producing set of activities such as "American sociology," we might first examine putative effects on knowledge (or "ideas") and knowledge-seeking in other scholarly and scientific specialities.

Of course, new ideas and methods often have little influence until there develops a cohesive set of professional workers who will use them (Cole and Zuckerman, 1975:156). To trace influence from sociology upon the understanding of American life means that one has to distinguish among many of the nearly 50 special subfields that are recognized in meetings of the national association. A more precise delineation produces 24 specialties defined by aggregating the smallest subunits—"research areas"—that are clearly recognized within the field. The collaboration and coupling among the specialties are highly important, over and above the conceptual and methodological proximities and similarities, in shaping the utilization of knowledge across subfields (Krause, 1972, 1974).

No detailed and systematic studies have come to our attention that specify the influences of these various special sociologies upon the other social sciences or upon history, literature, criticism and other arts and sciences. Some historical and literary studies do suggest that the influence has been pervasive and important (Parrington, 1930; Wellek and Warren, 1949; Commager, 1951). Suggestive documentation and commentary has been given by Odum (1950: ch. 24), who believes that the widespread teaching of sociology has produced a common language and common ground for social thought throughout the nation. It is clear at any rate that continuous interchanges with related fields have had important reciprocal effects.

Such reciprocal influence was conspicuous in the rise of "behavorial" political science, dating from Charles E. Merriam's role in the founding of the Social Science Research Council and including Pendleton Herring, V. O. Key, Jr., Harold Lasswell, David B. Truman, Herbert A. Simon, Gabriel A. Almond. Particular influence of Parsonian ideas can be traced in the works of Karl Deutsch, William Mitchell, David Easton, and Robert B. Holt, among others.

Anthropology and sociology were closely linked in the work of Sumner and many other early sociologists, and borrowings have remained important into the present time. Social psychology in America was first created by sociologists: E. A. Ross published the first book in the U.S. to bear the title "social psychology," and Cooley, Mead, Dewey and Baldwin formed a crucial interconnected set in the formative period of the field. (A section on social psychology within the American Sociological Association continues to have the largest membership of any sub-speciality.) Long-term collaboration between sociology and social psychology has been maintained at several major universities, including Michigan and Cornell.

A limited but significant interpenetration of history and sociology has occurred, and is continuing (e.g., Schneider, 1969; Galambos, 1969; Johnson, 1969). The influence of sociology of knowledge appears substantial (Tarascio, 1975:47-51).

The contributions of any social science to knowledge about the society within which it exists may be classified into these types: (1) providing specific facts about the society and its place among other societies; (2) developing and using effective methods for generating and analyzing data; (3) developing conceptual schemes for grasping social realities; (4) providing causal explanations; (5) providing analytic and empirical predictions, and explicating possible alternative future paths; (6) developing paradigms and master perspectives in terms of which events are conceived and evaluated.

American sociology, with its strong empiricist bent, has generated or organized from existing sources an enormous volume of information about many aspects of culture and society within the United States. Although it has not had the great good fortune of economics, blessed with vast data-gathering resources of government (and with a dollar-metric), it has made extensive use of the data provided by federal and state census and vital statistics; the record of sociological demography is clear and impressive in providing accurate and comprehensive descriptions and analyses.

The frequent and rapid movement of research methods and techniques across disciplinary lines makes it unrewarding to seek to attribute particular methods to sociology. However, it is evident that sociology has especially emphasized and developed methods of participant observation, surveys and survey analysis, some important types of scaling (Guttman, 1950; Laumann and Guttman, 1966; Lazarsfeld and Henry, 1968); sociologists have elaborated the use of multivariate methods (multiple regression; path analysis) and are beginning to borrow and adapt various econometric techniques. Use of these methods increasingly produces new and significant empirical findings, e.g., the surprisingly small independent effects of amount of education upon subsequent income.

The critical uses of sociology have been numerous. Thus in the 1920's L. L. Bernard's *Instincts: A Study of Social Psychology* delivered the *coup de grace* to a thriving academic industry. Bernard examined the works of 1,700 authors and found nearly 16,000 separate instincts (grouped under 6,131 types); he concluded, reasonably enough, that the number was excessive, that environmental factors were neglected, that the concept of instincts was unnecessary (Hinkle and Hinkle, 1954:29-30).

Many sociologists over a period of more than 70 years, starting with W.E.B. DuBois in 1896, helped to destroy the intellectual respectability of racialist theories. Further, the accumulating research on ethnic, racial and religious group relations not only debunked stereotypes and revealed the psychosocial and cultural sources of prejudices but also developed a body of research-derived rules of thumb for action programs to reduce discrimination (see summaries in Williams, 1947, 1957, 1964, 1975b).

In field after field, the main sociological influence has been to highlight the significance, and then to analyze the workings of social and cultural components of both individual and collective behavior. This influence was early apparent in "sociological jurisprudence," in sociology of work and of economic institutions, in political analyses, in studies of education. In later sub-fields it reappears. Thus social gerontology, not formally recognized until the 1940's, represented a shift from the earlier exclusive emphasis on individual physiological and psychological aspects of aging to the social, interactional and cultural aspects. Until a late stage, the study of aging had been " . . . dominated and guarded by biological and clinical scientists" (Streib and Orbach, 1968:616). The sociology of science is one of the latest specialities to develop (see Ben-David and Collins, 1966; Ben-David and Sullivan, 1975), and its similar influence on history of science is now widely seen (cf. Guerlac, 1974).

Much of sociological theory represents efforts to extend and modify the theories, inherited from classical political economy (Abrams, 1968:8), that dominated popular thinking until very recent times: a view of society as an automatic outcome of the self-interested behavior of rationalistic actors, either benignly guided by an Invisible Hand or properly put in their places by the ruthless sorting of the competitive struggle for survival. Although both Spencer and Sumner had said— neither quite consistently—that the best public policy was to do nothing, few American sociologists since 1929 have believed it. The critical rejection of atomistic conceptions was fully accomplished by Talcott

Parsons in *The Structure of Social Action* (1937), *The Social System* (1951), and many subsequent works.

In field after field, sociological work has pointed to the empirical importance of variations in social interaction, informal groupings, stratification, norms and sanctions, statuses and roles; it consistently has revealed the complexity of ordinary social events and processes, showing unrecognized connections and effects. By a skeptical insistence upon collecting first-hand data about "things everybody knows," sociological research repeatedly shows that what commonsense regards as "obvious" frequently is false or inaccurate. It thus continues to demonstrate the basic but continually neglected truth that the real enemy of well-informed social action is not mere ignorance but the much more deadly foe of entrenched misinformation.

As sociology, in company with anthropology and psychology, persistently showed the systemic effects on individual persons of one after another cultural element and social relationship or group membership, it necessarily challenged deep-seated traditional views of human nature and society. The assumption that individuals *qua* individuals are the only "ultimate reality" in society was squarely denied, and the interpenetration of society, culture and personality was demonstrated in numerous specific forms. "Society" was shown to be neither an organic unity nor a social contract but a much more ccmplex network of relationships of reciprocity, exchange, power, cooperation, and conflict. Individuals emerged, in the later sociological social psychology, neither as biophychic monads nor as oversocialized occupants of statuses (cf. Coser, 1975).

Modern sociology has contributed to a detached and critical awareness of irony, ambiguity and paradox (Schneider, 1975). In attending to latent functions and unanticipated consequences, it has described and analyzed many of the ways in which good intentions produce undesired results, and vice versa (Merton, 1957; Coser, 1975). It has shown how pervasive are instances in which systematic evasions become an unacknowledged part of institutional patterns (Williams, 1970: ch. IX). It has produced numerous studies of alienation (Seeman, 1975), has explored the sometimes strange workings of bureaucracies, has suggested that much "deviance" results from activities of agents of social control (Gibbs and Erickson, 1975), has indicated how ordinary political participation by the poor and less powerful can reinforce the control of the already powerful (Alford and Friedland, 1975). Such contributions may appear to some persons simply as explications of the "absurdity" of a particular social system or of human society in general (see Lyman and Scott, 1970). But in long-run and sober appraisal the result surely must be a more complex and steady view of social realities than can be found in either utopian or cynical orientations.

Our discussion already has implied that main influences upon understanding have come both from (1) *focused research findings* (e.g., Stouffer, *et al.*, 1949; J. Coleman, *et al.*, 1966) or practical diagnoses and (2) the *pervasive use of a few fundamental concepts and perspectives*.

The focused analyses of large data-sets in relation to important questions of social policy as in *The American Soldier* and *Equality of Educational Opportunity* have directly increased knowledge, and have stimulated debate and further illuminating research.

Examples of practical diagnosis include conditional predictions, which are not merely guesses later judged valid. A series of studies of intergroup relations between the late 1930's and the mid-1950's correctly anticipated the broad development of desegregation and the Civil Rights Movement. (A. L. Coleman, 1960; Pettigrew and Back, 1968: 700-701). The post-1964 urban civil disorders were not a surprise to the sociologists who were immersed in the field research during the 1950's and early 1960's (cf. Williams, 1964, 1965). Similarly Leonard S. Cottrell, Jr. was able to forecast with considerable specificity the responses of American troops to the defeat of Nazi Germany and to the end of World War II (Stouffer, *et al.*, 1949, Vol. II: 549-595).

The second type of influence has been the persuasive presentation of an altered or new view of the world through the medium of a small set of images and basic conceptual schemes.[7] This mode of affecting understanding has been massive, but also diffuse, slow, uneven, and often subtle. In the main, however, sociological analyses have shown human individuals as inherently members of groups. The relations of persons to one another are not to be understood as based upon an already given set of self-interests; rather, interests are culturally defined and include fraternal and communal commitments as an actual part of "self"-interests.

Emphasis upon culture, environment, learning, modifiability, open-system, internalization of social relations—all these lead to a conception of individuals as intimately, continuously, pervasively social. Personality is suffused with cultural content; social objects and relationships are "inside" as well as "outside" of the concrete person. "Society" is not only a matter of the Durkheimian exteriority and constraint; it is also marked by internalization and motivated expression.

To the extent that these conceptions have been taken seriously, it has become difficult to believe that moralistic condemnation and punitiveness toward individuals are the only or necessarily the best modes of dealing with normative deviance.

At the same time that sociology has been building an image of the interpenetration of personality, culture and society, it has steadily chipped away at the rock-bound fallacy that the properties of collectivities can be directly inferred from additive models of the characteristics of persons taken severally apart from the collective context. The empirical evidence for "contextual effects" is by now overwhelming (Williams, 1975a). And a *detailed* and *specific* understanding of the relational sources of collective phenomena means that one inevitably comes to recognize that social relationships and collectivities typically are not *ad hoc* entities but represent to an important degree real, empirical systems.

Yet the emphasis upon comprehensive concepts and system-properties has never submerged the strong empirical tradition. Granting many exceptions, it still seems clear that the main thrust of American sociology has been to insist upon data rather than to accept a priori beliefs or plausible assumptions; to be skeptical of sheer plausibility, no matter how eloquent or erudite or intuitively appealing; to reject dogmatic certainties in favor of probabilistic modes of thinking.

Influences of Sociological Work and Sociological Contributions upon American Life.

Whether or not sociology has affected American life in any important way, there is no doubt that many sociologists have earnestly tried to alter or maintain important features of that life. For example, concern about relevance of research and teaching to social policy and practical affairs has been continuously evident in the history of the field, from Ward's "telesis" to the "social R and D" of the 1970's (cf. Lazarsfeld, Sewell, Wilensky, 1967; Demerath, Larsen, Schuessler, 1975).

Appraisals by sociologists themselves of the uses of sociology constitute a continuous thread of commentary in the United States from the beginnings of the profession to the present. From the 1890's to the 1930's the commentaries for the most part necessarily dealt with potential rather than actual uses. There were, of course, some "applications," e.g., in social work, and in rural community programs, and in public education, but major efforts to "put sociology to work" can be dated roughly from the reports of the President's Research Committee on Social Trends (chaired by an economist, Wesley C. Mitchell; the director of research was a sociologist, William F. Ogburn). In more recent years, sociology has been one of the fields examined in several assessments of the status and prospects of the social sciences. Examples include: *The Use of Social Research in Federal Programs* (1967); *The Behavioral Sciences and the Federal Government* (1968); *The Behavorial and Social Sciences: Outlook and Needs* (1969); *Knowledge Into Action: Improving the Nation's Use of the Social Sciences* (1969).

Much has been learned from these (and from currently active) appraisals. Yet it is fair to say that specific causal knowledge of how particular social science activities affect the wider social scene still is scarce and uncertain. Pre-formed opinions on the matter are easier to find than factual descriptions or verified conclusions. Before we examine the fragmentary evidence, it may be useful to ask, what conceivable effects could occur as outcomes of sociological activities (such as research, teaching, advising and consulting, publishing)? Some of the possibilities are:

1. Sensitizing individuals *qua* individuals or as policy-makers and practitioners in various occupations and organizations to factors and relationships that otherwise would be unnoticed, unknown, or misjudged.

2. Providing factual descriptions and conceptual mapping of important features of social life, past and present, in our own society and elsewhere.

3. Pointing out erroneous assumptions and beliefs; exposing stereotypes and myths; "debunking."

4. Calling attention to hitherto unnoticed elements and relationships, e.g., latent functions, unanticipated consequences, counter-intuitive regularities, surprising outcomes, paradoxical relationships.

5. Re-conceptualizing the social world; providing new perspectives, e.g. white-collar crime, secondary deviance, "positive" features of conflict, cultural fictions, institutionalized evasion of institutional norms.

6. Specifying the location and prevalence of various beliefs, values, preferences and behavior patterns within and among organizations, communities, societies, or other collectivities.

7. Providing research methods, techniques and study designs for generating and analyzing information relevant to practical activities in medicine, education, industry, government, religion, and so on.

8. Providing accessible and suitably codified sociological information to decision-makers in all types of organizations and associations.

9. Measuring the outcomes of programs of action through sociologically informed research and assessment procedures (cf. Scott and Shore, 1974).

10. Analyzing ideologies and social programs to reveal logical structure, factual bases, relations to interests of various social formations, probable consequences.

11. Establishing systematic sets of empirical generalizations; establishing "laws" (nomothetic knowledge).

Once again, appraisal of influence requires a further disaggregation

of the types of research, teaching, consultation, and other applied activities. If we accept as sociology what it is that self-designated sociologists do, the field contains immense diversity of intellectual styles,
conceptual schemes, methodologies, and objectivities. That diversity
includes the three kinds of science described by Habermas (1971):
(1) *empirical-analytic*, aimed at law-like knowledge, (2) *historical
hermeneutic*, intending to influence practical affairs through communication of understanding, (3) *critical*, aimed at transforming society by
continuous skeptical and penetrating analysis of conditions blocking
emancipation (cf. Sherman, 1974). The empirical-analytic approach of
an O. D. Duncan (e.g., Duncan, Featherman, Duncan, 1972) surely is
poles apart from the "reflexive" sociology advocated by an Alvin Gouldner (1971). Obviously one cannot expect clear or consistent effects
upon the environing society from a field that itself incorporates practically the full range of political views and values and beliefs to be
found in that society.

As Odum has said, sociology answered to pervasive interests and
concerns in American society—if it had not existed something very like
it would have been invented. Sociological inquiries developed the
concepts to *identify* the aspects of the social world that entered into
the discourse of education, literature, history, and public debate. In
thus establishing basic categories of thought and action, " . . . sociology
has also contributed powerfully to the integration of American thought
and scholarship throughout the regions of the nation as well as to unifying the nation's efforts and ideologies in the major aspects of social
thought and social processes" (Odum, 1951:432-433). Part of this "integration" resulted from the gradual diffusion into semi-popular thought
of generic concepts applied across the whole range of concrete social life.

Sociology in America both reflects and shapes pervasive cultural
assumptions. "Reform" today is not the same as the nineteenth-century
reform and humanitarian movements in American cities, led and supported by merchants, other businessmen and professionals, who were
concerned with pauperism, vice, crime and the threat of social disorder
from the improverished urban masses. Consistently they defined these
social problems in terms of individual weakness and moral defect.
Through charity, moral indoctrination and organized discipline they
hoped to restore self-support and moral conformity, thereby maintaining urban order and the security of the established society. The narrow scope of their efforts reflected an individualistic-moralistic view
of society—a view which " . . . conveniently overlooked the social and
economic inequalities of the urbanizing, industrializing capitalistic environment" (Mohl, 1972:948). Although the orientations then dominant
are still present; their modification and attenuation surely stem in con-

siderable part from the facts and perspectives developed by social science.

Sociological research, even in the precursor form of the British social survey, sometimes had been a catalyst for legislation. Charles Booth's multi-volumed *Life and Labour of The People of London* (1889-1891) was " . . . the most detailed and large-scale social description ever achieved, which stirred up the contemporary social conscience and eventually led to the Old Age Pension Act of 1908, a legal minimum wage in the 'sweated' trades, state provision for the sick and disabled, and the start of unemployment insurance" (Lécuyer and Oberschall, 1968:44). In the United States, an example of equal clarity has not been put forward, but fairly direct relationships exist between descriptive studies of social problems and subsequent public actions aimed at melioration or reform (cf. Loomis and Loomis, 1968).

Sociologists have been active from the beginning of the profession in fact-finding and codification and interpretation of data for the use of many different kinds of agencies, groups and publics. The list of major cases is long, e.g., farm organizations; the Armed Services; school systems; religious denominations and interdenominational and interfaith associations; hospitals; prisons, business corporations; social service voluntary associations; federal and state and local departments and bureaus dealing with health and welfare; federal, state and local units of the Cooperative Agricultural Extension Service; legislatures; the courts. Data-gathering activities have ranged in scope from the U.S. Census to *ad hoc* local inquiries. Along with other fields of empirical social inquiry, sociology thus has had a part in the growth of public interest in and reliance upon the "facts of the case" as ascertained by relatively systematic and technically disciplined collection of data. To whatever extent American society now, more than in the past, esteems and relies upon objective evidence, the social sciences must be credited with much of the change.

The vague term "sociologists," of course, often serves to label a scapegoat or whipping-boy. The comment of Pettigrew and Back (1968:693) concerning the uses of sociological research on race relations in the 1960's seems generalizable to several other subfields: "The *disuse*, rather than the use, of sociology is more apparent; the attacks of segregationists upon the field are perhaps flattering in their assumptions, but are simply not valid. To paraphrase Churchill, seldom have so many abused one profession for so little." Yet as plausible as this interpretation is in the specific context indicated, it does not take into account the "elective affinity" (Weber) of ideas and knowledge with strong interests. Given the interests of all those who wished to end segregation, the record suggests that the cumulative effects of the sociology of intergroup relations are tangible and not trivial, even if the best research-based theories did consistently run ahead of either popular acceptance or effective use in public policy for most of the period of rapid change *circa* 1945-1975. For research, teaching, and consulting did affect public opinion and legislative, judicial and administrative conceptions and behavior in the fields of race relations and civil rights during the period from the mid-1930's to the 1970's (cf. Research and Technical Programs Subcommittee, 90th Congress, 1967:84).

The uses or influences of sociology sometimes have appeared in the emergence and development of new specialties in related fields. Thus in the case of social biology, the discrediting of the early "eugenics" (associated with some 31 state sterilization laws and with some extreme proponents of racialist doctrines) was a combined outcome of the newer scientific genetics and of the alternative interpretations supplied by anthropology, psychology, psychiatry, and sociology. Since the *Eugenics Quarterly* changed its name to *Social Biology*, in 1970, most of its authors have been social scientists [Markle and Fox, n.d. (c.1972):20].

On the other hand, there have been salient failures of attempted influence. For many years some sociologists have been pointing to the great empirical and theoretical importance of "noneconomic" factors in population mobility, e.g., noting social causes for the phenomenon of high rates of out-migration over long periods which do not remove high levels of under- and unemployment in depressed areas. Yet an apparently fixed belief that differentials in wages and other economic "opportunities" will produce adequate economically-adjustive mobility remains widespread (Sheppard, 1968:551-556; cf. Williams, 1940, 1941).

Along with workers in economics and political science, sociologists have been influential in improving both the collection and the analysis of important statistical data on a wide range of social phenomena, including population, race and ethnicity, education, employment, health, utilization of public services, income, expenditures, savings, trade, transportation, public lands, crime and delinquency, and welfare services (see Hauser, 1968).

A highly important development that largely dates from the early 1960's is the appearance of the statistically sophisticated analysis of large data-bases to reveal complex social processes. Especially noteworthy have been analyses of social stratification and mobility, population changes, educational outcomes, and organizational processes.

Many of the effects of sociology that informed observers believe have occurred have not been and cannot now be documented. One class of such putative effects results from numerous consultative and advisory relationships between sociologists and decision-makers—in education, religious organizations, the military, health and medical agencies, social work organizations, inter-group and minority action programs, unions, corporations, and so on. Anecdotal materials and personal observations suggest that influence through consultative processes has been fairly widespread, although only occasionally of decisive weight in such contexts (Demerath, Larsen, Schuessler, 1975; Lazarsfeld, Sewell, Wilensky, 1968; Stouffer, *et al.* 1949). (No quantitative estimates can be attached to "fairly widespread" or "only occasionally.")

Chapter 5 of *The Behavioral and Social Sciences: Outlook and Needs* (1969) gives an array of examples of contributions of behavioral sciences to practical affairs: city manager plans, the social security program, tests of abilities and aptitudes, the work of the Council of Economic Advisers. Sociologists are credited with helping devise the "point system" for Army demobilization after World War II and for policy-relevant appraisals of educational plans of veterans. Research on social stratification is noted as one example of how social science findings and concepts have permeated public understanding of social issues, resulting in more realistic and complex debates and appraisals.

For reasons that have been discussed extensively in sociology of knowledge, the social sciences necessarily are received with sharply different and often ambivalent appraisals by various audiences even within a generally permissive society. The very effort to carry out objective analysis is bound to be perceived as especially threatening by individuals and collectivities that engage in deception, secrecy, manipulation, and mystification. More importantly, all complex societies inevitably contain cultural inconsistencies, hypocrisies, cultural fictions, systemic evasions of institutionalized norms, symbiotic relations between vice and virtue, widespread inequities and injustices, e.g., well-rewarded violations of nominally dominant rules. A realistic, empirical sociology can not exist without bringing matters of this kind into the public domain.

Probably few social scientists who have had intensive experience in the federal or state governments doubt that a serious barrier to greater use of research in government is the sheer lack of knowledge about the actual relationships (a) between social knowledge and governmental policies and practices, and (b) between social scientific research and social knowledge. It is abundantly clear, however, that political processes represent struggles among diverse organizations, interest-groupings, decision-makers; it follows that sheer knowledge alone, or "disinterested search for truth," will never be determinative and often may be of minor significance.

If we desire to evaluate the outcome of some purposive social action —such as a statute, a court decision, an administrative program, a political appeal—it is easy to pose the research question in simple terms: did or did not the action produce a desired change in behaviour. But the whole history of the social sciences shows that such a question is grotesquely simplistic.

Leaving aside all the complex questions of defining independent variables and making causal inferences, the identification and measurement of the dependent variable ("behavior") always proves *necessarily* complex. For behavior may refer to both intended and unintended outcomes in the varied forms of changes in overt public conduct, private conduct, knowledge, beliefs, opinions, attitudes, values; any one of these may be considered in terms of many "formal" dimensions, e.g., prevalence, incidence, salience, intensity, congruence, consistency, closure, linkage, clarity, variability.

The first lesson of serious social science is, indeed, that things are more complicated than they seem at first appearance. The reason that this is not a banal lesson is that it has numerous nonobvious implications, e.g., that simple remedies will produce unanticipated and often undesired effects. A corollary of the main principle is that any particular social event or recurrent relationship is likely to have multiple connections with other events, relationships or structures. Not all the important connections will be evident to commonsense. Worse, some of the connections believed in the conventional wisdom to be obvious will not exist or will have effects opposite to those assumed. Because of extended linkages, indirect effects, multiple feedback loops and complex quantitative variations, social arrangements often have counterintuitive outcomes. Accordingly, unanticipated consequences and cognitive distortions are commonplaces in sociological analysis—but often come as surprises or "crazy notions" to common sense.

No matter how narrow or specific any one sociological study or any one sociologist may have been, the total sociological enterprise in the long run *was bound to make every aspect of society and culture problematic*. There could be no limits short of this for a discipline that conceived of a social reality *sui generis* and sought to explicate the structure and causal interconnections of the components of that reality.

Conclusion

Sociology is likely to remain for the foreseeable future a "multiple paradigm science" (Ritzer, 1974). Contrary to C. P. Snow's amazingly parochial image of Two Cultures, sociology along with its sister social sciences, represents a Third Culture. The Third Culture is one of pluralism, and change—of the democracy of diversity rather than the consensual establishment of Big Science or the traditional aristocracy of the Humanities. In the case of sociology, the diversity[8] arises, first, from the existence of three major kinds of *interests* in doing sociological work: (1) scientific interests in description, prediction and explanation of regularities in social behavior; (2) humanistic interests in appreciative, evaluative and expressive aspects; and (3) evaluative-action interests—*praxis* in the service of revolution, reform, or maintenance of social relationships. These interests partially coincide with and partially cut across major intellectual paradigms, e.g., Ritzer's (1974) classification of the images of (1) social facts, (structuralism, functionalism, conflict sociology); (2) social definitions (symbolic interactionism, action theory, labeling, phenomenological sociology); (3) social behavior (behaviorism, social exchange theory).

Two central problems of American society in the late twentieth and early twenty-first centuries are likely to be *the problem of externalities* and *the problem of collective action*. The first, of course, is the problem of social costs, of the "tragedy of the Commons," of the undesired aggregative consequences that result when each of a plurality of social units follows an individually advantageous course that entails a noxious side-effect, which cumulates to become severely disadvantageous to each severally or to all collectively (cf. Chipman, 1965). The second dilemma, "collective action," concerns the failure to engage in a collective action that entails a cost to each participant but will produce advantage for all—if enough members of the collectivity will participate. But if "enough" do participate, those who do not participate benefit disproportionately: this is the free-rider problem. The problem of externalities leads to collective disadvantages—the solutions for which are rendered even more difficult by the failure of collective action.

Both of these problems are empirically frequent and have large-scale and important consequences. The problem of externalities underlies environmental pollution and degradation, traffic congestion, overloads on energy-supplying systems (e.g., "brown-outs"), excessive population growth, depletion of fixed resources, and numerous specific social processes of interferences and congestion. The problem of collective action may arise in any effort to deal with any such problems by voluntary actions of individuals. Precisely *because* individually rational action *produces* the problems, individual rational action cannot be relied upon to solve them. The most obvious alternative often is seen as political, that is, legislative, judicial or administrative action invoking coercion. But as has been shown by sociological analyses from Durkheim to the present, sheer coercive power, unsupported by some substantial consensus, is costly and, in the extreme, largely unworkable. Limits of space preclude developing here the full argument, but it can be shown that coercion alone is not a solution. Enduring "solutions" require that both coercion and "individual" (unit) advantages be tied in with compliance with norms based on consensus and social identification generated through very pervasive and complex processes of interaction (Buckley, Burns, Meeker, 1974; cf. Parsons, 1951:29-45; 1967:3-34).

These processes require deepened understanding in the America of the future—and such life-and-death processes are not likely to respect academic disciplinary boundaries.

The successive separations of specialized fields of social science have occurred in diverse ways over a period of two centuries. What was initially an undifferentiated set of philosophical and scientific interests, slowly took the forms of "political economy," "moral philosophy," and "general social science." Anthropology from the first had the distinctive practical attributes that its practitioners traveled to foreign areas and studied exotic cultures. Economics separated from political science as the former developed an imposing formalization, a special accumulation of quantitative data, and distinctive foci of interest. History always had a secure traditional base as narrative, ideology, humanistic enterprise. Psychology had historical roots in both biological and social sciences. The interface of psychology and sociology is in principle a genuinely interdisciplinary field, similar in logical status to biochemistry but unlike the latter, uneasily pulled toward both poles.

Sociology often has seemed, to its own practitioners as well as to other observers, to be a residual field, dealing with the problems left aside by other special disciplines. This impression has been reinforced by the continuing emphases in sociology upon the study of topical social problems. Yet, anaytically considered, the impression is decidedly incorrect, even though partially descriptive as an image of the historical development. For many of the central concepts and analytical models now used in sociological research are increasingly of the kinds widely shared with other fields and essential to powerful empirical explanation. For all of our technical specialization, we find extensive use across disciplines of such concepts as norm, institution, social control (cf. Janowitz, 1976), stratification, deviance, or social values—in political science, economics of development, urban anthropology, welfare economics, and so on. The widespread interpenetration of ideas and methods of analysis is not primarily a manifestation of academic imperialism but of the logical pressures of requirements for comprehensive analysis of social systems. In terms of concepts, assumptions, explanatory paradigms and logic of investigation there are striking commonalities across cultural and social anthropology, welfare and developmental economics, social and cultural history, political science, social psychology, and sociology.

The special disciplines will, and should, remain. Indeed, new special-izations undoubtedly will develop separate organizational identities in the future. But at the same time there will continue a loosely-connected but increasingly coherent network of integrated, explanatory social sci-ence theory.

Notes

1. For instance: "The idea that social topics could be subjected to quantita-tive analyses first acquired prominence in England in the latter half of the seventeenth century" (Lecuyer and Oberschall 1968:36).

2. "From the Founding Fathers of the Republic to the founding fathers of sociology there is a straight line of compulsive hope" (Rosenberg, 1963:4).

3. The interweaving of American experience with exposure to European thought is nicely brought out in the autobiographical accounts of Thomas and Park; see Baker (1973).

4. "Thus an idea born in the sphere of politics migrated to economics, was specialized in demography, and taken over and applied to biology. It was now ready to return to the field of general sociology, serving as the basis for one of the main types of conflict theory in modern times" (Martindale, 1960:147).

5. ". . . the stalwarts of early American sociology—Sumner, Ward, Giddings, Small, Ross, Cooley—whatever else they may have been, were pretty well con-taminated by worldly affairs" (Odum, 1951).

6. Cf. Odum (1960:421): "If early sociology was ameliorative and practical and non-sophisticated in general, it still reflected the powerful struggle of the intellectuals of a new society with growing pains trying to evolve a social science that would help solve its problems."

7. The widespread and varying uses of the concept of "culture" in the social sciences are sketched in the several articles grouped under the heading "The Idea of Culture in the Social Sciences" in *Social Science Quarterly*, 1972, 53 (September): 221-392.

8. In this diversity arise some of the intense preoccupations with the soci-ology of sociology; as early as 1967 there were over 250 articles on the subject and the output continues. As Dynes says it seems astonishing "that one of the smallest occupational groups could command such inordinate attention" (Dynes, 1974:169).

References

Abrams, P. 1968. The Origins of British Sociology: 1834-1914 (Chicago and London: University of Chicago Press).

Advisory Committee on Government Programs in the Behavorial Sciences, National Research Council. 1968. The Behavorial Sciences and the Federal Government (Washington, D.C.: National Academy of Sciences).

Alford, R. R. and R. Friedland, 1975. "Political Participation and Public Policy," in A. Inkeles, J. Coleman, N. Smelser, eds., Annual Review of Sociology, 1 (Palo Alto, California: Annual Reviews, Inc.): 429-479.

Atkinson, D. 1971. Orthodox Consensus and Radical Alternatives: A Study in Sociological Theory (London: Heinemann Educational Books).

Baker, P. J. 1973, "The Life Histories of W. I. Thomas and Robert E. Park," American Journal of Sociology, 79 (September): 243-260.

Bash, H. W. 1974. Review of Dick Atkinson, Orthodox Consensus and Radical Alternatives, Contemporary Sociology, 3 (November): 484.

Ben-David, J. and R. Collins. 1966. "Social Factors in the Origins of a New Science: The Case of Psychology," American Sociological Review, 31 (August): 451-465.

––– and T. A. Sullivan. 1975. "Sociology of Science," in Inkeles, et al., 1975: 203-222.

Bernard, L. L. and J. Bernard. 1943. Origins of American Sociology: The Social Science Movement in the United States (New York: Thomas Y. Crowell).

Blackwell, J. E. and M. Janowitz, 1974. Black Sociologists: Historical and Contemporary Perspectives (Chicago: University of Chicago Press).

Bordua, D. J. and A. J. Reiss, Jr. 1968. "Law Enforcement," in P. F. Lazarsfeld, W. H. Sewell, H. L. Wilensky, eds., The Uses of Sociology (London: Weidenfeld and Nicolson): 275-303.

Bottomore, T. 1975. "Competing Paradigms in Macrosociology," in Inkeles, et al., 1975: 191-202.

Bowers, R. V. 1968. "The Military Establishment," in Lazarsfeld, et al., 1968: 234-274.

Buckley, W., T. Burns, L. D. Meeker. 1974. "Structural Resolutions of Collective Action Problems," Behavioral Science, 19 (September): 277-297.

Chipman, J. S. 1965. "The Meaning and Nature of Equilibrium," in D. Martindale, ed., Functionalism in the Social Sciences, Monograph No. 5 (Philadelphia: American Academy of Political and Social Science): 35-64.

Cole, J. R. and H. Zuckerman. 1975. "The Emergence of a Scientific Speciality: The Self-Exemplifying Case of the Sociology of Science," in L. A. Coser, ed., The Idea of Social Structure: Papers in Honor of Robert K. Merton (New York: Harcourt, Brace, Jovanovich): 139-174.

Coleman, A. L. 1960. "Social Scientists' Predictions about Desegregation, 1950-1955," Social Forces, 38: 258-262.

Coleman, J. S., E. Q. Campbell, C. J. Hobson, J. McPartland, A. M. Mood, F. D. Weinfeld and R. L. York. 1966. Equality of Educational Opportunity (Washington, D.C.: U. S. Government Printing Office).

Commager, H. S. 1951. Living Ideas in America (New York: Harper and Brothers.)

Coser, L. A., ed. 1975. The Idea of Social Structure: Papers in Honor of Robert K. Merton (New York: Harcourt, Brace, Jovanovich.)

Demerath, N. J. III, O. Larsen, K. F. Schuessler, eds. 1975. Social Policy and Sociology (New York: Academic Press.)

Deutsch, K. W., J. Platt, D. Senghaas. 1971. "Conditions Favoring Major Advances in Social Science," Science, 171 (5 February): 450-459.

DuBois, W. E. B. 1899. The Philadelphia Negro: A Social Study (Philadelphia: University of Pennsylvania).

Duncan, O. D., D. L. Featherman, B. Duncan, 1972. Socioeconomic Background and Achievement (New York: Seminar Press).

Dynes, R. R. 1974. "Sociology as a Religious Movement: Thoughts on Its Institutionalization in the United States," American Sociologist, 9 (November): 169-176.

Eisenstadt, S. N. 1968. "Sociology: Development of Sociological Thought," in D. L. Sills, ed., International Encyclopedia of the Social Sciences, 15 (New York: Macmillan and Free Press): 25-36.

Faris, R. E. L. 1970. Chicago Sociology: 1920-1932 (Chicago: University of Chicago Press).

Galambos, L. 1969. "Parsonian Sociology and Post Progressive History," Social Science Quarterly, 50 (June): 25-45.

Gibbs, J. P. and M. L. Erickson. 1975. "Major Developments in the Sociological Study of Deviance," in Inkeles, et al., 1975: 21-42.

Glenn, N. D. and D. Weiner. 1969. "Some Trends in The Social Origins of American Sociologists," American Sociologist, 4 (November): 291-302.

Gouldner, A. 1971. The Coming Crisis of Western Sociology (London: Heinemann Educational Books).

Guerlac, H. 1974. "History of Science: 3. The Landmarks of the Literature," The Times Literary Supplement (April 26): 449-450.

Gumplowicz, L. 1892. Die soziologishe Staatsidee (Graz, Austria: Leuschner & Lubensky).

Guttman, L. 1950. Chs. 2, 3, 6, 8 and 9 in S. A. Stauffer, L. Guttman, E. A. Suchman, P. F. Lazarsfeld, S. A. Star and J. A. Clausen. 1950. Studies in Social Psychology in World War II, Volume IV: Measurement and Prediction (Princeton, New Jersey: Princeton University Press): 46-90, 172-212, 277-361.

Habermas, J. 1971. Knowledge and Human Interests (Boston: Beacon Press).

Hauser, P. 1968. "Social Accounting," in P. F. Lazarsfeld, W. H. Sewell, H. L. Wilensky, eds., The Uses of Sociology (London: Weidenfeld and Nicolson): 839-875.

Hinkle, R. C., Jr. and G. J. Hinkle. 1954. The Development of Modern Sociology: Its Nature and Growth in the United States (Garden City, N. Y.: Doubleday and Company).

Hollander, P. 1969. American and Soviet Society: A Reader in Comparative Sociology and Perception (Englewood Cliffs, N. J.: Prentice-Hall).

Hyman, M. D. 1968. "Medicene," in Lazarsfeld, et al., 1968: 119-155.

Inkeles, A. 1964. What Is Sociology? An Introduction to the Discipline and Profession (Englewood Cliffs, NJ.: Prentice-Hall).

Inkeles, A., J. Coleman, N. Smelser, eds. 1975. Annual Review of Sociology, Volume 1 (Palo Alto, California: Annual Reviews, Inc.)

Janowitz, M. 1976. Social Control of the Welfare State (New York: Elsevier Scientific Publishing Company).

Johnson, H. M. 1969. "The Relevance of the Theory of Action to Historians," Social Science Quarterly, 50 (June): 46-58.

Krause, T. 1974. "Interspeciality Utilization in Sociology," Dissertation Abstracts International, 35 (2).

———. 1972, "Social and Intellectual Structures of Science," Science Studies, 2: 369-393.

Laumann, E. O. and L. Guttman, 1966. "The Relative Associational Contiguity of Occupations in an Urban Setting," American Sociological Review, 31 (April): 169-178.

Lazarsfeld, P. F. and N. W. Henry. 1968. Latent Structure Analysis (New York: Houghton Mifflin).

Lazarsfeld, P. F., W. H. Sewell and H. L. Wilensky, eds. 1968. The Uses of Sociology (London: Weidenfeld and Nicolson).

Lécuyer, B. and A. R. Oberschall. 1968. "Sociology: The Early History of Social Research," in D. L. Sills, ed., International Encyclopedia of the Social Sciences, 15 (New York: Macmillan and Free Press): 36-53.

Lehmann, W. C. 1968. "Ferguson, Adam" in D. L. Sills, ed., International Encyclopedia of the Social Sciences, 5 (New York: Macmillan and Free Press): 369-371.

Lengermann, P. M. 1974. The Definition of Sociology: An Historical Approach (Columbus, Ohio: Charles Merrill and Sons).

Lipset, S. M. 1963. The First New Nation (New York: Basic Books).

Loomis, C. P. and Z. K. Loomis. 1968. "Rural Sociology," in Lazarsfeld, et al., 1968: 655-691.

Lyman, S. and M. Scott, eds. 1970. A Sociology of the Absurd (New York: Appleton-Century-Crofts).

Markle, G. E. and J. W. Fox, n.d. "Paradigms on Public Relations: The Case of Social Biology," Center for Sociological Research, Western Michigan University; processed paper.

Marsh, R. 1967. Comparative Sociology (New York: Harcourt, Brace and World).

Martindale, D. 1960. The Nature and Types of Sociological Theory (Boston: Houghton Mifflin).

Merton, R. K. 1957. Social Theory and Social Structure (New York: The Macmillan Company).

Mitchell, G. D., ed. 1968. A Hundred Years of Sociology (Chicago: Aldine).

———. 1970. "Sociology—An Historical Phenomenon," in P. Halmos, ed., The Sociology of Sociology, Sociological Review Monograph 16 (Keele: University of Keele, September): 129-149.

Mohl, R. A. 1972. "Poverty, Pauperism and Social Order in the Preindustrial American City, 1780-1840," Social Science Quarterly, 52 (March): 934-948.

Odum, H. W. 1951. American Sociology: The Story of Sociology in the United States through 1950 (New York: Longmans, Green).

Parrington, V. L. 1930. Main Currents in American Thought, Book III (New York: Harcourt, Brace).

Parsons, T. 1951. The Social System (Glencoe, Ill.: Free Press).

———. 1967. Sociological Theory and Modern Society (New York: Free Press).

Pettigrew, T. F. and K. W. Back. 1968. "Sociology in the Desegregation Process: Its Use and Disuse," in Lazarsfeld, *et al.*, 1968: 692-722.

Reiss, A. J., Jr. 1968. "Sociology: The Field," in D. Sills, ed., International Encyclopedia of the Social Sciences, 15 (New York: Macmillan and Free Press): 1-23.

Research and Technical Programs Subcommittee of the Committee on Government Operations, 90th Congress, U. S. House of Representatives, 1967. The Use of Social Research in Federal Domestic Programs. Parts I, II, III, IV (Washington, D. C.: U. S. Government Printing Office).

Ritzer, G. 1975. "Sociology: A Multiple Paradigm Science," American Sociologist, 10 (August): 156-167.

Rocher, G. 1975. Talcott Parsons and American Sociology (New York: Barnes and Noble).

Rosenberg, Bernard, ed. 1963. Thorstein Veblen (New York: Thomas Y. Crowell Company).

Schermerhorn, R. A. 1970. Comparative Ethnic Relations (New York: Random House).

Schneider, L., ed. 1967. The Scottish Moralists (Chicago: University of Chicago Press).

———. 1969. "On Frontiers of Sociology and History: Observations on Evolutionary Development and Unanticipated Consequences," Social Science Quarterly, 50 (June): 6-24.

———. 1975. "Ironic Perspective and Sociological Thought", in L. A. Coser, ed., The Idea of Social Structure: Papers in Honor of Robert K. Merton (New York: Harcourt, Brace, Jovanovich): 323-337.

Seeman, M. 1975. "Alienation Studies," in Inkeles, *et al.*, 1975: 91-123.

Sheppard, H. L. 1968. "Unemployment, Manpower, and Area Development," in Lazarsfeld, *et al.*, 1968: 544-566.

Sherman, L. W. 1974. "Uses of the Masters," American Sociologist, 9 (November): 176-181.

Special Commission on the Social Sciences of the National Science Board. 1969. Knowledge Into Action: Improving the Nation's Use of the Social Sciences (Washington, D. C.: National Science Foundation).

Spengler, J. J. 1972. "Veblen on Population and Resources," Social Science Quarterly, 52: 861-878.

Stinchcombe, A. L. 1975. "Merton's Theory of Social Structure," in L. A. Coser, ed., The Idea of Social Structure: Papers in Honor of Robert K. Merton (New York: Harcourt, Brace, Jovanovich, Inc.): 11-33.

Stouffer, S. A., E. A. Suchman, L. C. DeVinney, S. A. Star and R. M. Williams, Jr. 1949. The American Soldier, Volume I (Princeton, New Jersey: Princeton University Press)

Stouffer, S. A., A. S. Lumsdaine, M. H. Lumsdaine, R. M. Williams, Jr., M. B. Smith, I. L. Janis, S. A. Star and L. S. Cottrell, Jr. 1949. The American Soldier, Volume II (Princeton, New Jersey: Princeton University Press).

Strieb, G. F. and H. L. Orbach. 1968. "Aging," in Lazarsfeld, *et al.*, 1968: 612-640.

Suchman, E. A. 1968. "Public Health," in Lazarsfeld, *et al.*, 1968: 567-611.

Tarascio, V. J. 1975. "Intellectual History and the Social Sciences: The Problem of Methodological Pluralism," Social Science Quarterly, 56 (June): 37-54.

The Behavioral and Social Sciences Survey Committee, National Academy of Sciences and Social Science Research Council. 1969. The Behavioral and Social Sciences: Outlook and Needs (Englewood Cliffs, N. J.: Prentice-Hall).

Wellek, R. and A. Warren. 1949. Theory of Literature (New York: Harcourt, Brace and Company).

Williams, R. M., Jr. 1940. "Concepts of Marginality in Rural Population Studies," Rural Sociology, 5 (September): 292-302.

———. 1947. The Reduction of Intergroup Tensions (New York: Social Science Research Council).

———. 1957. "Racial and Cultural Relations," in J. B. Gittler, ed., Review of Sociology: Analysis of a Decade (New York: John Wiley and Sons): 423-464.

———. 1965. "Social Change and Social Conflict: Race Relations in the United States, 1944-1964," Sociological Inquiry, 35 (Winter): 8-25.

———. 1968-1969. "Sociology and Social Change in the United States," Studies in Comparative International Development, IV (7): 151-161.

———. 1970. American Society: A Sociological Interpretation (New York: Alfred A. Knopf).

———. 1972. "Conflict and Social Order: A Research Strategy for Complex Propositions," Journal of Social Issues, 28 (No. 1): 11-26.

———. 1975a. "Relative Deprivation," in L. A. Coser, ed., The Idea of Social Structure: Papers in Honor of Robert K. Merton (New York: Harcourt, Brace, Jovanovich): 355-378.

———. 1975b. "Racial and Cultural Relations," in Inkeles, *et al.*, 1975: 125-164.

Zeitlin, M., ed. 1970. American Society, Inc.: Studies in the Social Structure and Political Economy of the United States (Chicago: Markham).

Understanding Political Life in America:

The Contribution of Political Science

HEINZ EULAU

Stanford University

Contemporary political science is a congeries of fields and subfields, of approaches and methods, of theories and discoveries. Its status as a "discipline" is largely a metaphor; its status as a "science" is a possibility.[1]

Within this heterogeneous enterprise, the study of *American* politics as a specialization has made the most progress toward valid and reliable knowledge. In this field, the quarter century following the end of the Second World War has been a period of such unprecedented creativity and productivity that much of the earlier work can be considered obsolete. There are "classics," of course, still deserving and, indeed requiring attention.[2] But in the decades through the tranquil 1950's and noisy 1960's, influenced by the interdisciplinary movement in the behavioral sciences generally, new and noteworthy contributions were made to scientific knowledge about political behavior, processes, institutions and policies in the United States. It is with this new knowledge that I shall deal in this essay.[3]

In reviewing what is an impressive record, my intent is not to be exhaustive in a bibliographic sense or to be exclusive in a disciplinary sense. But as this essay is to be an appraisal of the impact of distinctive major contributions by *American* scholars on our understanding of *American* society, I shall attend only to those research studies generally considered seminal or influential, that is, as having enlightened a particular topic either by way of novel theory, novel method or novel substance. At the same time, to give continuity in research its due, I shall occasionally refer to the work of both predecessors and successors where it seems appropriate. The approach will be mainly but not rigidly chronological; itemistic rather than systematic. The attempt is made to convey to the reader a feeling of how the last two decades and a half appeared to a participant observer.

Perhaps something should be said about what this essay will intentionally not do. First, it will ignore various intramural intellectual conflicts over theory or method that are of interest only to some (and usually few) political scientists. While these conflicts have at times been fierce, they have had very little effect on most of the research that seriously deals with American politics. Second, the essay will not take account of the professional and institutional development of political science in American colleges and universities, again because it is not directly germane to the task at hand. Of course, much of the research on American politics could not and would not have been carried out if it had not been for public and private support given to individual scholars, professional associations, research organizations and conferences; but detailed reference to these relationships is not needed in this connection. Third, much as I am tempted especially on this occasion, nothing will be said about the impact of political science as a learned profession or scientific discipline on practical politics or public policy. There are two reasons for this purposeful neglect: first, good empirical evidence for judging the impact of political science in the real world of politics is difficult to come by; and second, the normative issues are so complex that assessment would require an essay of a quite different sort than designed here. My concern is therefore exclusively with impact on understanding within disciplined inquiry.[4]

However, even in regard to this last restriction some disclaimer is in order. While I shall stress what are variously called seminal, pioneering or innovative studies, these works must be seen in context so that no undue expectations be entertained as to either their scientific value or practical usefulness. The question asked by the phantom politician of the phantom political scientist, "What have you discovered lately, and of what use is it to my district?," is sometimes taken only all too seriously, even by political scientists stung by the bug of "relevance."[5] I agree with John C. Wahlke (1975:9), speaking here of research on legislatures but addressing a wider issue, that

> the knowledge we have is exceedingly incremental. What we know has grown by accretion of numerous bits and pieces; we can point to no striking "breakthroughs" or major discoveries that have increased or changed our understanding in dramatic or revolutionary fashion. Although there are obvious differences of quality and value among the many studies extant, few represent critical turning points or major landmarks.

Moreover, because some works are characterized as turning points or landmarks, this need not mean that they are necessarily the "best" from the perspective of either research execution or literary merit. On one hand, it is sometimes the ironical fate of "bad" research or "bad" writing to be pioneering or even classical because it inspires, but is also overcome by, subsequent research or writing that corrects the original work's mistakes and failures. On the other hand, excellent or very good books may not have much impact at all in the sense of orienting research or thinking in new directions. Quite a few books

of this type were published in the years since World War II, but I shall
not examine them. Hopefully, their authors will forgive me.

I also hope to be forgiven by those scholars who, in the years covered here, produced significant research of a landmark character that
never reached the "book stage." I might mention Herbert McClosky's
important work on leaders and followers (McClosky, Hoffman and
O'Hara, 1960; McClosky, 1964); Warren E. Miller and Donald E.
Stokes' interesting work on representation (Miller and Stokes, 1963;
Miller, 1964); or Ralph Huitt's studies in the Congress (Huitt and
Peabody, 1969). These studies, and several others conducted on a more
modest scale, published in the journals of political science, contributed
to the changing perspectives on American politics but will elude the
wide net cast in this survey.

The Chicago Influence: 1947-1951

That the present is ever a continuation of the past, no matter how
modern it may appear to contemporaries, is evident in a number of
important contributions which in the post-war years initiated new
approaches to understanding in different sub-fields of American government and politics. Five of these works, published in yearly succession,
were penned by scholars who had received their training at the University of Chicago. There, from the mid-1920's on, Charles E. Merriam
and his colleagues, notably Harold D. Lasswell and Harold F. Gosnell,
had begun to teach a new "more scientific" political science (see Karl,
1974). V. O. Key, Jr. had received his Ph.D. at Chicago in 1934; C. Herman Pritchett in 1937; Gabriel A. Almond in 1938; David B. Truman in
1939; and Herbert A. Simon in 1943.[6]

Simon was the first to publish what in the short run was an out-
rageously disturbing and in the long run turned out to be an astound-
ingly suggestive work. *Administrative Behavior: A Study of
Decision-Making Processes in Administrative Organization* (Simon,
1947), influenced by Chester I. Barnard (1938), was a fundamental
critique of those "proverbs of administration" whose conventional acceptance and use had for long precluded realistic views and appraisals
of administrative and organizational processes. Insisting on the difference in the cognitive and empirical status of facts and values, Simon
seemed once more to introduce the separation of policy and administration that had been rejected as unrealistic and undesirable. In fact, Simon
clarified confused notions in both the older approach and the newer
trends. Rationality as a criterion of administrative decision-making is
predicated on the construction of means-ends chains that defy clean

and orderly distinctions between policy formulation and execution. Simonian concepts like "bounded rationality" and "satisficing" (rather than "maximizing") have become household words in a new field called "organizational behavior" that has largely replaced the old public administration as an autonomus theoretical enterprise. As I wrote some years ago,

> public administration was increasingly seen as merely an arena of public action where, just as in private arenas, it was possible to study generic processes of bureaucracy, decision-making, and organizational behavior. But most of the interesting work along these lines was not done by political scientists but by sociologists and social psychologists as well as by a new species of specialists called "organization theorists." When James G. March and Herbert A. Simon published their inventory of relevant hypotheses, *Organizations* (1958), only a handful of political scientists were listed in their comprehensive bibliography (Eulau, 1970: 194).

If Simon buried the conventional study of public administration and linked up with organizational analysis in other disciplines, just the opposite occurred in the sub-field of public law which, beginning with a pathbreaking study by C. Herman Pritchett, *The Roosevelt Court* (1948), gradually freed itself from bondage to the lawyers. Earlier, under the impact of "sociological jurisprudence" and "legal realism" the Supreme Court had come to be recognized as a political institution and a policy-maker in its own right. What Pritchett did in his first work and also in a later study of the Vinson Court (Pritchett, 1954) was to refine the view of the Court as a political institution by demonstrating, through a technique known as bloc analysis,[7] that the justices formed coalitions, and that their positions could be predicted from attitude-scaling their opinions in non-unanimous decisions. The influence of Pritchett's work on the next generation of researchers was pervasive.

Of those who, in the 1920's and 1930's, had made the Chicago Department unsafe for conventional political science, none had been busier and more productive than Harold F. Gosnell. In a series of studies, some using the most advanced statistical techniques available at the time, Gosnell had undertaken careful and minute, even experimental investigations of electoral and party behavior (Gosnell, 1927). He found a worthy successor in V. O. Key, Jr., probably the most widely respected student of American politics in the century (see Garceau, 1968). Key had already published the first edition of what would be the leading textbook in American politics for the next 25 years (Key, 1942). *Southern Politics in State and Nation* (Key, 1949) was a model of painstaking field research and commitment to factual detail; but it was also a work whose perspicacious analysis obliterated the stereotypic view of Southern as one-party politics. True, the Democratic Party was dominant, but Southern politics was by no means as monolithic as commonly believed. Key discovered great variations in party patterns and voting behavior among and within the Southern states. His regional approach was followed by regional studies elsewhere (Fenton, 1957, 1966; Lockard, 1959), and Key himself published a (more limited) sequel for the North (Key, 1956). *Southern Politics* remains a source of many hypotheses about the functioning of the American party and electoral systems, notably the impact of competition on public policies, that continue to occupy empirical researchers to this day.[8]

Lasswell's influence on the early post-war behavioralists became perhaps first apparent in Gabriel A. Almond's *The American People and Foreign Policy* (1950). Public opinion had been talked about a great deal since Walter Lippmann's famous book of the early 1920's (Lippmann, 1922), but its empirical study had to await the perfection of the survey interview and of sampling statistics. An analysis of the sociological and psychological factors influencing public opinion on foreign policy, Almond's study discovered the centrality of "attentive publics" in the flow of mass communications, described the opinion environment in which foreign policy decisions are made, traced historic trends in the American political culture for possible prediction of responses, and identified the public's shifting attitudes on foreign policy as "moods" having their roots more in affective than cognitive processes of the mind. Almond's study was the first in what became a long line of increasingly perceptive studies of the political participation potential of citizens. Almond himself subsequently made two other important contributions to this genre of research (Almond, 1954; Almond and Verba, 1963).

The monotony of the Chicago influence was broken by an impressive study of the legislative process, Stephen K. Bailey's *Congress Makes a Law: A Study of the Full Employment Act of 1946* (1950). It was the first comprehensive, and probably remains the best, of all the case studies that pursue, step by step, the progress of a piece of legislation from conception to enactment. Although Bailey referred to his approach as a "vector analysis"—the vectors being ideas, institutions, interests, and individuals whose interaction creates the legislative maze —*Congress Makes a Law* did not seem to be overtly influenced by the behavioral movement but was researched and written in the tradition of the mechanical pressure-group model of American politics.[9] Bailey presented an empirically rich description of the policy-making process in Congress that focused on all participants, those who pressured and those who were pressured, their presuppositions and conduct. The work was symptomatic of the changing character of political research beyond the Chicago circle.

Bailey's mechanical metaphor of the "vector" is absent from David B. Truman's enormously influential study of interest groups in American society, *The Governmental Process* (1951), which supports the view that the behavioral movement in political science was more a renaissance than a revolution (see Eulau, 1969a). Reaching back to where an obscure scholar, Arthur F. Bentley (1908), had left the study of social groups, but also relying on current group and attitude psychology, Truman painted a rich canvas of American associational life and its interface with the network of governmental institutions. So great was the persuasiveness of Truman's masterful synthesis that it had the paradoxical effect of (a) being widely accepted as a true description and viable interpretation of the American pluralist system of politics, and (b) not really stimulating as much or the kind of empirical research that one might have expected from so magisterial a work. Despite recent attacks on Truman's (and other pluralists') theory for not anticipating the revolt of black people in the ghettos, the resistance of the young to the Vietnam War, or the attempt at liberation of middle-class women, Truman's work has not been matched by any effort similar in analytic depth or in extent of substantive coverage.

With Truman's work closes the first phase of the post-war rejuvenation in the study of American politics. There were straws in the wind elsewhere that political science was undergoing profound changes in all of its fields. There were rumblings in comparative and international politics. Harold Lasswell, in collaboration with Abraham Kaplan, published *Power and Society* (1950), setting the tone of discourse for two decades. But the behavioral breakthrough had come in the field of American politics. It was a belated development. The war had temporarily silenced the Chicago message; yet it had also helped in bringing political scientists into closer contact with political reality and with other social scientists (see Dahl, 1961). Whatever might have been, the fact is that in the short period of five years the study of American politics had been reoriented in new directions by a few works that remain eminently modern.

The Deceptive Decade: 1952-59

Linear extrapolation and geometric progression are not reliable guides in estimating scientific research output. If they were, one might have predicted more significant research reporting than did actually occur in the years following the Chicago impact. Why it did not occur is a matter of speculation. Perhaps the Chicagoans had been so much ahead of the times that a gap was bound to develop; it would require time for their work to be emulated and extended. It is true that the Chicagoans had a jump on the rest of the profession, but there were some among the rest, not trained at Chicago, who were about to continue the discipline's innovative push. In fact, then, the quantitatively low output of the 1950's was deceptive and concealed the ferment of those years. There was much research planning, much research conferencing, much research "re-tooling" and, indeed, much researching.[10] The journals sometimes published preliminary or partial analyses of significant work in process. But few projects reached the stage where they could be reported in final form.

An impression not uncommon at the time, and a source of misunderstanding to this day, was that the post-war scientific movement in political science, initially referred to as "political behavior approach" and later as "political behavioralism,"[11] was an off-shoot of the "behaviorism" that had been the dominant mode in psychology during the 1920's; or that it was especially beholden to the influence of psychoanalysis.[12] In fact, it was sociology and to a lesser extent economic theory which, in the course of the 1950's, would influence the behavioral orientation in political science.[13] This is not to minimize the influence of psychology in general, and especially of social psychology, in the work on voting behavior that would soon become prominent; but precisely because the behavioral movement was influenced by social psychology, one must not neglect the impact of sociology and economics (and later, by way of the concept of culture, of social anthropology).

It seems to me that political scientists in appraising the state or development of their knowledge about American political institutions and processes have been most cavalier in their treatment of the contribution made by political sociology, and especially by the group of sociologists associated with Columbia University in the late 1940's and 1950's. However, the work of this group has never been seen as a whole.[14] This may be due to the fact that most of them subsequently moved into other subject-matter areas. But in a score of years or so, theoretically significant, methodologically sophisticated and substantively solid contributions highly relevant to an understanding of American political life were made by faculty members and students connected with the Columbia Department of Sociology.

There was Philip Selznick who, in a truly epochal work, *TVA and the Grassroots* (1949), explored the participatory potential of citizens in bureaucratic environments and introduced the concept of cooptation into political discourse. There was C. Wright Mills whose social-structural analyses (1951), and especially his *The Power Elite* (1956), were widely discussed. There came, in due course, *Union Democracy* by Lipset, Trow and Coleman (1956) which, by the indirect route of a deviant case analysis, examined the tendency of democratic organizations to turn into oligarchies. There were others in the Columbia group who dealt with explicitly political themes (Gouldner, 1954; Blau, 1955; Coleman, 1956, 1961; Coser, 1956; Sills, 1957; Rosenberg, 1957; Hyman, 1959; Selvin, 1960).

However, for political science the immediately most significant work to come out of Columbia was a study of citizen voting behavior conducted in the up-state New York city of Elmira during the 1948 presidential election campaign. *Voting*, by Bernard Berelson, Paul F. Lazarsfeld and William N. McPhee (1954), along with its famed predecessor study, *The People's Choice* (Lazarsfeld, Berelson and Gaudet, 1944), and a successor study, *Public Opinion and Congressional Elections* (McPhee and Glaser, 1962), remains unexcelled as a social-structural and contextual analysis of electoral decision-making. All three volumes introduced or pursued a variety of suggestive hypotheses about the factors influencing the voting act—the activation hypothesis (voters are activated and their preferences reinforced by the campaign rather than converted); the cross-pressure hypothesis (over-lapping memberships in social groups reduce political interest and commitment); the two-step flow of communication hypothesis (the effect of the mass media is channeled through opinion leaders rather than direct); the crystallization hypothesis (the voter's choice emerges gradually through time and is not a rational decision); the reference group hypothesis (voters follow in their vote choice significant others and especially those in their primary environment like family members, work associates, etc.); or the breakage effect hypothesis (voter perceptions and preferences are partly determined by structural or compositional effects, i.e., a person inclined to vote Democratic on other grounds will vote Republican if he is surrounded by Republicans).

Enormously significant for the changing focus of the discipline away from formal institutional to behavioral analysis was the series of biennial national election studies begun in 1952 by the Survey Research Center and later continued by the Center for Political Studies of the Institute of Social Research, University of Michigan. A first publication, *The Voter Decides* (Campbell, Gurin and Miller, 1954), introduced the trilogy of party identification, issue orientation and candidate image as the variables that remain basic in voting research. The book's importance as a source of new knowledge concerning citizen behavior is easy to underestimate because it was overshadowed, in due course, by a successor work (Campbell, Converse, Miller and Stokes, 1960), that was to have more of a landmark character. But, at the time of publication, *The Voter Decides* was by all odds the first national study of a single election that was based on a wide array of questions concerning citizen behavior.[15]

At an altogether different front there were the first rumblings toward a new "political economy" which, in the 1960's, gave rise to an interest in "public choice" and "public policy." Although not directly concerned with the American scene, political scientist Robert A. Dahl and economist Charles E. Lindblom, in *Politics, Economics and Welfare* (1953), undertook a theoretical but empirically grounded exploration of alternative types of societal decision-making: polyarchy, hierarchy, bargaining, and market pricing. Pursuing these themes from the point of view of both organizational control and policy consequences, Dahl and Lindblom not only laid the groundwork for their own individual prolific and erudite later work (Dahl, 1956, 1967; Lindblom, 1965) but also for an entire later generation. If this very important work no longer looms in contemporary discussion, it may be due to its having become a classic—its message so absorbed into contemporary scholarship that reference is no longer necessary.[16] This is a pity because the work seems to me insufficiently exploited as a source of ideas and hypotheses about the interface of politics and economics.

Compared with the complex and, one might say, leisurely argument of Dahl and Lindblom's work, Anthony Downs' *An Economic Theory of Democracy* (1957) had something of a shock affect, and the shock continues to reverberate through the discipline. An enthusiastic admirer, himself an innovator of note, referred to Downs' thesis as "one of the few significant attempts to develop a formal, positive political theory and certainly one of the half-dozen outstanding works of political theory in this century" (Riker, 1962: 33). As is the secret of theories that remain influential, Downs' model of citizen, politician and party behavior was sufficiently incomplete, even false, to stimulate a generation's efforts to correct and extend it.

What to political scientists was shocking was Downs' unabashed deductive, normative positivism. Downs sought to predict or explain what policies the government would actually follow after having been advised about what alternative policies were feasible. To this problem Downs applied simple, familiar assumptions about rationality, ordered preferences and utility maximization, and he speculated about the effects of uncertainty and information costs on government behavior. Even radical empiricists took note of Downsian theorizing and works of a similar genre, published in the sixties, that were based on assumptions of self-interested, rational conduct.

The 1950's were truly a deceptive decade. For a time it almost seemed that the new behavioral and scientific movement would be limited to the voting studies coming out of Michigan and Columbia. But it was really a decade of preparation and gestation. The sociologists were teaching the political scientists willing to learn a good deal of methodology; the economists were teaching theoretical modeling. As the next section will show, some large-scale research projects were actually in the field from the early fifties on. Their slow reporting suggests that political scientists had to learn by doing and by doing were learning. The harvest was yet to come.

The Great Avalanche: 1960-1964

It was as if a coin had been dropped into the slot machine and the jackpot had been hit. Books distinguished by the remarkable quality of the research and thought that had gone into them came tumbling off university and commercial presses alike. Were it not for books having a publication date, it would be difficult to recall just what volume reached one's desk when, for so rapid was the rate of publication in the early 1960's.

The decade began with a trilogy of works reporting research that had been incubated and completed in the 1950's. All three books dealt, in one way or another, with one or another aspect of American electoral politics. All three were large-scale collaborative efforts that had involved, for social science, considerable financial outlays. All three reflected the great confidence that research sponsors had placed in political science in the early fifties and belied the latter-day tale that massive social science research was riding on the coattails of the natural sciences after Sputnick had shattered the alleged complacency of the public and private foundations.

Heading the list was a book with the proud title *The American Voter* (Campbell, Converse, Miller and Stokes, 1960). Based on careful analyses of citizen responses to survey questions asked during the Eisenhower years, this work probed deeply into the motivational and cognitive aspects of the individual person's voting behavior but also sought to understand elections as aggregate change processes by way of a novel typology that distinguished between maintaining, deviating and realigning contests. *The American Voter* was a multi-directional sign-post that turned a generation of scholars in new and different directions, including the authors of the work itself (see Campbell, Converse, Miller and Stokes, 1966; Miller and Levitin, 1976). Voting research has become the kingpin in the scientific study of politics, and the number of studies taking off from the Michigan contribution can now be counted in the hundreds and will soon be counted in the thousands.[17]

Elections provide critical linkages between citizens and their leaders. By enabling citizens to choose among rival candidates, they empower and legitimate what is called democratic government. Complex as the electoral process is in a federal system like the American, it is better understood than the process by which candidates, especially aspirants to the Presidency, are nominated. *The Politics of National Party Conventions* (David, Goldman and Bain, 1960) was a historical account of the origin and development of one of America's unique institutions and a detailed analysis of contemporary nominating patterns.[18] The work laid to rest the stereotypic view of the presidential nomination invariably being the conspiracy of a small group of men meeting in smoke-filled rooms and imposing their choice on a helpless convention. Oligarchic selection is certainly one possible pattern, but there are other modes—confirmation, inheritance, factional insurgence and still others. In attending to both the broad patterns of convention behavior and the conduct of individual delegations and delegates, *The Politics of the National Conventions* stimulated later studies of the conventions that produced the candidacies of a Goldwater, Nixon and McGovern.

What makes the nominating and electoral mechanisms work, apart from the human actors involved, is money. Without financial support candidates cannot run and voters cannot choose. Alexander Heard's *The Costs of Democracy* (1960) was based on research in this most difficult of research areas that involved the help of over a thousand persons and was partly based on off-the-record conversations with more than 600 politicans. A participant observer as a Senate consultant, Heard examined the effect of expenditures on the outcome of elections, the nature of contributions as political action, the sources of campaign funds (corporate and labor as well as underworld), the modes of fund raising, legislative and administrative finance regulations, and so on. A solid empirical work, Heard's book also addressed reform and considered many of the alternative means of campaign funding which have been of much practical concern in the most recent past. *The Costs of Democracy* was not a narrowly conceived study of "money in politics" but a major contribution to an understanding of party politics in the United States.[19]

The drama of American politics centers in the drama of the Presidency. Of all the institutions of American government none is more visible to citizens and elusive to the researcher. It is difficult to gain access to an institution that is so highly self-protective and secretive in its operations. Until about 1960, most works on the Presidency were formal—historical or constitutional—analyses, although some of them were not without merit in their particular genre. Even today the institutionalized Presidency remains relatively unexplored, though political scientists are beginning to take it apart by studying such aspects as "decision-making in the White House" (Kessel, 1975) or the "presidential advisory system" (Cronin and Greenberg, 1969). This, in retrospect, makes Richard Neustadt's *Presidential Power: The Politics of Leadership* (1960) all the more significant. It has certainly been the most insightful work on the functioning the President as a component, and most important, part of the Presidency. In Neustadt's influential analysis— influential because generally accepted as accurate and not discredited by contrary evidence—the President does not simply sit at the apex of a submissive hierarchy of political appointees and bureaucrats (something Richard Nixon had failed to learn from his predecessors). Rather, he is at the center of a complex net of power relationships that require him to husband or spend his resources more like a clever broker than a haughty commander if he wishes to achieve his legislative and administrative goals. Neustadt's analysis is sometimes called "impressionist" (whatever this may mean); close reading reveals unobtrusive use of behavioral science concepts.

Inaccessible and inhospitable as the White House is to the political researcher, the Supreme Court is even more so. Neustadt had the unusual opportunity as an insider to observe White House operations. No political scientist has as yet been a Supreme Court clerk to have a similar opportunity for participant observation. What goes on in the judiciary as a political system and in the judicial as a political process must be inferred from the opinions and decisions of the justices. In general, the study of courts as behavioral phenomena and of law as a political process followed, from the middle 1950's, two lines of inquiry. One line followed a quantitative approach and applied ingenious statistical techniques to make relevant discoveries about judicial behavior. The other line took a more contextual view of what the justices are doing when they interpret or declare the law.

It is problematic which one of Glendon Schubert's books should be singled out as the landmark work of the judicial behavior movement that, following Pritchett, he did so much to foster. His books of the early 1960's appeared in such rapid succession that they could well be described as a single enterprise (Schubert, 1960, 1963, 1964, 1965). However, I shall mention only *Quantitative Analysis of Judicial Behavior* (Schubert, 1959), which is not his "best" book, but which, I think, was the most important programmatic statement of the political behavior approach in the judicial field. I am not qualified to assess the book's substantive merits, but a sympathetic reviewer emphasized some novel findings—that "an increasingly large proportion of the Court's time and energies is devoted to summary as distinguished from formal decision-making; the Supreme Court accepts jurisdiction in far more appeals cases coming from federal courts than from state courts because it feels greater responsibility for and authority over the federal courts; whether review is granted, especially when the Court's decision is announced per curiam, tends to be determined by the Court's approval in a psychological rather than in a legal sense of the decisions reached below; the currently crowded condition of the Court's docket gives law clerks greater weight in administering the Court's business than they had in the past" (Tanenhaus, 1961).

The contextual perspective on judicial conduct had been articulated as early as 1955 by Jack W. Peltason (1955) who now contributed an empirical study of the actions of Southern courts in the school segregation case in *Fifty-eight Lonely Men: Southern Federal Judges and School Desegregation* (Peltason, 1961). Referring to this new genre of research, the book was hailed by a respected public law scholar, the late Robert McCloskey (1963), as "an event in the development of that literature, one of the most significant events that has taken place so far . . . . The result is a study with important implications for a nation that has chosen to devolve major governmental responsibilities upon its courts . . . . We have here one of those rare books that should fascinate any layman who cares about public questions, yet satisfy the most exacting scholarly critic."

Legislatures, it is said, have lost in "power" over the last hundred years (though there is no theoretically satisfying explanation of just what this means), but one would not know it to judge from the great amount of research done on legislative behavior and processes since the early 1960's. Legislative bodies are of course as "open" as executive offices or courts are "closed" and, therefore, natural hunting grounds for data-happy political scientists. Once the survey had been accepted as the standard tool for studying the electorate, systematic or purposive interviewing of legislators no longer seemed to be the formidable task it was once assumed to be. Legislators were accessible and all too willing to talk.

Three works of quite different character led the way to reorienting legislative research in the years of the Great Avalanche. One was a study of the Senate of the United States; a second was a genuinely comparative study of four state legislatures; and a third was a study of Congressional handling of foreign trade legislation. Each of these studies, in its own way, led to a flowering of research on legislative institutions.[20]

The parade was led by Donald Matthews' *U.S. Senators and Their World* (1960), the first composite portrait of the 180 Senators who had served between 1947 and 1957, as well as a detailed account of the ways in which Senators live and behave. Of particular interest was Matthews' analysis of Senate norms, happily called "folkways," and constituency relations. *U.S. Senators and Their World* remains the standard work on the Senate and continues to be widely used to introduce students to the peculiar ways of a peculiar institution.

The Legislative System: Explorations in Legislative Behavior (Wahlke, Eulau, Buchanan and Ferguson, 1962) was an ambitious effort by a team of researchers not only to compare legislative behavior and processes in the four American states of California, New Jersey, Ohio and Tennessee, but to capture all of the components of the "legislative system" as a whole, at least as seen through the eyes of legislators. The original plan to interview systematically all participants in the legislative arena—legislators as well as lobbyists, staff members, executive officials, constituents, and so on—could not be carried out for lack of funds. Nevertheless, the finished work covered a wide range of topics: the legislative career, legislative roles, legislative norms, interpersonal relations, constituency relations, the place of party, and many other aspects of legislative conduct. The final section of the work sought to reconstruct the legislative maze out of the itemistic role orientations and to move the analysis from the micro to the macro level. Conceived in 1955, researched in 1956-57 and limited by the state of the research technology at that time, the volume's multi-dimensional perspective came as close as one could hope for to a comprehensive view of the legislative system; and it stimulated many partial replications and extensions of its theoretical design and empirical questions in subsequent research both in the United States and abroad (see Hirsch and Hancock, 1971; Patterson and Wahlke, 1972; Kornberg, 1973).

The third work of note dealing with legislative politics during the Great Avalanche was *American Business and Public Policy: The Politics of Foreign Trade* (Bauer, Pool and Dexter, 1963). Like the authors of *The Legislative System*, Bauer and his colleagues rejected the mechanical model of pressure politics as well as the even older model of rational decision-making. Unlike the Wahlke-led team, Bauer and associates relied on more free-wheeling interviewing in their pursuit of "what actually happened" in foreign trade legislation. Yet, they too focused on Congressmen's career choices, professional identities and activities rather than on choices about particular alternatives. Though they dealt with a single area of legislation, the authors of *American Business and Public Policy* overcame the limitations of a case study and developed generic conceptions about the relationship between interest groups and Congress, creating new hypotheses for independent and systematic testing.[21]

The focus shifts from national and state to local politics in a monumental study by Wallace S. Sayre and Herbert Kaufman, *Governing New York City* (1960). Written by two scholars usually considered to be "in" public administration, *Governing New York City* was an eminently "political" study. Nowhere is the dichotomy between politics and administration less appropriate than in the country's largest metropolis which the authors felicitously described as a multi-centered system composed of separate and numerous "islands of power" competing with each other in the making of public policy and the distribution of the stakes of politics. By never losing sight of the fact that a pluralistic system contains both elements of resistance as well as innovation as it adapts itself to changing conditions, Sayre and Kaufman transformed what might otherwise have been a tedious compendium of information about city institutions and processes into an insightful study of urban complexities.

Governing New York City as evidence of the pluralistic multiverse that American politics is and continues to be has never been properly appreciated. This is probably due to the appearance, a year later, of two works which, precisely because they were less burdened by evidence and more explicitly theoretical, would become the targets of praise or criticism in the controversy over pluralism that flared up in later years. Interestingly, of these two works "conservative" Edward C. Banfield's study of decision-making in Chicago, *Political Influence* (1961) has remained less controversial that "liberal" Robert A. Dahl's New Haven study, *Who Governs? Democracy and Power in an American City* (1961).[22] This has probably been due to Dahl's self-conscious repudiation of sociologist Floyd Hunter's earlier study of Atlanta, *Community Power Structure* (1953), which had claimed to find an oligarchic control structure in that Southern city. Though highly germane, Banfield's study seemed immune to the ensuing controversy. Like Sayre and Kaufman in New York, Banfield discovered a great variety of urban decision processes and a multiplicity of participants taking diverse roles in connection with concrete policy issues. Chicago's structure of influence seemed to him largely reflected in the decentralized formal structure of city government. Political fragmentation resulting from multiple and overlapping jurisdictions was intensified by competition between the political party organizations and interest groups, and, on particular issues, quite different persons were found to influence the decision process.

Dahl's *Who Governs?* combined historical analysis of elite transformation, case analyses of several policy-making arenas, and cross-sectional analysis of citizen resources in a complex, conceptually elegant description of competitive politics. Although the study became the center of controversy over "power"—a rather hopeless concept and subject—it is much more fruitful to view it as a study of the twin problems of political stability/change and democratic consensus. The study *is* concerned with influence patterns which involve coalition formation and bargaining, but they are of interest not as ends in themselves but as evidence of the contribution they make to social change and the resolution of conflicts.

While Banfield and Dahl did not miss the role of the political parties in the local politics of their cities, Samuel J. Eldersveld made them the heart of his investigation into the relationships within and between party cadres, and between the latter and the citizenry, in Detroit. The result of intensive survey research on party personnel and voters conducted in 1956-57, *Political Parties: A Behavioral Analysis* (1964) corrected the simplistic view of the party as a hierarchy. Focusing on the characteristics, perceptions, attitudes, communications and intraorganizational relationships of party leaders on all levels of party organization, Eldersveld examined the resulting interrelationship and transactions at a level of detail that no national survey has as yet matched. The party does not appear simply as an object of identification or support as it usually does in election studies, but as a very complex structure of vertical and horizontal relationships and activities—a "stratarchy," as Eldsveld called it, of sometimes competing, sometimes conflicting, and sometimes cooperating interests.

The research discussed so far used data about individuals but was not interested in individuals as such. Even such explicitly "behavioral" studies as *The American Voter* or *The Legislative System*, being based on relatively large numbers of cases, were essentially aggregative and interested more in the conditions, processes and consequences of collective behavior than in the unique behavior of any one individual. Concentration of attention on the political person as such requires more intensive procedures than the population survey can use. In *Political Ideology: Why the American Common Man Believes What He Does* Robert E. Lane (1962) used tape recorder and depth-analytic interviewing to probe into the personality-based attitudes and beliefs of 15 working- and middle-class men. What he found was, in essence, that their psychic processes were so preoccupying these men that there was little energy left for political participation. Unfortunately, the intensive study of political personality, pioneered by Harold D. Lasswell (1930, 1948) and here continued by Lane, has remained so underdeveloped that one must take any conclusions reached in this scarce literature with a grain of salt.

The individual person as a rational actor—something difficult to swallow for anyone who has sipped on the Freudian bottles of a Lasswell or Lane—becomes the basic theoretical unit of analysis in William H.

Riker's *The Theory of Political Coalitions* (1962) which presented an elegant and subsequently influential, but by no means uncontested, model of the minimum winning coalition in politics. Riker's work is only indirectly related to the concerns of this essay, but it included an epilogue on the United States in world affairs, nothing less, in which Riker tried to spell out the practical implications of his abstract theory. I am not sufficiently informed on what impact, if any, Riker has had on American statesmen, but in the academy his theoretical work has had some influence in thinking on topics like citizen participation, collective choice, aspects of power, public policy or electoral competition (see also Riker and Ordeshook, 1973). Riker argued and continues to argue for the use of axiomatic and deductive procedures in the study of politics. At the moment, the empirical requirements of axiomatic theory still seem to outdistance the data-gathering capabilities of political science.

Although written by two economists, James M. Buchanan and Gordon Tullock, *The Calculus of Consent: Logical Foundations of Constitutional Democracy* (1962) contributed to the intellectual ferment of the Great Avalanche and remains an important source for future research. More passionate in commitment to methodological individualism than others writing in the deductive genre, Buchanan and Tullock elaborated an unexpurgated model of constitution-making in a democracy. That the collective decisions made under constitutional rules themselves not neutral will also not be neutral had long been recognized, but rarely had the logic of the constitutional process been spelled out so conclusively. Recent Marxist-inspired students asking "who benefits?" would do well in heeding this compelling analysis. Along with a later work of the same genre, Mancur Olson's *The Logic of Collective Action* (1965), the work of Buchanan and Tullock is a critical contribution to theorizing about democratic processes.

Some of the greatest works on American political life were written by foreign scholars (de Tocqueville, 1838-40; Bryce, 1888) who brought to their task the enlightening perspective that comes with comparison. Nowadays the comparative approach to politics has become enormously more complicated because no single scholar has the necessary competence. It is unfortunate that disciplinary specialization has reached a point where no expert on, say, Soviet or African politics would dare to do research on and write about some aspect of American politics. The subfield of "comparative politics" is only rarely thought to include American politics (which, for academically parochial and politically chauvinistic reasons is treated as a separate field of study).[23]

Fortunately, the situation is gradually changing. As scholars studying abroad include in their analyses aspects of American politics as points of reference, aspects of political behavior abroad become in turn points of comparison enlightening American politics. This changing focus of comparative research was perhaps first evident in Gabriel A. Almond and Sidney Verba's massive *The Civic Culture: Political Attitudes and Democracy in Five Nations* (1963). One would not ordinarily include this work in a review of books on American politics, but it should be there for it was based on surveys conducted in Germany, Italy, Great Britain, Mexico and the United States—at the time of its research execution in 1959-60 by far the most ambitious cross-national research project ever undertaken. *The Civic Culture* remains a point of departure for a great number of studies concerned with political participation, apathy, alienation and citizen orientations. Its contribution to the understanding of American political behavior is both expansive and restrictive—expansive because at the national level of aggregation comparison with other countries is indeed conducive to insight; restrictive because it does not capture the fascinating local and regional variations in citizen attitudes and beliefs that have more recently been uncovered in more detailed studies of political behavior in America. But it is only fitting to complete this section with *The Civic Culture*, for it symbolized the ebullience of the research enterprise in political science in the years of transition from the Chicago Impact to the New Establishment.

The New Establishment, 1965-1969

By the middle 1960's the discipline's movers and shakers of the behavioral movement had become the New Establishment. Pritchett served as president of the American Political Science Association in 1964, Truman in 1965, Almond and Dahl in 1966 and 1967. Not surprisingly, by the middle of the 1960's, the sons of the New Establishment began to be heard from. New names and new topics came into prominence. The topics fell into a wide range—from the political socialization of grammar school children and the functioning of very small political groups to aggregative public policy analysis in the states and dissection of the federal system as a whole. The call for new themes had of course been made earlier—the suggestion to study children's political learning had first come from Merriam (1925) of the Chicago school; the promotion of policy analysis had been a persistent quest of Lasswell (1941); or the need for fresh study of federal relations had been pointed out by Arthur Maas (1959) and others. What was new in the middle 1960's was the empirical fulfillment of vaguely conceived ideas that had been around for some time but had yet to be tried.

It would be a case of gross over-determination, therefore, to attribute the character of the research output of the period to the times of trouble that began to envelop the country from 1965 on. The criticism is sometimes made that the difficulties of the period—the rebellions in the ghetto, the draft resistance of the young, the belligerence of middle-class women, or the alleged unresponsiveness of the "system"—caught political scientists and social scientists generally unaware, as if prophecy were a criterion of scientific decisions what to study and when. The theoretically-oriented, empirical researcher is always "behind the times," for his mission is not prophecy or forecasting but explanation and prediction. Even if research is inspired by some contemporary problem, the lead-time required before research can actually begin and the lag-time that follows prior to publication of findings are usually counted in many years. This is why the "cry for relevance" is so adolescent and, in fact, so serious a threat to a serious political science.

It is doubtful that when Fred I. Greenstein executed his field work in 1958, he could have anticipated that the elementary school pupils he studied would, eight or more years later, constitute the politically volatile Vietnam generation that saw in "protest" a way of life. And one finds nothing in his *Children and Politics* (1965) that would help one understand the protest generation of the middle and late sixties. Yet, Greenstein's research was path-breaking and inspired many younger scholars to follow his lead into the study of political socialization.[24]

Even prior to Greenstein's work, two scholars at the University of Chicago, social psychologist Robert D. Hess and political scientist David Easton, had launched a national political socialization study. One report of this project (Hess and Torney, 1967) was written from the perspective of the psychology of child development. The other, *Children in the Political System: Origins of Political Legitimacy* (1969) was co-authored by Easton and Jack Dennis. The study drew on questionnaire responses from 12,000 students in grades two through eight collected in eight cities of four regions of the country, a very large undertaking. The analysis was concerned with children's cognitive and affective views of political authorities, from the President down to the policeman, and of governmental institutions generally, on the assumption that the processes involved in the acquisition of images of authority have implications for the stability of the political systems over time. These processes—politicization, personalization, idealization and institutionalization—are presumably not immune from intervention and manipulation. What distinguished the Easton and Dennis study was its attempt to analyze their respondents' answers in terms of the senior author's macro-political categories such as "system stress" or "diffuse support." There is reason to believe that linking individual and polity in one fell swoop by way of such conceptualization is not sufficient to solve the methodological issues involved in what is sometimes called the level-of-analysis problem. There are intervening structures that can be ignored only at the risk of committing various fallacies associated with aggregate or global analysis (see Eulau, 1969b).

Recognition of the importance of small groups as intervening structures is basic to a highly imaginative experimental laboratory study of 12 local Connecticut boards of finance by James D. Barber, *Power in Committees: An Experiment in the Governmental Process* (1966). Politicians and political scientists alike have long known, of course, that much politics takes place in and much policy is made by small groups which, if associated over any length of time, assume the character of cohesive "primary groups." Until Barber's work, the systematic study of small decision-making groups had been of concern to political scientists only marginally, though much work along this line had been done by sociologists and social psychologists. By the time of Barber's study, the small-group literature had been reviewed and assessed by two political scientists (Verba, 1961; Golembiewski, 1962). But the difficulty of gaining access to natural-setting decision-making groups had evidently discouraged political scientists. Bringing boards of finance into the small-group laboratory and observing interaction patterns among their members was a courageous departure (which, so far, has not been followed up by distinguished similar work).[25] Barber found a great deal of internal stratification and role specialization as well as dispersion of power going along with norm consensus and integrative behavior.

If Barber's experimental study has not as yet had the influence it should have, this is not the case with what in some ways is also a small-group study, Richard F. Fenno's weighty *The Power of the Purse: Appropriations Politics in Congress* (1966). To call Fenno's research a small-group study is something of a falsehood, for his book is much more than simply a study of Congressional appropriations committees. Marshalling a great amount of information from documents and interviews over a period of six years, Fenno demonstrated that the committees' internal processes and external relations affected decisional outcomes. In the mode of the time, Fenno relied on structural-functional conceptions to explain why it is that the committees' structural integration is not matched by an equally integrated product. This is due, Fenno found, to specialization within the appropriation process on the one hand, and the guardian function of the committees on the other hand. The appropriation committees' non-partisanship is not present, for instance, in the House Committee on Ways and Means reported on by John F. Manley in *The Politics of Finance* (1970), a worthy successor to Fenno's study. This committee was controlled at the time by a powerful chairman; partisan considerations made for quite different behavorial patterns and suggested the utility of exchange theory in explaining decisional outcomes. What Fenno's and Manley's as well as other committee researches show is that Congress is a very complex organization which defies, for the time being, conventional models of either politics or organization.[26]

That small groups were significant Congressional actors even in simpler times was shown in a historical study by James S. Young, *The Washington Community, 1800–1828* (1966). This rich contextual study of the "establishment" found in the boarding houses around Capitol Hill deftly probed, in the author's own words, into "the governing group as entity: legislators, executives, judges, and all who gather around them at the seat of power; their inner life as a group; their special world as a governing fraternity; the lifeways and workways, the outlooks and values, the organizational patterns, that distinguish this unique group in American society." (Young, 1966: VII). As Nelson Polsby (1967: 165) has pointed out, *The Washington Community* was "a major critique and revision of current conceptions of the growth of American political institutions. It will be a long while before the insights of this book are thoroughly digested, mastered, debated and superseded by further research." In fact, Young's findings were contested sooner than Polsby had probably anticipated (see Bogue and Marlaire, 1975). But this does not detract from the pioneering quality of Young's work. Its skillful use of statistical and anthropological modes of research made it a leader in the emerging field of political cliometrics.

Much of Congressional politics is federalistic politics—a function of the dispersion of power in the American political system. Speaking of American government and politics as a system is something of a sobriquet—unless, as in Morton Grodzins' posthumous *The American System* (1966), one appreciates the incredibly labyrinthine nature of this system. Grodzins' "American system" is not the disembodied system of the "general systems" theorists. What Grodzins presented was a new model of American federal arrangements which looked more like a marble cake—a model that had evolved out of a variety of empirical studies launched in a federalism workshop he had conducted at Chicago from 1955 on. *The American System* was based on these studies and presented a new view of government in the United States as one of antagonistic, and hence intrinsically political, cooperation between the different levels of government, including shared activities and services. Yet, though chaotic, Grodzins found the American system both responsible and responsive. This sober view has yet to penetrate the myopically monocratic image of American politics of those who see in the struggle between **President** and Congress the crucible of American policy-making. Grodzins work was edited by his student Daniel J. Elazar whose own works have extended the modern federalistic conception of the American system (Elazar, 1962, 1966; also 1970, treated below).

If proof were required to underline the continuing need for federalistic arrangements, one would easily find it in Donald R. Matthews and James W. Prothro's *Negroes and the New Southern Politics* (1966). A worthy successor to Key's *Southern Politics,* this magnificent volume made use of a huge array of data: aggregate registration statistics as of 1958, random sample survey materials collected in 1961, a 1964 Survey Research Center poll with an extra Negro quota sample, and local sub-sample surveys and a special poll of Negro students. Enlightened by psychological and sociological concepts, the study examines levels of black participation, presents profiles of the participants, places the problem of participation in its community contexts, studies Negro leadership and the role of the political parties, treats the student protest movement and, more generally, the relationship between conventional and unconventional politics in the South as it appeared in the early and middle 1960's. The richness of the materials gathered by Matthews and Prothro as well as meticulous analyses of the data made *Negroes and the New Southern Politics* an exceptionally vital diagnosis of the American dilemma. As this dilemma appears today to be truly national—in the North as well as the South—one would want other regional studies patterned on the Matthews-Prothro model, for national sample surveys are not sufficient to capture the sub-cultural and geographical diversity of white-black relations. In providing the model Matthews and Prothro struck a happy balance between Key's state and sub-state and their own regional and community analysis.

What is impressive about the studies of the "class of '66" is the wide range of approaches to what is basically the same problem—the relationship between politics and policy. This was the concern of Barber's experimental study of finance boards, of Fenno's structural-functional study of the appropriations process, of Young's historical analysis of the Washington establishment, and of Grodzins' institutional description of the American federal system. It is the problem also of the policy output studies of an aggregative character that began in the early 1960's, originally inspired by some observations by V. O. Key about the relationship between political competition and social policies in the states. These observations were picked up by a number of scholars, amended and extended and finally tested in various states even before the appearance of Thomas R. Dye's *Politics, Economics, and the Public: Policy Outcomes in the American States* (1966).

Dye's work is notable less for the originality of its design or execution than for the extent to which it pursued what has turned out to be a troubling dilemma of these studies. Conducted at the macro level of the states with aggregate indicators of policy (largely budget data) and of politics, the policy output studies seemed to show that political variables such as party competition, malapportionment, formal institutional differences and even interest-group strengths do not explain differences in policy results among the states; that, in fact, physical resources and demographic factors explained both governmental processes and policy outputs. Dye, painting the widest canvas at the time, came to a similar conclusion: "Economic development shapes both political systems and policy outcomes, and most of the association that occurs between system characteristics and policy outcomes can be attributed to the influence of economic development. Differences in the policy choices of states with different types of political systems turn out to be largely a product of differing socio-economic levels rather than a direct product of political variables" (Dye, 1966: 293). The difficulties noted by Dye and his predecessors in the early 1960's did not discourage their successors. There has been a veritable flood of studies in the same genre and a growing critical literature.

The face validity of the policy output studies is doubtful not only because, as has recently been argued, they were based on inappropriate theory and perhaps on inappropriate data (Munns, 1975), but also because they left out what is perhaps the most significant variable in the equation that links politics and policy—the motivations and conduct of those who make policy, the politicians. Important as structural and institutional conditions are in channeling the policy process, the policy product is not independent of the purposes that politicians pursue; and the purposes of politicians are not unrelated to their ambitions. An adequate theory of political ambition would seem to be highly relevant to explaining politicians' choice-making behavior and the results of their behavior.

Given the lead-time needed for major research to mature, one can not fault Joseph A. Schlesinger for not being directly concerned, in *Ambition and Politics: Political Careers in the United States* (1966), with the fascinating question of whether and to what extent policies made by incumbent politicians are at least in part determined by the recruitment and career paths open to them in the political arena. Schlesinger introduced the valuable concept of "opportunity structure," and there is indeed reason to assume that this structure is itself not independent, in a federal system, of the policies enacted in the states. Of course, this speculation is not the main reason for citing Schlesinger's work here, though one might have wished for its appearance in 1960 rather than in 1966. As a meticulous description of the political opportunity structure at the state and national levels between 1914 and 1958, under-girded by an interesting "ambition theory," the work has already had considerable impact on subsequent studies of party politics and political recruitment.

Cutting points in a time series may be willful but must not be arbitrary. What changed in the late 1960's was the expectation to which one had become pleasantly accustomed in the early and middle years of the decade that there would be at least one annual publishing event to be taken note of. Not that political science suddenly atrophied (and it must be remembered that this essay is limited to studies about American politics; there was a good deal of significant publishing activity in other fields of the discipline). Indeed, perusal of the increasing number of journals indicates continuing discovery and development. By 1970 the political science profession had grown considerably beyond its numbers in the forties, fifties and early sixties. But, apart from the works mentioned here, there was only one of the landmark class after 1966, so that making 1969 the breaking point does not violate the principle of non-arbitrary classification.

The Continuing Quest: 1970-1975

The fact that fewer works of an innovative or landmark character came off the presses in the late 1960's did not mean that there was less research activity in those years. On the contrary, the sons of the New Establishment were better trained and more research-minded than their mentors. What happened was that this new generation deepened and extended the research enterprise, and in doing so essentially elaborated and revised the themes that had been introduced earlier. The vehicles for reporting this research were likely to be shorter monographs, symposia and journal articles rather than reports of long-term studies, for the reward structure of the academy is such that younger scholars, in order to make a reputation, must publish as soon as they can (and sometimes much). Although no count is available, I am inclined to believe that the profession's research output probably tripled in the decade of the 1960's. There were few nooks and crannies of American government and politics that were not explored by the growing cadre of younger scholars.

Nevertheless, there continued to be published in the 1970's a small number of works likely to leave a mark on the future development of research in American politics and, increasingly, in the study of public policy. Just as in the earlier periods, most of this research had been planned and executed several years prior to publication. What distinguished the output of the first half of the seventies from the equivalent period of the sixties was the progress that had been made in the intervening years at the technical and methodological fronts. Most important perhaps was the coming of the high-speed digital computer. Within a few years analysis moved from the counter-sorter into an altogether new computing environment. Not only much easier data manipulation but also the application of more refined statistical techniques and other methodological inventions became possible. Scale and factor analyses, laborious to conduct for a long time, became routine, and by the middle of the sixties regression analysis and causal modeling had become firmly established. As a result, the new research following the Great Avalanche and the New Establishment was even more demanding in its insistence on theoretical explicitness and methodological sophistication.

It is all the more interesting, therefore, that the first work to be mentioned here coped with its topic by digging deep into the historical roots of the phenomenon of right-wing extremism in the United States, suggesting that there is no necessary conflict between synchronic and diachronic analysis, and indeed setting an example of how historical and cross-sectional approaches can be combined. In the preface to their masterful synthesis, *The Politics of Unreason* (1970), Seymour M. Lipset and Earl Raab described the evolution of their project and its many tributaries from history and survey research. The work demonstrated that dispassionate and disinterested scholarship need not be passive if it comes to the examination of those values that make scholarship possible in the first place, and that an "objective" piece of research can be politically salient without being a piece of propaganda. It is not easy to say just where Lipset and Raab came out in regard to the future of right-wing extremism. On the one hand, they discovered tendencies that may be immanent in the American experience, denying the pluralist and tolerant vision of American democracy. On the other hand, they found that the American social structure may be just sufficiently productive of change to countervail the status and class anxieties which seemed to be the psychological and sociological groundings of right-wing politics. It is certainly to be expected that *The Politics of Unreason* will stimulate research into all forms of political extremism, left and right, that threaten the promise of American life.

Just where that promise can be best fulfilled remains a political question that has been agonized over from the country's very beginning. Extremism has been sometimes identified as a small-town phenomenon, but small-town America is no more. As Daniel J. Elazar shows in his profoundly perceptive *The Cities of the Prairie: The Metropolitan Frontier and American Politics* (1970), local America has become so tied into the federal system that treating cities as isolated units makes little sense. This is a study of what Elazar called "civil communities"—

17 of them— in ten "lesser" metropolitan areas of the Midwest: cities of the prairie like Pueblo, Colorado, or Duluth-Superior, Minnesota. By "civil communities" Elazar meant areas that have many governmental institutions on several formal levels of federalistic organization that must be treated as wholes if the resulting "system" is to make sense. On the basis of research conducted as long ago as 1959 to 1962 and involving a variety of techniques—historical probes, documentary and quantitative evidence, unobtrusive measures, and extensive interviews with significant participants in the political process—Elazar created an ethnographic profile of the cultural diversity that is the American system and that Morton Grodzins had more broadly sketched at an earlier time. *Cities of the Prairie* was a unique work not likely to be easily emulated, for it was not simply a work in social science but also, in many respects, a work in the humanities. In other words, it was a work more closely associated with its author's sensitivity to local Americana than one normally encounters in the study of metropolitan politics.

Novel theoretical and methodological preoccupations distinguish four works on very different topics published in yearly succession from 1972 to 1975. Political participation, more broadly conceived than in any previous study, occupied Sidney Verba and Norman H. Nie in their remarkable *Participation in America: Political Democracy and Social Equality* (1972). Citizen participation consisted, for Verba and Nie, not only in the selection of government personnel but also in the influence on governmental decisions. Hence, contact between citizens and public officials loomed large in their analysis. Moreover, they were interested in more than the individual citizen as participant; rather, citizen participation seemed crucial from the perspective of the country's functioning as a democratic polity. To shed light on the problem of participation so defined and also from the perspective of social equality, Verba and Nie interviewed over two thousand persons and several hundred community leaders in 64 communities. The complexity of the sample design was matched by the complexity of the analysis, both described in great detail. No summary can do justice to their analysis which consisted of three major parts—the participation input, the process of politicization, and the consequences of participation, each divided into some seven chapters. Most noteworthy was their effort to establish the degree of "concurrence" in citizen and leader perspectives, and their effort to conduct parts of the analysis at the aggregate level of the communities rather than at the individual level of persons. If their conclusions were contrapuntist, it was because the nature of participation in a heterogeneous political structure is multimelodious. Participation, they concluded, "looked at generally, does not necessarily help one social group rather than another. . . . It could work so that lower-status citizens were more effective politically and used that political effectiveness to improve their social and economic circumstances. Or it could work, as it appears to do in the United States, to benefit upper-status citizens. . . . It depends on who takes advantage of it" (Verba and Nie, 1972: 343). And the final sentence: "Citizens may be participating more, but enjoying it less" (Verba and Nie, 1972: 343).

Originally conceived as a replication on the city level of the research reported by Wahlke and his associates in *The Legislative System* (1962), the project described in *Labyrinths of Democracy: Adaptations, Linkages, Representation and Policy* (Eulau and Prewitt, 1973) turned into an altogether different enterprise. An intensive study of 82 city councils in the San Francisco Bay region conducted from 1962 on, and based on 435 interviews with members of the councils and much other information, this work stands almost alone as a group-level analysis of decision-making behavior.[27] Tightly written and tightly integrated, the analysis concerned the decision-making group's internal and external adaptations; its linkages with significant actors in the environment—voters, constituents, interest-group spokesmen, administrative officials; problems of responsibility, responsiveness and representation; and the relationship between these structural aspects of the political process and the public policies that emerge as collective properties of the cities for which the councils legislate. A variety of analytic techniques—causal analysis, contextual analysis, structural analysis, and configurative analysis—were used to come to grips with the labyrinthine nature of the legislative manifold. In its concern with public policy *Labyrinths of Democracy* proposed a new behavioral definition and applied the definition in an analysis that culminated in the construction of an "eco-policy" typology as a fruitful means to observe policy in a development perspective.

There is something to be gained from the lag between the time when research is conducted in the field and when it is written up. No doubt, M. Kent Jennings and Richard G. Niemi, doing their research in 1965 but not publishing their full report, *The Political Character of Adolescence* (1974), until nine years later, benefitted from the experience which they, as college teachers, must have had in the intervening years. For the high school seniors of 1965-66 were the cohort that, perhaps more than any other of recent vintage, carried the burden of exposure to America's first unpopular war. Although the research itself came at a time when it was not as yet clear what would happen to this cohort, Jennings and Niemi had the advantage of hindsight in interpreting their data. What became clear—something previous socialization studies had less occasion to observe—was that analysis of political learning is well advised to attend to both changes in the individual exposed to various

socialization experiences as well as to the changes in politics and society
that take place simultaneously. Jennings and Niemi's study was by far
the most broadly designed study of its kind, involving interviews with
1,669 students, 1,992 parents of these students, 317 social studies teachers and 96 principals, as well as relying on 20,833 mass-administered
questionnaires. The study explored a great variety of political characteristics of the students—party preferences, opinions on issues, political
knowledge and attitudes, and so on—in terms of the relationship existing
between parents and child and in terms of the school context, including
the impact of curriculum, teachers and peers.

Many years ago, when Harold Lasswell bluntly defined the study of
politics as the study of influence and the influential, and the influential
as those who get more of what there is to get, he called those who get
the most "elite" and the rest "mass" (Lasswell, 1936). Political scientists have paid much attention to institutionalized governmental and
political elites—legislators, judges, executives, party leaders, lobbyists,
and so on—but have generally left the study of other societal elites,
with the exception perhaps of lawyers, to the sociologists (see, for instance, Janowitz, 1960). A political scientist, Everett C. Ladd, Jr., and
a sociologist, S. M. Lipset, joined forces in a study of academic elites,
The Divided Academy: Professors and Politics (1975), that was truly
gigantic in the size of the sample of respondents on which it was based
—over 60,000 faculty members in more than 300 institutions queried by
mail in 1969, and about 500 respondents queried by telephone and
subsequently by mail in 1972. While many of the study's "internal"
findings are undoubtedly of great interest to those who work in, control
or benefit from the academy, the work's political significance stems
from the university world's intimate relationship to the "world outside"
—government and business—that has become a fact of life in the years
since the Second World War. Academic personnel have become pervasive as advisers, consultants and, quite often, employees of public and
private decision-making institutions. Although, as Ladd and Lipset
found, the academy is highly divided in political orientations that are
not unrelated to academic specialization, the general tendency of the
professoriat to be left of center on most issues is significant for the drift
of American public policy. For, in this age of high technology, public
policy making has become increasingly dependent on the best technical knowledge that physicists, biologists, economists or sociologists can
provide. While both government and industry have their in-house
experts and specialists, they draw on the academy, and especially the
elite universities, where the very best scholars are located. And these
scholars, more than their less-achieving colleagues, are the most liberal
on the political issues confronting American society. Understanding the

modern academy is conducive to understanding the direction of political, economic and social change in America. It is for this reason that *The Divided Academy* is of critical importance as a work in political science.

It is too early to say with confidence whether the works of the 1970's will have the impact that their predecessors had, but there is every reason to think so. Ideological extremism, the future of the metropolis and federalism, citizen involvement in governance, governance itself from its structural moorings in small decision-making groups to policy development, the continuing socialization of the young in a rapidly changing political culture, and the role of the intellectual elites in public life are likely to remain current concerns. Each of the works reviewed here was an important landmark in the process of contemporary research development in the broad field of American politics.

Conclusion

What of the future and its promises? An intensive interest in public policy had emerged by the middle 1960's. However, it is still quite unclear just what "public policy" means to different investigators. As different meanings are given to the concept, different things are being investigated by way of very different theories and methods. There are those who see in studying policy a way of expressing their ideological spleen; those for whom a policy provides the arena in which to study the political process; those for whom the study of public policy is a kind of cost-benefit and econometric analysis; those who try to establish causal connections between surrogate policy variables like budget outlays and political patterns; those for whom the policy arena is a place to build and test models of rational private and public choice; those who believe that policy analysis should be concerned with evaluating the impact of policies on people at the grass roots; and those who see in policy study a way of becoming government policy advisers and consultants.

Public policy is the rage,[28] but it has not jelled as a "field" that may have autonomous status across disciplinary boundaries or within a single discipline, or that may simply be another specialization within the sub-field of American politics. If no widely accepted paradigm for the scientific study of public policy has emerged, it is probably due to there not having appeared a truly integrative work of landmark character that could give direction. I have recently read two excellent works by Charles O. Jones (1975) and Aaron Wildavsky (1975) which should be hailed as contributions to the policy literature. But I am hard put to think of them as something different, in spirit or kind, from the works on the political process or budget process with which most political scientists are familiar. I have a hunch that the new public policy is the old public administration in contemporary (and temporary) disguise.

Just about 20 years ago I had an opportunity to review the literature of political science—not alone of studies in American politics but in all of the discipline's sub-fields. I am now taking the privilege of quoting from that review to place this conclusion into context. Referring to the intellectual conflicts within the discipline, I indicated there that if, "at midcentury, political scientists are agreed on anything, it is probably on the muddled state of their science. Political scientists are riding off in many directions, evidently on the assumption that if you don't know where you are going, any road will take you there" (Eulau, 1970: 131-132).[29] And lamenting the discipline's failure to cumulate its findings, I suggested that it is impossible to say "that anything has been disproven as long as conventional tests of proof—the requisites of scientific status in any field of knowledge—are not commonly accepted by political scientists, or, in fact, are rejected by some as altogether irrelevant in political inquiry" (Eulau, 1970: 135).

There are two things to be said today about these judgments. First, they still hold for the discipline *as a whole*. In fact, from the perspective which I try to represent, the situation may have worsened in the intervening years as the discipline's scope expanded and ever more specializations were added. Second, the judgments are no longer true of the sub-field generally called "American Politics" whose landmark and innovative contributions I have presented in this essay. The great bulk of these contributions meets the criteria and standards of scientific investigations—scientific not in some narrow, parochial sense, but in the sense that particular topics or subjects require different forms of scientific inquiry. There are different ways of doing science in the study of electoral behavior, of legislative decision-making, of the judicial process, of executive policy-making, and so on. Moreover, Americanists do not go off in any direction they please; and they are also pretty much agreed on what tests of proof are appropriate in regard to particular subjects. There is both much cumulation and replication going on in the study of American politics. An article dealing with innovative or exceptional research can hardly demonstrate this. On the whole, Americanists in political science have reason to be proud of the development and current status of their sub-field.[30]

Notes

1. There is a great deal of writing on the state and development of political science. For an overview, see Eulau (1970); Somit and Tanenhaus (1964, 1967); Irish (1968). For an Englishman's assessment, see Crick (1959).

2. I am not sure how a "classic" is to be defined. For all practical purposes, it presumably is a book worth reading even though "dated." I would include such works as Holcombe (1924); Gosnell (1927); Odegard (1928); Herring (1929, 1940); Peel (1935); Schattschneider (1935); McKean (1940).

3. An image of pre-World War II political science as legalistic and anecdotal is only partly true. Just as pre-World War I political science was also reformist, so post-World War I political science was not unaffected by philosophical pragmatism and realism which provided the foundations for the emergence of scientific empiricism as the dominant mode of studying American politics.

4. For a discussion of the problems involved, see Eulau and March (1969). This is the report of the Behavioral and Social Sciences Survey Political Science Panel, sponsored by the Social Science Research Council and the National Research Council—National Academy of Sciences.

5. This is a story all of its own. The contemporary case of the theoretical scholar stung by the bug of relevance, admittedly under trying conditions, is David Easton (1969).

6. All of these scholars except Simon subsequently served as presidents of the American Political Science Association. I have it on good authority that Simon was once offered the nomination but rejected it.

7. Bloc analysis was first developed in connection with the study of legislative behavior. For the first extensive use of this method, see Beyle (1931).

8. Key (1961) later published a book on public opinion and democracy. This work was largely based on survey data collected by the Michigan Survey Research Center. It did not have the acclaim or impact of *Southern Politics*. A posthumously published study (Key, 1966), in which he argued on empirical grounds the basic rationality of the electorate, remains controversial.

9. Bailey received his Ph.D. from Harvard University where E. Pendleton Herring had been teaching. The influence of Herring's *The Politics of Democracy* (1940) on Bailey's work and especially on his formulation of vector analysis is unmistakable.

10. I am a victim here of my self-imposed injunction not to write about professional and institutional developments in political science; for the period from about 1950 on was one of considerable organizational growth and intellectual stimulation, especially by two committees of the Social Science Research Council then headed by E. Pendleton Herring. For a "personal view" of the ferment of the 1950's, see Eulau (1967).

11. As far as I know, the notion of "behavioral science" as an interdisciplinary experience was first articulated in *Report of the Study for the Ford Foundation on Policy and Program* (Ford Foundation, Study Committee, 1949). Also see Ranney (1962). As far as I can determine, the "ism" attached to "behavioral" first appeared in Charlesworth (1962).

12. This impression probably stemmed initially from the influence that Lass-

well's explicitly "psychiatric" writings (Lasswell, 1930, 1948) were believed to have on the emerging behavioral orientation in political science. It probably also stemmed from the influence that the Freud-and-Marx-inspired work on the "authoritarian personality" in fact had in the 1950's (Adorno *et al.*, 1950). See Lane (1953).

13. For instance, in 1951 appeared a quantitative study by a political scientist of the relationship between party and constituency as factors in Congressional rollcall voting (Turner, 1951). This study provided new and reliable information in a matter of long interest, but was also something of a bridge between the work in the same field by an earlier sociologist (Rice, 1928) and a later sociologist (MacRae, 1958).

14. There has been recognition of the work of particular individuals of the Columbia group in particular areas of study, and some like Selznick, Mills or Lipset have had a continuing influence on research by political scientists. Needless to say, perhaps, I am not suggesting that the Columbia group were of one mind in regard to theory, method or judgment. On the contrary, they were a very diverse lot. That Columbia spawned so distinguished a group is not an accident but, as in the case of the "Chicago school" in political science, a profound aspect of scientific development. For autobiographical reports on their work by some of the Columbia group, see Hammond (1964).

15. The National Opinion Research Center conducted a national survey of voting during the 1944 election, but the write-up by Sheldon J. Korchin (1946) remained an unpublished Harvard doctoral dissertation known only to the few students of elections who have been diligent enough to consult it. It is probably quite forgotten today but must be consulted by anyone who, in due time, prepares to write an exhaustive history of voting studies.

16. For instance, I find no reference to the Dahl-Lindblom work in the volume on "Policies and Policymaking" of the recently published *Handbook of Political Science* (Greenstein and Polsby, 1975). And I count only five isolated and incidental references to Dahl-Lindblom elsewhere in this eight-volume work.

17. For an appraisal of the Michigan research, see Prewitt and Nie (1971); for an appraisal by one of the Michigan researchers, see Converse (1975). I am again victimized by my self-imposed limitation not to discuss institutional developments. What made possible the great influence of the Michigan school of electoral analysis was the continuance of the biennial election surveys, their dissemination through the archival activities of the Inter-University Consortium for Political Research under the leadership of Warren E. Miller, Richard I. Hofferbert and Jere Clubb, and the improved methodological training of the new generation of students stimulated by the Consortium's summer programs.

18. The work was partly based on a prior study of the 1952 conventions which, despite its five volumes, failed to impress, largely because of its atheoretical character (see David, Moos and Goldman, 1954). The 1960 study corrected for this failing.

19. It deserves mention that since Heard's work the study of "money in politics" has been systematized and institutionalized. Heard (1968:237–238) writes: "In 1958 an organization devoted exclusively to the study of campaign

finance was established in Princeton, New Jersey. The Citizens' Research Foundation, with a small staff under the direction of Herbert E. Alexander, extended some of Heard's approaches and initiated new ones of their own. Through its publications series, its own research, its assistance to anyone studying the subject, and the accumulation and dissemination of information, the Foundation kept a steady focus of attention on political finance in the United States and contributed in many significant ways to the continuity and development of its study."

20. It should be pointed out, however, that there were a number of sophisticated, if less extensive, studies in the late 1950's that contributed to this flowering. Beginning in 1954, Ralph K. Huitt had begun to publish perceptive studies about aspects of the Senate of the United States, finally brought together in a single volume (Huitt and Peabody, 1969). These essays had a great deal to do with rejuvenating the study of legislative institutions. And David B. Truman (1959) had published an intensive study of partisan behavior during the Eight-first Congress, based on bloc analysis of roll-call votes. For a survey of legislative research through the early 1960's, see Eulau and Hinckley (1966); for an up-date, see Peabody's essay in Huitt and Peabody (1969); also Eulau and Abramowitz (1972).

21. The book had an inadvertent pay-off shortly after publication. It was reviewed in a lengthy article in the prestigious journal *World Politics* by Theodore J. Lowi who introduced his own typology of policies—distributive, redistributive and regulatory—that had some influence, even if found wanting, on later policy research (see Lowi, 1964).

22. No invidious meaning is to be given to my use of the terms "liberal" and "conservative." I don't know whether and how Banfield or Dahl would label themselves. But there is a difference between them. It is this difference that makes it all the more remarkable that they formulated very similar conceptions of the political process in the cities they studied. The controversy concerning the shape of "power structures" was not only over substantive questions but even more over theoretical and methodological issues. The literature has become legion (and somewhat boring). For an enunciation of the position taken by the New Haven researchers, see Polsby (1963). For a leftist critique, see Bachrach (1967).

23. That is, Ph.D. candidates may offer both "comparative politics" and "American politics" as separate fields. The absurdity of this is evident when, for instance, a student takes examinations in comparative politics and international politics but not in American politics, thereby depriving himself of an observational standpoint that is probably critical for his understanding of an politics in foreign countries. For some reason, "America" is not part of the world in which the comparative scholar generally moves.

24. At the very time of Greenstein's field work appeared Herbert Hyman's *Political Socialization* (1959). Despite its title, it had more to do with the learning of religious, ethnic and other social norms and values than political ones. Hyman's book was useful to political scientists but not decisive in directing the course of research.

25. However, there exists today a journal, *Experimental Study of Politics*,

now in its sixth year of publication, that seeks to stimulate experimental studies and, in fact, has published some articles of high quality.

26. Fenno's influence on Congressional committee studies antedates his 1966 book and stems from his original article on the House Appropriations Committee (Fenno, 1962). More recently, Fenno has published a comparative study of several Congressional committees (Fenno, 1973).

27. The project also produced a number of specialized studies by some of its collaborators involving mostly individual-level analyses (Black, 1970, 1972, 1974; Eyestone, 1971; Loveridge, 1971; Prewitt, 1970; and Zisk, 1973).

28. It is difficult to pinpoint chronologically what I call "the rage," for counter to much contemporary impression an interest in public policy has always been, in my view, at the base of political science. Policy issues were studied in electoral and legislative researches as well as in public administration case studies from the late 1940's on. The most immediate stimulus probably was institutional: in 1964 the Social Science Research Council appointed a Committee on Governmental and Legal Processes to succeed its Committee on Political Behavior. Headed by Austin Ranney, the new committee soon sponsored a series of conferences and funded some policy resarch. See Ranney, ed. (1968).

29. I should point out here that though first published in 1959 and republished in 1970, the essay from which I am quoting was actually written in December, 1956, and reflects my impression of the state of the discipline at that time.

30. As I reflect on this review of the landmark literature, I am embarrassed for not having mentioned some of the very fine studies that, through the years, have made an impression on me, from which I have learned, and which I certainly expect my graduate students to read. Excellent though they are, these books do not fit my definition for inclusion in this particular survey. As many of their authors are acquaintances or friends of long standing, I'm doubly embarrassed. To assuage my conscience, I shall mention a few here—but again only to illustrate rather than to exhaust the list, for there are many other excellent research studies that have made significant contributions to an understanding of the whole of American politics. But see the following (Wood, 1959; Kaufman, 1960; Wilson, 1962, 1973; Cohen, 1963; Edelman, 1964; Price, 1964; Barber, 1965; McConnell, 1966; Sharkansky, 1969; Sundquist, 1969; Allison, 1971; Pressman and Wildavsky, 1973; Kirkpatrick, 1974; George and Smoke, 1974; Mayhew, 1974; Wolfinger, 1974; Zeigler and Jennings, 1974). And many more.

References

A. THE LANDMARKS

Almond, G. A. 1950. The American People and Foreign Policy (New York: Harcourt, Brace).
——— and S. Verba. 1963. The Civic Culture: Attitudes and Democracy in Five Nations (Princeton: Princeton University Press).

Bailey, S. K. 1950. Congress Makes a Law: A Study of the Full Employment Act of 1946 (New York: Columbia University Press).

Banfield, E. C. 1961. Political Influence (New York: Free Press).

Barber, J. D. 1966. Power in Committees: An Experiment in the Governmental Process (Chicago: Rand McNally).

Bauer, R. A., I. de S. Pool and L. A. Dexter. 1963. American Business and Public Policy (New York: Atherton).

Berelson, B., P. F. Lazarsfeld and W. N. McPhee. 1954. Voting (Chicago: University of Chicago Press).

Buchanan, J. M. and G. Tullock. 1962. The Calculus of Consent: Logical Foundations of Constitutional Democracy (Ann Arbor: University of Michigan Press).

Campbell, A., P. E. Converse, W. E. Miller and D. E. Stokes. 1960. The American Voter (New York: Wiley).

David, P. T., R. M. Goldman and R. C. Bain. 1960. The Politics of National Party Conventions (Washington: Brookings Institution).

Dahl, R. A. 1961. Who Governs? Democracy and Power in an American City. (New Haven: Yale University Press).

————— and C. E. Lindblom. 1953. Politics, Economics and Welfare (New York: Harper).

Downs, A. 1957. An Economic Theory of Democracy (New York: Harper).

Dye, T. R. 1966. Politics, Economics, and the Public: Policy Outcomes in the American States (Chicago: Rand McNally).

Easton, D. and J. Dennis. 1969. Children in the Political System: Origins of Political Legitimacy (New York: McGraw-Hill).

Elazar, D. J. 1970. Cities of the Prairie: The Metropolitan Frontier and American Politics (New York: Basic Books).

Eldersveld, S. J. 1964. Political Parties: A Behavioral Analysis (Chicago: Rand McNally).

Eulau, H. and K. Prewitt. 1973. Labyrinths of Democracy: Adaptations, Linkages, Representation and Policies in Urban Politics (Indianapolis: Bobbs-Merrill).

Fenno, R. F. 1966. The Power of the Purse: Appropriations Politics in Congress (Boston: Little, Brown).

Greenstein, F. I. 1965. Children and Politics (New Haven: Yale University Press).

Grodzins, M. 1966. The American System (Chicago: Rand McNally).

Heard, A. 1960. The Costs of Democracy. (Chapel Hill: University of North Carolina Press).

Jennings, M. K. and R. G. Niemi. 1974. The Political Character of Adolescence: The Influence of Families and Schools (Princeton: Princeton University Press).

Key, V. O. Jr. 1949. Southern Politics in State and Nation (New York: Knopf).

Ladd, E. C. Jr. and S. M. Lipset. 1975. The Divided Academy: Professors and Politics (New York: McGraw-Hill).

Lane, R. E. 1962. Political Ideology: Why the American Common Man Believes What He Does (New York: Free Press).

Lipset, S. M., M. Trow and J. Coleman. 1956. Union Democracy (Glencoe, Ill.: Free Press).

——— and E. Raab. 1970. The Politics of Unreason: Right-Wing Extremism in America, 1790-1970 (New York: Harper and Row).

Matthews, D. R. 1960. U.S. Senators and Their World (Chapel Hill: University of North Carolina Press).

Neustadt, R. 1960. Presidential Power: The Politics of Leadership (New York: Wiley).

Peltason, J. W. 1961. Fifty-eight Lonely Men: Southern Federal Judges and School Desegregation (New York: Harcourt, Brace and World).

Pritchett, C. H. 1948. The Roosevelt Court (New York: Macmillan).

Riker, W. H. 1962. The Theory of Political Coalitions (New Haven: Yale University Press).

Sayer, W. S. and H. Kaufmann. 1960. Governing New York City (New York: Russell Sage Foundation).

Schlesinger, J. A. 1966. Ambition and Politics: Political Careers in the United States (Chicago: Rand McNally).

Schubert, G. 1959. Quantitative Analysis of Judicial Behavior (Glencoe, Ill.: Free Press).

Simon, H. A. 1947. Administrative Behavior: A Study of Decision-Making Processes in Administrative Organization (New York: Macmillan).

Truman, D. B. 1951. The Governmental Process (New York: Knopf).

Verba, S. and N. H. Nie. 1972. Participation in America: Political Democracy and Social Equality (New York: Harper and Row).

Wahlke, J. C., H. Eulau, W. Buchanan and L. C. Ferguson. 1962. The Legislative System: Explorations in Legislative Behavior (New York: Wiley).

Young, J. S. 1966. The Washington Community, 1800-1828 (New York: Columbia University Press).

B. OTHER WORKS:

Adorno, T. W., E. Frenkel-Brunswik, D. J. Levinson and R. N. Sanford. 1950. The Authoritarian Personality (New York: Harper).

Allison, G. 1971. Essence of Decision (Boston: Little, Brown).

Almond, G. A. 1954. The Appeals of Communism (Princeton, N. J.: Princeton University Press).

Bachrach, P. 1967. The Theory of Democratic Elitism: A Critique (Boston: Little, Brown).

Barber, J. D. 1965. The Lawmakers: Recruitment and Adaptation to Legislative Life (New Haven: Yale University Press).

Barnard, C. I. 1938. The Functions of the Executive (Cambridge: Harvard University Press).

Bentley, A. F. 1908. The Process of Government (Bloomington: Principia Press, 1935 reissue).

Beyle, H. C. 1931. Identification and Analysis of Attribute-Cluster Blocs (Chicago: University of Chicago Press).

Black, G. S. 1970. "A Theory of Professionalization in Politics," American Political Science Review, 64 (September): 865-878.

———. 1972. "A Theory of Political Ambition: Career Choices and the Role of Structural Incentives," American Political Science Review, 66 (March): 144-159.

———. 1974. "Conflict in the Community: A Theory of the Effects of Community Size," American Political Science Review, 68 (September): 1245-1261.

Blau, P. M. 1955. The Dynamics of Bureaucracy (Chicago: University of Chicago Press).

Bogue, A. S. and M. P. Marlaire. 1975. "Of Mess and Men: The Boardinghouse and Congressional Voting, 1821-1842," American Journal of Political Science, 19 (May): 207-230.

Bryce, J. J. 1888. The American Commonwealth (New York: Macmillan), 2 vols.

Campbell, A., G. Gurin and W. E. Miller. 1954. The Voter Decides (Evanston: Row-Peterson).

———, P. E. Converse, W. E. Miller and D. E. Stokes. 1966. Elections and the Political Order (New York: Wiley).

Charlesworth, J. C., ed. 1962. The Limits of Behavioralism in Political Science (Philadelphia: American Academy of Political and Social Science).

Cohen, B. C. 1963. The Press and Foreign Policy (Princeton: Princeton University Press).

Coleman, J. S. 1957. Community Conflict (Glencoe, Ill.: Free Press).

———. 1961. The Adolescent Society (New York: Free Press).

Converse, P. E. 1975. "Public Opinion and Voting Behavior," in Greenstein and Polsby, eds. Handbook of Political Science, 4: 75-169.

Coser, L. 1956. The Functions of Social Conflict (Glencoe, Ill.: Free Press).

Crick, B. 1959. The American Science of Politics (Berkeley: University of California Press).

Cronin, T. E. and S. D. Greenberg, eds. 1969. The Presidential Advisory System (New York: Harper and Row).

Dahl, R. A. 1956. A Preface to Democratic Theory (Chicago: University of Chicago Press).

———. 1961 "The Behavioral Approach in Political Science: Epitaph for a Monument to a Successful Protest," American Political Science Review, 55 (December): 763-772.

———. 1967. Pluralist Democracy in the United States: Conflict and Consent (Chicago: Rand McNally).

David, P. T., M. Moos and R. Goldman. 1954. Presidential Nominating Politics in 1952 (Baltimore: Johns Hopkins University Press), 5 vols.

Easton, D. 1969. "The New Revolution in Political Science," American Political Science Review, 63 (December): 1051-1061.

Easton, D. 1953. The Political System: An Inquiry into the State of Political Science (New York: Knopf).

Edelman, M. 1964. The Symbolic Uses of Politics (Urbana, Ill.: University of Illinois Press).

Elazar, D. J. 1962. The American Partnership (Chicago: University of Chicago Press).

———. 1966. American Federalism: A View from the States (New York: Crowell).

Eulau, H. and K. Hinckley. 1966. "Legislative Institutions and Processes," in J. A. Robinson, ed., Political Science Annual (Indianapolis: Bobbs-Merrill), 1: 85-189.

———. 1968. "The Behavioral Movement in Political Science: A Personal Document," Social Research, 35 (Spring): 1-29.

Document," Social Research, 35 (Spring): 1-29.

———. 1969a. "Tradition and Innovation: On the Tension between Ancient and Modern Ways in the Study of Politics," in H. Eulau, ed., Behavioralism in Political Science (New York: Atherton): 1-21.

———. 1969b. Micro-Macro Political Analysis: Accents of Inquiry (Chicago: Aldine).

———. and J. G. March, eds. 1969c. Political Science (Englewood Cliffs, N.J.: Prentice-Hall).

———. 1970. "Political Science," in B. F. Hoselitz, ed., A Reader's Guide to the Social Sciences (New York: Free Press): 129-237.

———. and A. Abramowitz. 1972. "Recent Research on Congress in a Democratic Perspective," Political Science Reviewer II (Fall): 1-38.

Eyestone, R. 1971. The Threads of Public Policy: A Study of Policy Leadership (Indianapolis: Bobbs-Merrill).

Fenno, R. F., Jr. 1962. "The House Appropriations Committee as a Political System: The Problem of Integration," American Political Science Review, 56 (June): 310-324.

———. 1973. Congressmen in Committees (Boston: Little, Brown).

Fenton, J. H. 1957. Politics in the Border States (New Orleans: Hauser).

———. 1966. Midwest Politics (New York: Holt, Rinehart and Winston).

Garceau, O., ed. 1968. Political Research and Political Theory (Cambridge: Harvard University Press).

George, A. L. and R. Smoke, 1974. Deterrence in American Foreign Policy: Theory and Practice (New York: Columbia University Press).

Golembiewski, R. T. 1962. The Small Group: An Analysis of Research Concepts and Operations (Chicago: University of Chicago Press).

Gosnell, H. F. 1927. Getting Out the Vote (Chicago: University of Chicago Press).

Gouldner, A. W. 1954. Patterns of Industrial Democracy (Glencoe, Ill.: Free Press).

Greenstein, F. I. and N. W. Polsby, eds. 1975. Handbook of Political Science (Reading, Mass.: Addison-Wesley), 8 vols.

Hammond, P. E. 1964. Sociologists at Work: Essays on the Craft of Social Research (New York: Basic Books).

Heard, A. 1968. "Political Financing," in D. A. Sills, ed., International Encyclopedia of the Social Sciences (New York: Macmillan and Free Press), 12: 235-241.

Herring, E. P. 1929. Group Representation before Congress (Washington: Brookings Institution).

Herring, E. P. 1940. The Politics of Democracy (New York: Rinehart).

Hirsch, H. and M. D. Hancock, eds. 1971. Comparative Legislative Systems: A Reader in Theory and Research (New York: Free Press).

Holcombe, A. N. 1924. Political Parties Today (New York: Harper).

Huitt, R. K. and R. L. Peabody. 1969. Congress: Two Decades of Analysis (New York: Harper and Row).

Hunter, F. 1953. Community Power Structure (Chapel Hill: University of North Carolina Press).

Hyman, H. 1959. Political Socialization: A Study in the Psychology of Political Behavior (Glencoe, Ill.: Free Press).

Irish, M., ed. 1968. Political Science: Advance of the Discipline (Englewood Cliffs, N. J.: Prentice-Hall).

Janowitz, M. 1960. The Professional Soldier (Glencoe, Ill.: Free Press).

Jones, C. O. 1975. Clean Air: The Policies and Politics of Pollution Control (Pittsburgh: University of Pittsburgh Press).

Karl, B. D. 1974. Charles E. Merriam and the Study of Politics (Chicago: University of Chicago Press).

Kaufman, H. 1960. The Forest Ranger (Baltimore: Johns Hopkins University Press).

Kessel, J. H. 1975. The Domestic Presidency: Decision-Making in the White House (North Scituate, Mass.: Duxbury).

Key, V. O., Jr. 1942. Politics, Parties and Pressure Groups (New York: Crowell).

———. 1956. American State Politics: An Introduction (New York: Knopf).

———. 1961. Public Opinion and American Democracy (New York: Knopf).

———. 1966. The Responsible Electorate (Cambridge: Harvard University Press).

Kirkpatrick, J. 1974. Political Woman (New York: Basic Books).

Korchin, S. J. 1946. Psychological Variables in the Behavior of Voters (Harvard University: unpubl. Ph.D. dissertation).

Kornberg, A., ed. 1973. Legislatures in Comparative Perspective (New York: McKay).

Lane, R. E. 1953. "Political Character and Political Analysis," Psychiatry, 16 (November): 387-398.

Lasswell, H. D. 1930. Psychopathology and Politics (Chicago: University of Chicago Press).

———. 1936. Politics: Who Gets What, When, How (New York: McGraw-Hill).

———. 1941. Democracy through Public Opinion (Menasha, Wis.: Banta).

———. 1948. Power and Personality (New York: Norton).

———. and A. Kaplan. 1950. Power and Society (New Haven: Yale University Press).

Lazarsfeld, P. F., B. Berelson and H. Gaudet. 1944. The People's Choice (New York: Duell).

Lindblom, C. E. 1965. The Intelligence of Democracy (New York: Free Press).

Lippman, W. 1922. Public Opinion (New York: Macmillan).

Lockard, D. 1959. New England Politics (Princeton, N. J.: Princeton University Press).

Loveridge, R. O. 1971. City Managers in Legislative Politics (Indianapolis: Bobbs-Merrill).

Lowi, T. J. 1964. "American Business, Public Policy, Case-Studies, and Political Theory," World Politics, 16 (July): 677-715.

Maas, A., ed. 1959. Area and Power: A Theory of Local Government (Glencoe, Ill.: Free Press).

MacRae, D., Jr. 1958. Dimensions of Congressional Voting (Berkeley: University of California Press).

Manley, J. F. 1970. The Politics of Finance: The House Committee on Ways and Means (Boston: Little, Brown).

March, J. G. and H. A. Simon. 1958. Organizations (New York: Wiley).

Mayhew, D. R. 1974. Congress: The Electoral Connection (New Haven: Yale University Press).

McClosky, H., P. J. Hoffmann and R. O'Hara. 1960. "Issue Conflict and Consensus Among Party Leaders and Followers," American Political Science Review, 54 (June): 406-427.

———. 1964. "Consensus and Ideology in American Politics," American Political Science Review, 58 (June): 361-382.

McCloskey, R. G. 1963. Review of J. W. Peltason, Fifty-eight Lonely Men, American Political Science Review, 57 (December), 960-961.

McConnel, G. 1966. Private Power and American Democracy (New York: Knopf.)

McKean, D. D. 1940. The Boss: The Hague Machine in Action (Boston: Houghton Mifflin).

McPhee, W. N. and W. A. Glaser. 1962. Public Opinion and Congressional Elections (New York: Free Press).

Merriam, C. E. 1925. New Aspects of Politics (Chicago: University of Chicago Press).

Miller, W. E. 1964. "Majority Rule and the Representative System of Government," in E. Allardt and Y. Littunen, eds., Cleavages, Ideologies and Party Systems (Helsinki: Transactions of the Westermark Society): 343-376.

——— and D. E. Stokes. 1963. "Constituency Influence in Congress," American Political Science Review, 57 (March): 45-56.

———. and T. E. Levitin. 1975. The New Liberals: Political Leadership and Generational Change in American Politics (mss., in press).

Mills, C. W. 1951. White Collar (New York: Oxford University Press).

———. 1956. The Power Elite (New York: Oxford University Press).

Munns, J. M. 1975. "The Environment, Politics, and Policy Literature: A Critique and Reformulation," Western Political Quarterly, 28 (December): 646-667.

Odegard, P. H. 1928. Pressure Politics: The Story of the Anti-Saloon League (New York: Columbia University Press).

Olson, M., Jr. 1965. The Logic of Collective Action (Cambridge: Harvard University Press).

Patterson, S. C. and J. C. Wahlke, eds. 1972. Comparative Legislative Behavior: Frontiers of Research (New York: Wiley).

Peel, R. V. 1935. The Political Clubs of New York (New York: Putnam).

Peltason, J. W. 1955. Federal Courts in the Political Process (New York: Random House).

Polsby, N. W. 1963. Community Power and Political Theory (New Haven: Yale University Press).

———. 1967. Review of J. S. Young, The Washington Community, American Political Science Review, 61 (March): 164-165.

Pressman, J. L. and A. B. Wildavsky. 1973. Implementation (Berkeley: University of California Press).

Prewitt, K. 1970. The Recruitment of Political Leaders: A Study of Citizen-Politicians (Indianapolis: Bobbs-Merrill).

———. and N. Nie. 1971. "Election Studies of the Survey Research Center," British Journal of Political Science, 1 (October), 553-576.

Price, D. K. 1965. The Scientific Estate (Cambridge: Harvard University Press).

Pritchett, C. H. 1954. Civil Liberties and the Vinson Court (Chicago: University of Chicago Press).

Ranney, A., ed. 1962. Essays on the Behavioral Study of Politics (Urbana, Ill.: University of Illinois Press).

———, ed. 1968. Political Science and Public Policy (Chicago: Marham).

Rice, S. A. 1928. Quantitative Methods in Politics (New York: Appleton).

Riker, W. H. and P. C. Ordeshook. 1973. An Introduction to Positive Political Theory (Englewood Cliffs, N. J.: Prentice-Hall).

Rosenberg, M. 1957. Occupations and Values (Glencoe, Ill.: Free Press).

Schattschneider, E. E. 1935. Politics, Pressures and the Tariff (New York: Prentice-Hall).

Schubert, G. 1960. Constitutional Politics: The Political Behavior of Supreme Court Justices and the Constitutional Policies that They Make (New York: Holt, Rinehart and Winston).

———, ed. 1963. Judicial Decision-Making (New York: Free Press).

———, ed. 1964. Judicial Behavior: A Reader in Theory and Research (Chicago: Rand McNally).

———. 1965. The Judicial Mind: The Attitudes and Ideologies of Supreme Court Justices, 1946-1963 (Evanston: Northwestern University Press).

Selvin, H. C. 1960. The Effects of Leadership (Glencoe, Ill.: Free Press).

Selznick, P. 1949. TVA and the Grassroots: A Study in the Sociology of Formal Organization (Berkeley: University of California Press).

Sharkansky, I. 1969. The Politics of Taxing and Spending (Indianapolis: Bobbs-Merrill).

Sills, D. L. 1957. The Volunteers: Means and Ends in National Organization (Glencoe, Ill.: Free Press).

Somit, A. and J. Tanenhaus. 1964. American Political Science (New York: Atherton Press).

——— and J. Tanenhaus. 1967. The Development of American Political Science (Boston: Allyn and Bacon).

Sundquist, J. L. 1969. Making Federalism Work (Washington, D. C.: Brookings Institution).

Tanenhaus, J. 1961. Review of G. Schubert, Quantitative Analysis of Judicial Behavior, American Political Science Review, 55 (March), 171-172.

Tocqueville, A. de. 1838, 1840. Democracy in America (New York: Harper, 1945, reissue).

Truman, D. B. 1959. The Congressional Party (New York: Wiley).

Turner, J. 1951. Party and Constituency: Pressures on Congress (Baltimore: Johns Hopkins University Press).

Verba, S. 1961. Small Groups and Political Behavior: A Study in Leadership (Princeton: Princeton University Press).

Wahlke, J. C. 1975. "Introduction," in S. C. Patterson, R. D. Hedlund and G. R. Boynton, Representatives and Represented (New York: John Wiley & Sons): 1-20.

Wildavsky, A. 1975. Budgeting: A Comparative Theory of Budgetary Processes (Boston: Little, Brown).

Wilson, J. Q. 1962. The Amateur Democrat (Chicago: University of Chicago Press).

———. 1973. Political Organizations (New York: Basic Books).

Wolfinger, R. E. 1974. The Politics of Progress (Englewood Cliffs, N. J.: Prentice-Hall).

Wood, R. C. 1959. Suburbia: Its People and Their Politics (Boston: Houghton Mifflin).

Zeigler, H. and M. K. Jennings. 1974. Governing American Schools: Political Interaction in Local School Districts (North Scituate, Mass.: Duxbury).

Zisk, B. H. 1973. Local Interest Politics: A One-Way Street (Indianapolis: Bobbs-Merrill).

Anthropology and America

WALTER GOLDSCHMIDT

University of California, Los Angeles

Western civilization has long had a love-hate relationship with the primitive. He represents both our suppressed desires and our frightening impulses. He represents both our fear of want and our freedom from wanting. He represents for us both the crudities and hardships of an uncivilized world and an escape from civilization and its discontents. The word "savage" used naked means cruel, harsh, unrelenting and unlettered; the same word clad in the adjective "noble," has reference to the finest qualities of mankind. Our annual Thanksgiving rite expresses appreciation for the generosity of the very savage with whom we fought bitter wars and from whom we wrested our land. The great, largely unsung anthropologist, George C. Engerrand, who taught for nearly four decades at the University of Texas, used to speak of the pendulum motion from good to bad in the history of our view of primitive man. Such a pulsation inevitably derives from a deep-seated ambivalence.

The matter is intellectually and philosophically important because the character of the primitive has been seen as a window to the nature of man. If primitive man, *Naturmensch*, as the German language so aptly puts it, can tell us what we really are—whether we are *Homo economicus* or Rousseau's noble savage—then the understanding of primitive behavior becomes a central and necessary element in the formulation of the metaphysical system that will underlie our moral philosophy. As we have been in search of such a system since the Enlightenment, having progressively discarded theological explanations, the issue is incandescent and perduring.

Anthropology inevitably is at the center of this issue. In the public mind, anthropology is the study of primitive peoples, dead or alive. While this is not the case (and never has been), it *is* true that anthropology (1) is the only discipline regularly to study unlettered peoples, and (2) derives its basic insights and orientations from the study of tribal and peasant communities. The anthropologist cannot, therefore, escape the emotional dilemma created by the Western ambivalence toward the savage.

The fundamental mandate of anthropology is the study of human nature. Most anthropologists would not agree. Anthropology conscientiously destroyed the old, ethnocentric notions of human nature and turned to situational factors—culture and society—as explanatory elements, leaving the impression, at least, that the infant is a *tabula rasa* on which anything could be imprinted. Important as these situational elements are, and important as their illumination has been, we still cannot understand the workings of culture or the form of society without taking cognizance of man the animal. (This, incidentally, is why the continued association between physical and cultural anthropology has been so valuable.) The very boast inherent in anthropology's eponym—the study of man—is an assertion of this mandate. Of all the social disciplines, anthropology is the only one that has no particular subject matter, no delineated focus such as characterizes economics (the market), political science (the institutions of authority), etc. Its subject matter is not primitive people, *per se*, for anthropologists have from the beginning concerned themselves with modern and Western societies; it is not the study of social behavior, but of man. If anthropology ceases to be the study of man it will dissolve into the meaningless examination of trivia—a danger by no means remote, as a sampling of its literature will reveal.

It was the quest for understanding man that led anthropologists to examine the diversity of customs, the physical and biological varieties of man, the evidences for his antiquity in the caves of Europe and the middens throughout the world, the manner of his speech and the formulations of his symbolic systems. These diverse orientations, involving very different kinds of research activities and capacities, direct attention to the three fundamental dimensions of anthropological explanation: the biological, the historical-evolutionary, and the social-cultural. Hence, the anthropologist not only faces the moral-philosophical dilemma inherent in the symbolic meaning of the savage, but also stands at the point of intersection between the biological formulations of the natural sciences, the sociological explanations of the social sciences, and the problems of meaning, symbol, and change of such humanistic studies as linguistics, aesthetics and history. When C. P. Snow formulated the notion of two cultures, anthropologists immediately recognized they had a foot in each—and feared they might fall between two stools. In this age of specialization, such broad disciplinary scope leads naturally to a kind of intellectual agoraphobia, so that it is not surprising that the anthropologists seek the security of specialization, with its constant threat of trivilization.

Beginnings

Anthropology as a discipline had its origin deep in the nineteenth century. That was the century of biology, the century in which the

great advance in biological knowledge transformed Western metaphysics from theology into science, culminating with Darwin's unequivocal establishment of man's place in nature. Anthropology had deep
roots in this biological tradition, but from its very inception it took
cognizance of that other, peculiarly human quality: man the myth-
maker; man the creator; man the prisoner of habit and custom. Alfred
Kroeber, for many years the dean of anthropological studies, has
pointed out that while anthropology today is perceived as a social
science, its origins lay in the amalgamation of humanistic studies (history, philology, mythology) and science (biology, geology, geography.)
It became a social science by default or predilection, yet it is not a
social science like the others.

Anthropology in America is an old tradition. This is not surprising,
for the Americans were concerned with exotic cultures from the first
landing—at the outset with the "native races," later with the issue of
slavery and the problem of "race," and ultimately, with the assimilation of immigrants. In each of these relationships there was exploitation, expropriation and prejudice, and in this there was a conflict with
the self-image of America as independent, democratic and egalitarian.
The question as to whether the manifest behavioral attributes of these
variant populations was a product of biology or the end result of other
causes was therefore a political and moral issue as well as a philosophical one. An early inspiration to anthropological studies came from that
remarkable product of the Enlightenment, Thomas Jefferson, who
not only is credited with one of the first stratigraphic excavations in
archeology, and with investigations in American Indian languages, but
whose instructions to Lewis and Clark were a model for ethnographic
investigation. Early in the century the American Antiquarian Society
was established, and one of its main problems was an effort to discover
who the mound-builders had been. In 1842 the American Ethnological
Society was established, one of the oldest scholarly organizations in
America still extant, and by mid-century the New York lawyer and
financier, Lewis Henry Morgan, had made his classic study of the Iroquois and later opened up the cross-cultural investigation of kinship
—that hardy perennial of anthropological investigation.

There emerged in anthropology essentially two lines of thought, one
holding that behavioral patterns were expressive of biological differences; the other that they were products of cultural evolution. Both
theories were essentially ethnocentric, taking progress as a given element in human history, seeing Western civilization as the finest product
of cultural evolution just as man was viewed as the finest product of
biological evolution. But they were different in their social implications, for a racist orientation was a rationale for social discrimination

and the disadvantaged status of the poor, while a cultural orientation, as we would now put it, was a mandate for bringing light to the benighted.

We can illustrate these two lines of thought by referencing two widely read works of this period. The more durable of these is Morgan's *Ancient Society* (1877). This work developed the thesis of cultural evolution in its most explicit form. Morgan had, as already indicated, begun his interest with an ethnographic study of his Iroquois neighbors in up-state New York, followed by the detailed examination of the varieties of kinship organizations. In *Ancient Society*, he sees the formulation of the diversity of kinship, marriage and political organizations as a result of the evolution of modes of economic production. It is a thesis that, properly reformulated, is still viable if not universally accepted. Morgan's close association with the Iroquois, his appreciation of their remarkable government as well as the quality of individuals personally known to him, resulted in a permanent concern for the welfare of these native populations (a pattern of sentiment that many subsequent anthropologists have followed). Morgan's thesis was picked up by Friedrich Engels in his influential work, *The Origin of the Family, Private Property and the State* (1884:9), in the preface of which he made it clear that Marx credited Morgan with having "discovered anew the materialist conception of history." Morgan was important to Marx because he found the institution of private property to be a recent evolutionary development, not characteristic of societies at the higher stages of savagery and of barbarism—that "its dominance as a passion over all other passions marks the commencement of civilization" (Morgan 1963:5). That Morgan finds this passion self-destructive to civilization endeared him to Marx and Marxists and has made him a figure of controversy. But what interests us is that he represents man's behavior as a product of socioeconomic conditions.

The second work is Nott and Gliddon, *Types of Mankind* (1854:56): "One of the main objects of this volume is to show that the diversity of races must be accepted by Science as a *fact*, independent of theology . . ." (his stress). "A small trace of white blood in the Negro improves him in intelligence and morality; and an equal trace of Negro blood, as in the quadroon, will protect such individuals against the deadly influence of climate which the pure white man cannot endure," they write later (p. 68). While Morgan's work became politically important because of its endorsement by Marx and Engels, Nott and Gliddon were from the outset concerned with political matters. Early in the Introduction, Nott and Gliddon make extended reference to discussion in 1844 with John C. Calhoun, Secretary of State, over the matter "that England pertinaciously continued to interfere with our inherited Institution of Negro Slavery . . . " (p. 50). As a result of their conversations, and ensuing correspondence, Calhoun was condemned for having "intruded *Ethnology* into diplomatic correspondence" by the British press, though "a communication from the Foreign Office promptly assured our Government that Great Britain had no intention of intermeddling . . . with our internal affairs" (p. 51). Though Nott and Gliddon have been forgotten, their viewpoint is by no means erased from modern thought.

These two works exemplify the diverse meanings that the primitive can have for an understanding of mankind. They also demonstrate that these philosophical concerns, however much rooted in the science of the day, had important political and social involvements.

As the stockmen followed the mountain men into the arid west and they in turn were replaced by the landlappers, American relations to the aboriginal inhabitants of these lands reflected the ambivalence toward the savage. It is not necessary here to go over the sordid history (for there was no ambivalence among those who coveted the lands), but only to note that a scholarly interest followed the march westward. This interest was essentially of the natural history variety, of writers like Schoolcraft, painters like Catlin and naturalists like Marin. The American Museum of Natural History in New York, the Peabody Museum at Harvard and particularly the United States National Museum associated with the Smithsonian Institution developed collections of artifacts, photographs and other data relevant to American Indian life. A great impetus in this direction came with the organization of the Bureau of American Ethnology under the direction of John Wesley Powell. Powell had been raised on the western rim of American settlement, lost an arm in the Civil War, became a teacher in Illinois whence he began to explore the West. Not only was he the first to descend the Colorado River by boat, but he developed an interest in Indian culture. Influenced by Morgan, he was impressed with the degree to which these cultures were adapted to the arid lands they inhabited—a kind of environment that earlier Americans and Northern Europeans had had little experience with or understanding of. For nearly a quarter of a century he directed the Bureau, under the aegis of which great monographic studies of Indian tribal life were published. This period, when the remaining Indians were being reduced to reservation life by governmental edict, was one in which self-taught anthropologists recorded the details of tribal life and customs—only lightly touched with theoretical issues. Though those who did so were concerned with the fate of the Indians, there is little evidence of significant impact on policy during this rapacious period in American history.

From Natural History to Science

Though anthropology had long been recognized by the scientific community (established as a separate section of the American Association for the Advancement of Science in 1882), it was not an academic discipline, and those few who taught it and identified themselves as such were trained in other fields. Nor was there any real coherence; the museum anthropologists of the Peabody, the biologists concerned with race, and the ethnographers of Washington had very little in common.

On to this scene came a young German of Jewish extraction with a doctorate in physics, a rich background in geography, a field investigation among the Eskimo and a calling for anthropology: Franz Boas. This liberal intellectual man of scientific training and prodigious energy turned the nineteenth century combination of philosophizing and natural history into twentieth century science. It is perhaps no paradox, though a bit ironic, that this quintessentially German middle-class immigrant should have given a peculiarly American shape to the field.

Of all the remarkable qualities Boas possessed, the manifestations of which we shall examine shortly, the most unusual lies in his breadth of viewpoint. Most men of genius who shape or reshape a whole field of thought do so through some clearly defined set of ideas. We have no difficulty in perceiving what it was that Darwin or Freud or Einstein said and did; such men brought forward an explicit new thesis with which they transformed a field of learning. There is no such thesis from Boas. Instead, there was a broad, integrative, internally consistent *viewpoint*. Indeed, many of Boas' detractors viewed him as atheoretical or even anti-theoretical, for he had little patience for the "arm-chair" theorizing that characterized anthropology during this epoch of sparse data. He had even less patience for racism, having seen the effects of prejudice from the short end of the stick. This outlook was compounded by (1) a liberalism in which the individuality of each person was respected and the institutions of power were distrusted, (2) an empiricism which demanded a careful and close look at the data and distrusted premature or monolithic theorizing, (3) a cultural relativism that demanded the examination of each social system in its own terms, (4) an eclecticism that recognized that the subjects of anthropological investigation were the result of many forces, which, in turn, made him see (5) the behavior of individuals as a product of cultural context and (6) the character of culture as the product of its unique history. Because of this last item, his was called the historical (or diffusionist) school, but that is a false narrowing of Boas' outlook, though it did characterize much of the work of the first generation of his students.

How was it possible for a person of such eclectic and apparently atheoretical outlook to have such influence that it has dominated American anthropology throughout the twentieth century? Aside from being in the right place at the right time and his own self-conscious recognition of this mission, it was done through prodigious labor. Consider only the following of his active achievements:

He was the first professor of anthropology (Clark University, 1888-92) to turn out an American anthropological doctorate, and when he went to Columbia began producing the students that were to spread his outlook over the land. The names of those of the first quarter century include Kroeber, Lowie, Goldenweiser, Radin, Cole, Spier, Herskovitz and Mead, to name a few of the most influential.

He had the major responsibility for installing the anthropological exhibit at the World's Columbian Exposition in Chicago, insisting on presenting materials in the context of cultures rather than as arrays of artifacts of common type. This not only set the pattern for the Field Museum, which developed out of the Chicago fair, but influenced museum displays throughout the country, particularly the American Museum of Natural History, where he later held an appointment.

He took an active role in forming or reforming anthropological organizations. He was an active member of Section H (the anthropological section) of AAAS; he organized the American Folklore Society (1888); he revitalized the moribund American Ethnological Society (1889-1890); was one of the major founders of the American Anthropological Association (1901-2), and was a prime mover in organizing the American Association of Physical Anthropologists (1918) and the Linguistic Society of America (1924).

He established and later edited the *Journal of American Folklore* for 18 years, was responsible for reorganizing and professionalizing the *American Anthropologist* (1898-99); he edited the *International Journal of American Languages* and was largely responsible for establishing the *American Journal of Physical Anthropology.* He also edited the two volume *Handbook of American Indian Languages* published by the Bureau of American Ethnology.

He organized one of the first two major scientific expeditions, the Jessup North Pacific Expedition, ever to be undertaken by anthropologists and was a prime mover in establishing the International School of Archaeology and Ethnology in Mexico.

He engaged in extensive research in physical anthropology and linguistics as well as spending a cumulated two and a half years of ethnographic field work on the Northwest Coast and wrote literally hundreds of papers and monographs based on such first-hand research.

He presented his ideas in popular form, notably in his *The Mind of*

Primitive Man (1911) and *Anthropology and Modern Life* (1928) but also on occasion in the mass media.[1]

I think that two specific pieces of work represent best how his ideas shaped American thought. The first of these was a major anthropometric undertaking sponsored by the United States Immigration Commission, which apparently wanted to determine whether the influx of immigrants was resulting in the "deterioration" of the American population. Boas' (1912) findings were that the children of immigrants changed toward a mean: "The East European Hebrew, who has a very round head, becomes more long-headed; the South Italian, who in Italy has an extremely long head becomes more short-headed; so that in this country both approach a uniform type." These still somewhat enigmatic findings were a source of extended and acrimonious controversy. First, they questioned the importance of that most sacred of anthropometric measurements, the Cephalic Index. More important, they undermined the whole notion of the fixity of racial features, and with it much of the then prevalent physical anthropology. Both he and his critics were clear on this. Since head shape had always been considered one of the most stable elements in racial typology, he wrote: "We are compelled to conclude that when these features of the body change, the bodily and mental make-up of the immigrants may change." This study of physical anthropology thus became one of the strongest blows in favor of a cultural approach to understanding man's behavior. It was not calculated to please those who were worrying about the deteriorating influence of East Europeans and Italian peasants.

The second work is Boas' Introduction to the *Handbook of American Indian Languages* (1911). Long recognized as one of the pivotal essays in the development of the science of linguistics, the essay makes two major points of interest here. First, it made quite clear that race, language and culture, which had so often been confused with one another, were entirely separate phenomena. A classification of peoples based on racial features does not coincide with one based upon language, nor would either coincide with one based upon customs, social systems, or religious belief. The confusion is still not entirely eliminated from popular thought, though it is unequivocal. The second is the recognition that each language must be understood in its own terms as an internally coherent but more-or-less unique structure. Linguistic studies—philology—had largely been limited to the Indo-European languages, with their fundamentally similar structure, and scholars had endeavored to force all languages into the procrustean bed of Latinate grammatical categories. Boas taught that grammars must be evoked through examination of paradigms, establishing the phonetics and the grammatically relevant particles of meaning through paradigmatic questioning. Thus each grammar emerged in terms of its own structure. The importance of this approach to the development of the science of linguistics cannot be overestimated. But what is more important to us is that it represents—at first unconsciously, but later as a matter of explicit philosophy—the model of the Boasian approach to ethnography. Each culture must be understood in its own terms rather than in terms of some theoretical universalistic structure. This is the genesis of cultural relativism. It is a difficult lesson to keep in mind.

I have cited these two works less for their substantive interest than as examples of the emerging anthropological approach to human behavior: the unimportance of biological elements as determinants of human variation, the plasticity of humans as natural elements, the force of culture in shaping the character of the individual, the examination of this behavior in terms of its inherent consistency, with the further implication of the impropriety of approaching exotic behavior from an ethnocentric bias. At a deeper level, this evokes a holistic approach, a pattern of cultural relativism, and the necessity for a unified science of man, encompassing physical anthropology, archeology, linguistics, and ethnology. It is symbolic to the character of American anthropology that one should cite works in physical anthropology and linguistics to establish the significance of cultural theory.

Empty Empiricism

For the first third of this century, anthropologists concentrated on the study of the disappearing American Indian cultures. Boas insisted that his students engage in field research, and the investigation of an exotic culture became the hallmark of the anthropologists. These investigations were made with a studious avoidance of any theoretical predilections, a naiveté with respect to methods, an investigation into the whole range of cultural phenomena, including language and folklore, and often also physical measurements, and a painstaking attention to detail. The intellectual stance appeared entirely negative. Early post-Boasian anthropology was against racial explanation of behavioral diversity; it was anti-cultural-evolutionist, condemning evolution with the epithet "arm-chair anthropology"; it was against environmentalism and materialistic explanations; it countered numerous European historical schools. The absence of a positive theory or an explanatory approach, rendered the work essentially sterile. The detailed investigation of cat's cradles or moccasin forms and the lengthy texts of native tales, taken down phonetically and so laboriously that all spontaneity and affect was lost in the telling, were, nevertheless, contributions to our knowledge of the diversity of human behavior. They built up the corpus of knowledge that constituted the natural history of man—later characterized as butterfly collecting.

Such theorizing as was done was in the examination of the geographical distribution of diverse elements. Controversy centered on whether items that were similar in character were examples of cultural "diffusion" or were independently invented. Cultural "complexes" and specific cultural elements or traits were mapped to demonstrate the independent movement of these items in the hope that it would be possible to reconstruct the history of nonliterate peoples. The cultural viewpoint became a historical viewpoint and the post-Boasians came to be known as the American historical school of anthropology. Even the investigation of the politically potent and psychologically significant Plains Indian Sun Dance, in the hands of the intellectually powerful Leslie Spier, was reduced to an analysis of the history of its formal elements. Anthropologists were quoting with approval Maitland's dictum that anthropology had the choice between becoming history or nothing, and it appeared to be opting for the latter course.

But to view this period as intellectually sterile is to misunderstand the peculiar strength of the Boasian view of man and to make it impossible to appreciate what was to follow. Something very important was being established through these detailed empirical investigations salted away in the long, dull monographic series published by museums and universities. It was the recognition of cultural complexity, richness, and diversity of tribal peoples; it was an appreciation of the depth of their institutionalized fantasy life, and the patterned, internally consistent quality of tribal community existence. Under the minutiae of such ethnographic reportage there lay hidden a latent model of human social behavior—latent, for even today it has not been given adequate explicit formulation. Such a model was necessary to refute the still popular and then scientifically reputable explanations of human diversity in terms of genetic variations, i.e., race. A sense of wholeness and of interrelatedness, of temporal and spatial continuities, of environmental forces impinging upon needs of humanity, of language formulating thought even as it was formed by it, of the whole complex web of social systems and ideological systems and their mutual effects upon one another was necessary to an outlook that would counteract continuing racist assumptions in the social sciences.

The eighteenth century search for the savage within us had been converted into a nature versus nurture opposition in the nineteenth. The continuing search for that savage in the twentieth, undertaken under a sterile empiricism, had the profound effect of destroying the validity of the search itself—or at least changing the nature of the game. For even as tribal cultures were being killed off or fading away, the cold scientific eye designed by a renegade physicist was destroying the mythical savage. The new anthropology sought not to find the quintessential man within a tribal community. Only a careful examination of the range and diversity of human behavior, only the detailed examination of the conditions and concomitants of such diversity could offer adequate triangulation on the phenomenon that was at the heart of the anthropological quest: human nature.

Theoretical Ferment

The second quarter of this century saw the fruits of this peculiarly American stance, even as furthur complexities developed. For one thing, anthropologists began turning their thoughts homeward. Margaret Mead returned from Samoa, wrote her popular and appealing *Coming of Age in Samoa* (1928) and her *Growing Up in New Guinea* (1930)—("These can go on like the Elsie Dinsmore books," said one reviewer)—and began discussions in the popular press and on the podium of the characteristics of the American culture. Robert and Helen Lynd (1929) made sociological history by examining in ethnographic terms a town in what is now called Middle America (with a foreword by the eminent anthropologist, Clark Wissler). Lloyd Warner (1941) returned from his ritual field trip to Australia and began an intensive study of Newburyport, Massachusetts, and then a series of other cities. It turned out that we were just one more tribe, that our behavior could as well be studied as that of the Hopi. And if towns, why not factories,[2] hospitals, schools? Acculturation studies—investigation of the product of Western influence on tribal life—became stylish, and anthropologists began to have some influence on the administration of Indian affairs. We will return to these matters later.

For another thing, anthropologists began to formulate theoretical statements. As a generation of anthropologists grew up who had not experienced first hand the Boasian tabu on theorizing, as European influences grew in this country, and as methodological sophistication borrowed from sociology and psychology increased, anthropologists more often sought to test hypotheses and develop theoretical positions rather than merely "let the facts speak for themselves."

There were in this period three major theoretical movements that impinged upon American anthropology and which have subsequently been absorbed by it. Though individuals tend to be of one persuasion or another, and often are vehemently opposed to its alternative, it is an expression of the holistic spirit of anthropological thought in the

United States that they can all be accommodated within the discipline. These three streams are Durkheimian sociology, Freudian psychology, and an (American born) cultural ecology.

A. R. Radcliffe-Brown's functionalism was an adaptation into anthropology of ideas developed by Durkheim and his associates before World War I. Its powerful central idea is the recognition of the salience of social relationships as an element in understanding human behavior. Social anthropology, Raymond Firth (1968: 320) has written, "aims at understanding and explaining the diversity of human behavior by a comparative study of social relationships over as wide a range of societies as possible." While there was an indigenous American sociological influence upon anthropology, the real impact of sociological thought was imported by Radcliffe-Brown when he taught in Chicago from 1930 to 1937 and trained many of the leading scholars of that generation.

The movement filled a serious hole in Boasian anthropology. Despite Boas' breadth and the intellectual calibre of his first generation students, the Boasian orientation was singularly devoid of a sociological sense. Given a focus on culture as bags of customary procedures and beliefs, with a secondary but important concern with the inner life of individuals, there was little recognition that communities were made up of individuals in potential conflict and competition. When, for instance, I analyzed Yurok Indian "protestant ethic" in terms involving a "capitalistic" social structure in which status mobility was a prime element (Goldschmidt, 1951), Kroeber, on whose data I was deeply dependent, agreed with most of my analysis, but could not see social mobility operant under native conditions. Yet for a tribal people, Yurok society was uniquely designed for social mobility. When Ruth Benedict described Pueblo Indian life in terms of harmony and unity, it took the Chinese anthropologist Li An-che (1937) to point out the Zuni use of ritual organization as instruments of status and power. To be sure, most American anthropologists had studied cultures under reservation conditions where social relations were dominated by the demands and constraints imposed upon them from the outside. American anthropology remained a quest for the traditional, the customary and the ideal; ongoing interpersonal relations were seen as a product of Westernization. For this reason, the infusion of sociological perceptions was an important addition to American anthropology.

American and British social anthropology, as this stance came to be called, were quite different, and this difference is itself instructive. Here we must make a characteristically anthropological kind of analysis, seeing the difference in terms of the social structure and "national character" of the two populations. First, the manifest differences. In England social anthropology became virtually synonymous with anthropology. Everything was placed on the theoretical formulations of social systems, and everybody adhered, with greater or lesser degrees of conviction, to the Radcliffe-Brownian banner. Since Radcliffe-Brown had denounced both history and psychology as admissible elements in the explanations promulgated in the name of anthropology, this meant not only recognizing the salience of social systems, but renouncing the relevance of those other factors. (A verbal tabu was placed on the word culture. I remember the embarrassed silence that fell over the congregation at the Association of Social Anthropology meeting in the Tylor Library of Oxford when some member let "culture" slip from his tongue—as if it were a dirty word.) Sometimes this resulted in remarkable *tours de force*, as when Mary Douglas (1966) explained the cultural phenomenon of pollution without recognizing any psychological component. Dirt, she says, is matter out of place; pollution results from the disarrangement of social relationships. In the United States as I have said, the sociological dimension was incorporated into on-going anthropological thought. Individual scholars, in an era of increased specialization, might concentrate on such problems and even adopt the negative attitudes toward others, but for the most part, they saw sociological phenomena in an historical and psychological context—as does American anthropology in general.

There are, as I have said, both social structural reasons for this difference and cultural ones. (Both must, in turn, be seen in their historical and ecological contexts, but this would take us too far afield.) In England and Europe, teaching units—departments—are generally small, concentrated in subject matter, with a single professor who exerts a great deal of influence on the selection of lower ranking colleagues. Such a situation means that subjects as broad as anthropology are broken into their natural minimal components. By contrast, American institutions have larger departments, with several members of the same rank, and the democratizing influence of rotating chairmanships. For a relatively small field like anthropology, there are economic and political advantages in American universities for larger groups to remain unified. Thus the basic unit of collaboration contains the diverse subfields; archeologists, linguists, physical anthropologists live and work together with cultural anthropologists in what admittedly is often an uneasy collaboration. Furthermore, American colleges teach much larger and intellectually less mature undergraduate student populations, rendering lower level teaching a more important aspect of the professor's job. In the process of working out curricula and manning the large introductory classes, these departmental members are forced to keep in mind the broader arena of intellectual discourse, even while engaging in their narrow specialities as scholars. If this is true on the wide canvas of anthropological inquiry it is even more important to the narrower range of ethnological, or socio-cultural investigations and theories.

The second reason why the British have opted for the social thesis relates to British national character. After World War I there emerged in England two dominant theoretical figures, Radcliffe-Brown and Bronislaw Malinowski. Though both called their theories functionalist (in contrast to the diverse evolutionary and historical schools of thought) they differed widely in their perceptions of the world, of man, and of the role of anthropology. The spare, polished, restrained and extremely limited writings of R-B (as he inevitably came to be known) stood in contrast to the rich, flamboyant speculative and voluble writings of the ex-Polish scholar who wrestled with Freud (through Ernest Jones) over the universality of the oedipal complex and who invoked human needs and other psychological and physiological aspects of man in his theoretical outlook. He was a teacher of great power and drew to him, when he was professor at the London School of Economics between the wars, many of the subsequent leaders of British anthropology. Yet England turned its back on his ideas in favor of the more ascetic and controlled thesis propounded by R-B. Whatever other forces were at work, I believe that British temperament played a large part in the natural selection that took place. Well-known English reticence, the restrictions on expression of emotion amounting to virtual denial made them uncomfortable with Malinowski's affect-laden formulations.

The great diversity of the American population from which anthropologists were drawn did not involve such characterological limitations, while the larger departments, the greater geographical dispersion and the far larger total number of practitioners encouraged diversity of outlook.

FROM PSYCHOLOGY

If the true task of anthropology is the search for human nature, psychology is inescapable. Anthropologists were both strongly attracted to Freudian thought and repelled by it. Freud's expeditions into the dark recesses of the mind brought back ethnographies of private fantasy lives that were, after all, not so very different from some of the institutionalized fantasy encapsulated in religious ritual and myth. But on the other side, Freud built his theory on the assumption of instincts and a universal formula for the human psyche and this was something that anthropologists had been fighting against in their explanations of the diverse manifestations of human behavior. Here again we may cite Malinowski's description of father-son relations in the matrilineal Trobriand society as an example of the reaction to elements in psychodynamic theory. Matters were not helped by Freud's one excursion into quasi-anthropology in his *Totem and Tabu* (1962) which substituted a belief in aboriginal sin for a belief in original sin. Yet the fascination remained, the influence on Mead was clear—as well as on Ruth Benedict, whose *Patterns of Culture* (1934) was to become one of the first true anthropological best-sellers in this country. Edward Sapir, who had developed the Boasian notion of the influence of linguistic structure upon the thought patterns of a community, wrote an article for the first issue of *Psychiatry* under the title "Why Cultural Anthropology needs the Psychiatrist," in 1938.

In order for anthropology to absorb psychiatry it had first to transform it, and this it succeeded in doing. It was the neo-Freudians who were born in or came to this country and worked here that the anthropologists found congenial: Harry Stack Sullivan, Karen Horney, Erich Fromm and particularly Erik Erikson. What these have in common is their perception of the force of culture in shaping psychodynamics, their awareness that the particulars of Freudian theory were derivative from middle-class Austrian Jewish culture, and their avoidance of too quick a delineation of a universal human nature. Given this alteration, anthropologists began increasingly to examine the dynamics of human growth in the formulation of cultural attributes. After all, if the French and English were not separate "races," as the nineteenth century expression had it, they were nevertheless very different in temperament, and this could be "explained" by the manner in which they reared their children, the dynamic interaction between parents and child, the process of enculturation. Erikson's (1963) investigations among the Sioux and the Yurok had a deep impact on both fields. Ralph Linton, the anthropologist, collaborated with Abram Kardiner, a psychiatrist, on in-depth analyses of exotic cultures, including the materials Cora DuBois brought back from the tiny island of Alor. The more orthodox Freudian anthropologists like Geza Roheim and George Devereaux were largely ignored, if not actually rejected in this process of amalgamation. (Similarly, while orothodox Freudian therapists exist in plenty, it is the anthropologically modified neo-Freudians whose public utterances are listened to outside therapists' circles.)

Methodological naiveté still characterized anthropological investigations and methodology was subordinate to persuasive literary abilities. Some attempt to redress this was made in the use of "projective tests"

—instruments designed to uncover aspects of the unconscious, notably the Rorschach ink-blots and the Thematic Apperception Test. A. I. Hallowell (1942) pioneered in the use of the former of these, demonstrating that traditional Ojibwa responses were different from Westerners' yet were integrated and "healthy," while those who had lost their native culture demonstrated a disintegrated personality structure in their Rorschach responses.

FROM ECONOMICS

The third major development during this period was indigenous—a reformulation of evolutionary theory. Boas' rejection of nineteenth century cultural evolutionism was in part a rejection of premature theorizing and in part a result of his maiden field expedition to the Baffinland Eskimo. Though his doctorate was in physics, he had been much influenced by geography and he thought he could explain Eskimo behavior as a response to geographical conditions. He found he could not. I think, but cannot substantiate, that ideological considerations were also relevant, that this anti-evolutionism was also a rejection of both materialism and Marxism—at least among many of Boas' students. Robert Lowie, in his *Primitive Society* (1920) wrote the obituary for evolutionary theory. Prematurely, as is often the case.

Environmentalism never had much influence on American anthropological thought. Though efforts to define "culture areas" were a part of the task of organizing anthropological data, there was surprisingly little recognition of the fact that these areas coincided closely with zones of geographical uniformity. In this, Powell, influenced by Morgan's evolutionism and impressed with the adaptive character of Western Indian cultures, was more right than Boas.

There were during the 1930's two voices favoring the older evolutionary point of view—both generically Marxist in tone. One was the eminent British archeologist, V. Gordon Childe (the social anthropologist in England had a studied indifference to historical matters), whose analysis of social change in conjunction with the neolithic and urban "revolutions" of antiquity was most telling (e.g., Childe, 1939). The archeological record was clear; there was a progression in the development of technology and quite clearly also a developmental sequence in the size if not the shape of human communities. Since institutions were, in part at least, instrumentalities for getting the world's work done, it made sense to assume an evolutionary development of these less tangible elements in human culture. The second was Leslie A. White (1949), who developed a theoretical analysis based upon increments of non-human energy sources available through technological growth. His theorizing was largely devoid of ethnographic reality while his excellent ethnographic work on eastern Pueblo culture was entirely devoid of theory. But it was Julian Steward (1938, 1949) who was responsible for the effective introduction of a neo-evolutionary theory. His early work on the ecological elements as they formed the social organization of Western Utes and Shoshonean communities was an empirical investigation of an essentially evolutionary hypothesis. His and White's many students have carried on this tradition.

It was, as a matter of fact, the introduction of the concept of ecology that was necessary to the formulation of a neo-evolutionary stance. With a recognition of the dynamic interaction between the forms that a culture displays and the opportunities and problems an environment provides, this more materialistic line of investigation could be developed on an empirical rather than merely a philosophical basis. Evolution is too slow a process to be observed in the course of a sabbatical year, but one can examine the degree to which institutions are adaptive to local conditions and can make comparisons among cultures with diverse economies to establish the general validity of ecological explanations.

These considerations bring us back to economics and hence the problem of rationality. Karl Polanyi (1947), an economic historian, picking up an old Morgan/Marx theme, argued that tribal and early cultures did not have a "market mentality." There developed out of this a controversy in the anthropology of economic institutions between the "formalists" and the "substantivists"; that is, between anthropologists examining tribal economies in terms of formal economic models based on the operations of the "market," and those who argued that exchanges in tribal communities are social "prestations," obligatory gifts without consideration of profit. This narrowly defined issue has broad implications; it involves the materialist interpretation of history, the dichotomy between primitive and civilized, and a perception of human "rationality." It is an explicit example of the meaning of the savage, of human nature, of the virtue inherent in man and the evils of industrial economies.

Hunting peoples cannot have individual rights to land, for game does not respect the arbitrary limits man imposes on nature. Many tribal cultivators have some kind of community (usually kin-based) land holding systems and social ties (again usually defined in the idiom of kinship) are of utmost significance in the orderly production of goods. Hence the notion of "primitive communism" and with it, by extension, the belief that tribal peoples do not engage in activities for personal gain.

This is a controversy to which I have recently contributed and my own experience with it is worth a brief recounting. I was impressed, in my investigations of the Sebei of Uganda (among whom I have done extensive research), with the variation in payments men made for their wives, and undertook a careful examination of them. Now brideprice is a widespread phenomenon and has, because of its deep moral implications, evoked a good deal more controversy than well-formulated research. We have even been enjoined to call it "bride wealth" as a verbal rejection of the "debasing" thought that these exchanges have the character of a purchase. Without here trying to present the supporting data, let me say simply that such market phenomena as price differentials and "flow of goods" (here wives and cattle) from areas of relative abundance to areas of relative scarcity are clearly demonstrated in a detailed examination of actual payment contracts among the Sebei. Since the Sebei display the operation of a "market mentality" in an area where, if anywhere, affective ties should dominate over economic considerations, the implications go beyond the marital contract to support a pattern of economic rationality. Though, with proper academic caution, I made it clear that these conclusions applied only to the Sebei, I was privately convinced that this behavior could be generalized to all societies having bride payment customs. As I was dissatisfied with my semi-popular presentation in *Scientific American* (1973), I asked the editor of a more academic journal to publish a revised version (1974).[3] He asked me to expand my article with comparative material and I therefore examined brideprice data among diverse East African tribes. The results were startling. I found that there were two models of brideprice in this limited area of highly comparable cultures. Some ethnographers reported that the amount of goods was standardized, that it was a symbolic transfer of goods not subjected to bargaining, and hence in fact a prestation. When I removed such tribes from my sample, the remainder (who did engage in haggling) reflected "market" conditions. The others clearly did not.

There are several lessons to be derived from this anecdote, not the least of which is the tendency for anthropologists to continue their ethnocentric biases—ethnocentric to the cultures to which they have become attached by virtue of studying them. It also makes it clear that the distinction between market and non-market "mentality" is not a distinction between primitive and civilized, but between cultural definitions of the situation. Finally, of course, it demonstrates the fallacy of the dichotomy between rational and irrational. The Sebei are no more rational in handling their marriages in terms of economics than the Masai are in handling theirs in terms of social ties. Behind all this lies the still greater issue of human morality, of man's self-interestedness in his relations with others as against his sense of community and identity—all the moral questions that the quest for the savage evokes.

The Public Arena

These three elements—the sociological of Durkheimian cast, the psychological of Freudian persuasion, and an evolutionism that involved the role of economics and rationality—all entered into anthropological discourse during a brief span between the late twenties and the mid-forties. All of them continued to be vital theoretical strains in post-war American anthropology and, indeed, some of the examples I used are products of that later period. American anthropology has accommodated all three and many anthropologists as individuals accept elements from each, but there has been no real integration of these theoretical orientations.

Meanwhile, during the difficult and intellectually turbulent years of the depression and the Second World War, anthropologists began to examine our own culture and to apply their anthropological insights to current problems.

Anthropologists began to investigate American communities, factories, hospitals and schools. This cultural outlook was in tune with the liberalism of the New Deal era. Anthropological influence on the Bureau of Indian Affairs and on the Department of Agriculture was direct. Less direct influences on racial attitudes began to be felt throughout government and reached the Supreme Court, as anti-racist policies drew support from the intellectual stance. Margaret Mead brought back the essential lesson that apparently physiological disabilities—such as the discomforts of the menarche—were culturally formed. A generation grew up with a new model for child care, as Spock began to replace the old labor department bulletin of advice on child care (which had been written by doctors more influenced by chemists than anthropologists). The depression was in some measure responsible for the anthropologists' turning inward, as academic opportunities did not keep pace with the production of doctorates in the field. By the time the war broke out, there were many young scholars who had had non-academic experience ready to bring anthropology into the service of the nation. The long period of isolationism in America had rendered us ignorant of the world, and anthropologists were in a position to supply much needed information on such exotic places as North Africa, the South Pacific, the Philippines, and above all Japan. Anthropologists were brought into the OSS (precursor of the CIA); they developed programs of linguistic

training based upon Boasian understanding of language structures,
physical anthropologists designed airplane seats and escape hatches,
cultural anthropologists wrote handbooks on tropical survival and summaries of native cultures for occupying forces. Probably the most significant—and certainly the most "anthropological"—of these programs
was "the study of culture at a distance" organized by Ruth Benedict
and Margaret Mead (e.g., Mead, 1955). Here was a classic application
of Boasian anthropology to an urgent problem. The years of examining
the minutiae of cultures, of perceiving the community as an entity, of
seeing individual behavior shaped by institutional settings, of seeking
the central pattern, gestalt and *geist* of a population made it possible
to piece together the character of a nation from the fragments of information available from diverse sources. The perception of culture—
despite the manifest difficulties in defining the word or even using it
with consistency—that had emerged in the detailed reports on the
Winnebago, the Kwakiutl and the Crow, could be used to enlighten
policy decisions. The classic study of "National Character" was Benedict's *The Chrysanthemum and the Sword* (1946), and the formulation
of this program was generally credited with responsibility for our successful policies in post-war Japan.

All this intellectual ferment and practical activity involved but a few
hundred individuals (The American Anthropological Association—not
limited to professionals—had fewer than 1,000 members in 1930 and but
about 1,150 in 1944.) Anthropology was almost as exotic as the normal
subjects of anthropological investigation and most universities found
they could get along without an anthropologist, or at best have one
attached to the sociology department who would teach a course on
"the Indians" and, hopefully, engage in local archeology.

Expansion and Specialization

Things changed rapidly when the war was over. The backlog of anthropologists who had found jobs in government during the depression and
service in the war returned to the academies to teach GI's who had
had experience in the exotic places these anthropologists had studied
and yearned to see. As the Cold War replaced the hot, opportunities
for research in distant lands developed more rapidly than departments
could supply scholars. The Social Science Research Council and American Council of Learned Societies collaborated in organizing means to
preserve the international effort that the war had engendered. Remote-
ness became irrelevant with intercontinental air transport. Anthropologists began to do what they had originally entered the field to do:

engage in the anthropological experience, become involved with and seek to understand alien people, escape their middle-class lives, get back to "basics," and, of course at the same time, enjoy the prosperity that growing academia provided. (Between 1944 and 1966, membership in the AAA increased from about 1,150 to nearly 6,000—more than five-fold in 22 years.)

Though anthropology was growing at its greatest rate ever, anthropologists were removing themselves from the American scene. They were neither studying the American culture, as they had been before the war, nor engaging in the practical uses to which anthropology had been put by government and private industry. The Society for Applied Anthropology, which was formed in 1941, continued but the anthropology was rarely applied. It was not until the late 1960's that anthropologists began again to discover the lost tribe known as the U.S.A., now under the catch-prase "urban anthropology." The expansion that took place was an expansion overseas—to Micronesia, Southeast Asia, Japan, Africa and Latin America. "Area studies" in American universities were the center of growth; the cold war afforded overseas opportunities for this intellectual exodus.

Anthropology was not ready for this expansion. It had, as I have just recounted, absorbed widely diverse elements into its intellectual armamentarium. Anthropologists were thinking these diverse thoughts and publishing them in anthropological journals, but different anthropologists were thinking different kinds of thoughts. The image of the blind man and the elephant leaps to mind. The separate points of view were so new and ill-formed as hardly to be dignified by the term "schools." The rapid expansion of anthropology created intellectual chaos, a chaos compounded by the information explosion that resulted when returned doctoral candidates transformed their theses into books and articles.

For the field experience continued to be the hallmark of the anthropologist, and field experience now meant work in distant lands that would provide the neophyte scholar with a cross-cultural perspective as well as the necessary cachet to enter its diminishingly esoteric circles. It also required the search for the novel, the special—not in the old sense of odd or unusual, but in the new sense of displaying intellectual virtuosity. For the decades of new theorizing meant that it was not enough to return with notebooks full of descriptive data, texts, etc., as had been true in the early decades. It was now necessary to emerge from the experience, from the exquisite hardships of ethnographic investigation, with some new perception, some new vision. Since cultures are infinitely complex and highly diversified, and as anthropologists became increasingly sensitized to new subtleties in the human scene, the literature became richer, more intricate—and totally chaotic.

The inevitable result of this development was an increased specialization. Where a Boas not only taught in all the subdisciplines of anthropology (linguistics, archeology, physical anthropology, and ethnology) but also made significant contributions to most of them, the cultural anthropologist increasingly narrowed his interest to law or economics or medicine. Hyphenated fields (ethno-semantics, socio-linguistics) and specialized societies express this growing tendency.[4]

In the era of expansion of the past 30 years, it would seem that nothing is safe from anthropological enquiry. After each annual conclave of anthropologists, the press reports such studies as those of strippers or hippies, of the social relations among garbage collectors or of analyses of the garbage they have collected. Certain major fads developed: increasingly more detailed analyses of kinship systems, studies of "acculturation" and culture change in general, the character of peasant communities. Perhaps the most important of these movements has involved a rapprochement between the physical and cultural anthropologists in primatology. The rejection of biological explanation of behavioral difference and the essential irrelevance of "race" reduced the physical anthropologists' importance in the discipline. Some turned to the study of human genetics and physiologic adaptation; others to the detailed examination of monkeys and apes. If the quest for human nature could not be satisfied by examining primitive man, perhaps it could be uncovered by finding the common element in our closest phylogenetic relatives. Here too, commonalities remain elusive. The easy conclusions on the nature of man promulgated by the ethologists extrapolating from studies of stickle-back fish and herring gulls are dissipated when we discover how variantly two closely related species of baboons play out their social lives (e.g., Kummer, 1972).

Specialization is both necessary and desirable. The difficulty in anthropology lay not at the flanks, but at the center. The failure to consolidate the theories of culture into some coherent and integrated whole has deprived anthropology of a formalized frame of reference. A global concept such as the concept of culture served adequately as a blanket term during the nascent period of scholarly development but has in and of itself no analytic power. To say that "culture" is the reason that Hopi initiate their children in Kiva ceremonies in groups while Plains Indian youths are transformed into adults through a vision sought in isolation is to say nothing more than that you believe biology is not responsible. Indeed, it is no better an explanation than those the natives give when they say they do so "because it is our custom." To explain such matters in terms of either social organization, child rearing practices or economics generally leads to more-or-less well-elaborated tautologies. The fact is that the various anthropological orientations—the concern with

the material and with the spiritual, with the dynamics of child development and the social definition of the situation—all play a part in understanding the phenomenon subsumed under the term culture. Despite
the oppositions cited above, there is really no inherent conflict among
the diverse orientations that enter into anthropological discourse. Man
is both rational and irrational; economic considerations do influence
culture; history is a factor and time a dimension of culture; man is
highly plastic but within the bounds of physiology, anatomy, and psychological predisposition, and so on.

The exuberant years of anthropological exploration were undertaken
when the Boasian outlook had been confounded by complex theoretical
accretions inadequately assimilated. There had been neither time nor
talent to construct a theoretical model that accommodated the diverse
elements. Scientific fields generally center around a central model—a
working model that is not taken as gospel, but as point of departure,
a model that accommodates the known data. The evolution of the scientific investigation of any phenomenon results in the model becoming
increasingly complex; consider our models of the atom, of the gene,
the brain, sleep. Anthropology did not proceed from a model, however
simplistic, but from an outlook. Expanded information makes us aware
that the model must be more complex than the formulation a Boasian
might have made, but the model was not formulated. Those who perceive a model of man, who construct in their minds some relationships
that enter into an explanation of human behavior, see it at best through
a glass, darkly.

The Continuing Quest

Meanwhile, antiquated ideas that seemed dead rise up again in new
dress. Biological explanations, so comforting as a rationale for groups
with power and status, are surfacing once more. The ethologists argue
for the territorial imperative in beast and in man; Lorenz justifies
human aggression in naturalistic terms; and Jensen trots out worn-out
statistics in the long outmoded frame of reference of racism. Neo-
Marxists, forgetting the complicated fantasies on which man builds
elaborate structures of imaginary reality, reduce human motivation to
simplistic economic formulae and reawaken old images of the Arcadian
myth of the propertyless primitive. Lévi-Strauss becomes an international savant by exhuming the savage mind, reminiscent of the pre-
logical mentality that his compatriot, Lucien Lévy-Bruhl created and
then renounced before his death. (I doubt that any reputable anthropologist had seriously used the word "savage" in a title since the death

of Malinowski; even the word "primitive" is now used with caution.) And a young population discontent with the materialistic civilization and enamored with the ancient myths of a world of special meaning and supernatural experience follow the recurrent teachings of Don Juan, hoping to gain insight into the nature of humanity through the magical chemistry of hallucinogens. The savage that the post-Boasian anthropologists had buried under the dry pages of their empirical monographs stirs in his grave.

The myth of the savage endures. Or, better, the myths. For the myth takes on variant form, both for the philosopher and the layman. For the savage is in the minds of each of us a projection of our ideals or our fears, of our impulses and our discontents; a window to the soul. Three quarters of a century of assiduous, rationalistic, empirical investigations in every quarter of the globe, from the beginnings of time to the present, from the businessman to the bushman, have not succeeded in allaying this mythic character. Meanwhile the savage of reality, the tribal man, is rapidly dying out—being slaughtered in twentieth century Brazil as he was in nineteenth century America, being drawn into the modern world that is becoming increasingly homogenized through commercial and political exploitation.

Anthropologists, particularly American anthropologists, have tried to examine the people of the world, their physique, their past, their language, their convictions, their customs, their beliefs, and their daily lives, on the assumption that this would reveal the nature of man. They did so on the assumption that mankind everywhere was constituted alike and that the historical, the situational, or the circumstantial factors were responsible for the differences they discovered. In order to proceed they had to suspend their own culturally biased evaluation of human conduct and human nature. Indeed, they had to suspend judgement on the very existence of something that could be called human nature—though they could not in fact, engage in any discourse regarding what they found without covert but powerful presuppositions about the nature of that human nature. However much individually each anthropologist sought in his field experience in tribal communities the revelation of his own soul, anthropology as a profession was engaged in a larger enterprise. People vary in their character, their aspirations and their daily conduct. It was essential to understand how widely they varied, which could not be done within the constricted limits of Western man. It was essential to understand these variations in terms of diversity of circumstances in order not only to know what was universal, but what extraneous elements might account for the manifest variations that human conduct displays, and this could not be done within the limits of industrialized societies.

As anthropologists probed deeper and deeper, each into his own special area of competence and each in terms of his own predilections (his own quest?), they discovered how complex was this phenomenon of man. They learned that there were a few universals in human society (or so near to universals that the exceptions offer test cases): family and kinship regulations that tied people together, ideas of the soul that expressed universal concern with the individual, social dimorphism between the sexes, ritualized restraints on conduct, collaborative aims for self-preservation. They learned also that, however variantly these universals were played out in actuality, there was also regularity in their diversity. In the process they learned also that the simple dichotomy that had brought them into this quest, the savage versus the civilized, was a false one.

The quest has not been in vain. Though the quest for *the* savage is chimerical, the understanding of what man is emerges from the comparisons among the varieties. This is not a conceptual "least common denominator"; it is rather an emergent in the discovery of the intricately interrelated circuitry between the elements that enter into his existence. How people feel about themselves relates to what they do; what they do relates to the technology they are heir to and the environment in which they exist; how they utilize that environment relates to the patterns of collaborative arrangements; collaborative needs require emotional reinforcements; sentiments publicly expressed define how people feel about themselves. The circle completed can be retraced in a myriad of different ways. The elements are far more numerous and the lines of interaction far more complex than can be developed here.

The American, perhaps more than any other, needs the formulation of this model in a cogent form to replace the sloganesque. America needs it first because it is heir not to a single self-reinforcing tradition, but to diverse, often antithetical cultural sources. Having no generally accepted mythic systems, it is especially adapted to the synthetic formulation of a scientific outlook. It needs it also because, in the absence of cultural reinforcement, it is peculiarly vulnerable to simplistic formulae. It needs it also because, more than most countries, it must accommodate peoples of diverse orientations and bring them to common purpose. Public policy is in the hands of the economists, whose vision of man is dominated by rationality and greed, and the political scientists, whose vision of man is dominated by practicality and lust for power. But human motivation is far more complex. Social institutions have been created in diverse forms from time immemorial, both by tribal and urban man, to balance these needs with more humane ones. The anthropologists, having studied mankind, can bring the lessons learned from the real savages they found in their quest for the eternal savage within to bear on matters of public policy.

Notes

1. For a more complete discussion and references to other works see Tanner (1959).
2. A major impact was provided by anthropologists in the famous Hawthorne Studies (Roethlisberger and Dickson, 1939).
3. For a full background, see Goldschmidt (1976).
4. Special interests within cultural anthropology have developed rapidly. The Society for Medical Anthropology and the Council for Anthropology and Education each have more members today than there were members of the American Anthropological Association at the close of World War II.

References

Benedict, R. 1934. Patterns of Culture (Boston and New York: Houghton, Mifflin).
———. 1946. The Chrysanthemum and the Sword; Patterns of Japanese Culture (Boston: Houghton, Mifflin).
Boas, F. 1911. "Introduction," in F. Boas, ed., Handbook of American Indian Languages, Bulletin of the Bureau of American Ethnology, No. 40, Part 1 (Washington, D. C.): 5-83.
———. 1912. Changes in Bodily Form of Descendants of Immigrants (New York: Columbia University Press).
———. 1945. Race & Democratic Society (New York: J. J. Augustine).
———. 1962. Anthropology and Modern Life (New York: W. W. Norton). First published in 1928.
———. 1963. The Mind of Primitive Man (Rev. ed.; New York: Free Press). First published in 1911.
Childe, V. G. 1939. Man Makes Himself (New York: Oxford University Press).
Douglas, M. 1966. Purity and Danger: A Comparative Study of Pollution and Danger (London: Routledge & Kegan Paul).
Engels, F. 1907. The Origin of the Family, Private Property and the State (Chicago: Chas. H. Kerr). Translated by Ernest Untermann; first published 1884.
Erikson, E. H. 1963. Childhood and Society, (2nd ed.; New York: W. W. Norton). First published in 1950.
Firth, R. 1968. "Social Anthropology," International Encyclopedia of the Social Sciences, 1 (New York: Macmillan): 320.
Freud, S. 1962. Totem and Tabu: Some Points of Agreement between Mental Lives of Savages and Neurotics (New York: Norton Library). Translated by James Strachey; first published in Imago in 1912 and 1913.

Goldschmidt, W. 1951. "Ethics and the Structure of Society, An Ethnological Contribution to the Sociology of Knowledge," American Anthropologist, 53(Oct.-Dec.): 506-524.

———. 1973. "The Brideprice of the Sebei," Scientific American, 229(July): 74-85.

———. 1974. "The Economics of Brideprice Among the Sebei and in East Africa," Ethnology, 13 (October): 311-331.

———. 1976. Culture and Behavior of the Sebei (Berkeley and Los Angeles: University of California Press).

Hallowell, A. I. 1942. "Acculturation Processes and Personality Change as Indicated by the Rorschach Technique," Rorschach Research Exchange, 6: 42-50.

Kardiner, A. 1945. The Psychological Frontiers of Society (New York: Columbia University Press).

Kumer, H. 1972. Primate Societies (Chicago: Aldine).

Li An-che. 1937. "Zuni: Some Observations and Queries," American Anthropologist, 39(January-March): 62-76.

Lowie, R. H. 1920. Primitive Society (New York: Liveright).

Lynd, R. S. and H. M. Lynd. 1929. Middletown: A Study in Contemporary American Culture (New York: Harcourt).

Mead, M. 1939. From the South Seas: Studies of Adolescence and Sex in Primitive Societies (New York: William Morrow).

———, ed. 1955. Culture Patterns in Technical Change (New York: Mentor Books). Originally published by UNESCO.

Morgan, L. H. 1963. Ancient Society: or, Researches in the Lines of Human Progress from Savagery through Barbarism to Civilization (Cleveland and New York: Meridian Books, World Publishing Company). First published in 1877.

Nott, J. D., M.D., and G. R. Gliddon. 1854. Types of Mankind; or Ethnological Researches Based upon the Ancient Monuments, Paintings, Sculptures, and Crania of Races, and upon their Natural, Geographical, Philological and Biblical History (Philadelphia: Lippincott, Grambo).

Polanyi, K. 1947. "Our Obsolete Market Mentality," Commentary, 13 (September): 109-117.

Roethlisberger, F. J. and W. J. Dickson. 1939. Management and the Worker: An Account of a Research Program Conducted by the Western Electric Company, Hawthorne Works, Chicago (Cambridge, Mass.: Harvard University Press).

Sapir, E. 1949. "Why Cultural Anthropology Needs the Psychiatrist," in David Mandelbaum, ed., Selected Writings of Edward Sapir in Language, Culture and Personality (Berkeley: University of California Press): 569-577. First published in Psychiatry, 1938.

Steward, J. 1938. Basin-Plateau Aboriginal Sociopolitical Groups (Washington, D. C.: Bureau of American Ethnology, Bulletin 120).

———. 1949. "Cultural Causality and Law: A Trial Formulation of the Development of Early Civilization," American Anthropologist, 51 (January-March): 1-27.

Tanner, J. M. 1959. "Boas' Contribution to Knowledge of Human Growth and Form," American Anthropologist, 61 (October): 76-111. Reprinted in Walter Goldschmidt, ed., The Anthropology of Franz Boas (Memoirs of the American Anthropological Association, no. 89).

Warner, W. L. and P. S. Lunt. 1941. The Social Life of a Modern Community (New Haven: Yale University Press).

White, L. A. 1949. The Science of Culture (New York: Farrar Strauss).

American Geography:

Social Science Emergent

KEVIN R. COX

The Ohio State University

Very broadly this paper is concerned with two major issues: the emergence of geography as a social science; and the nature of the geographic contribution to an understanding of American society.

To the founding fathers of academic geography in the U.S.A. such a brief might have seemed, at the very least, a trifle odd. To a marked degree academic geography within this country gained its initial nourishment within the womb of geology: the first American geographers had largely been trained as geologists. Although this legacy is now a rapidly diminishing one the slow emergence of geography as a social science is inexplicable without it. In the early days, for instance, much geographic research was in the area of what is now regarded as physical geography—climatology, biogeography and geomorphology—and the output of work dealing with man and society was correspondingly less. But the influence was also apparent in human geography. Those concerned with the geography of social or economic life, for example, nurtured what seem now to have been very primitive behavioral assumptions: the idea, that is, that human behaviors immediately responsible for the patterns geographers observed on their ubiquitous maps were controlled, if not determined, by forces of a natural environmental nature—soil fertility, climate, natural vegetation, etc. The idea of processes in society at large, existing independently of the natural environment of that society, were not regarded as falling even indirectly in the geographer's sphere of interest.

It is a mark of the changes that have occurred within geography over the last 75 years that the discipline is seen more and more as a social science. Judging from the degree to which geographers now contribute to social science journals and from the titles of their textbooks (Fielding, 1974; Morrill, 1974) this is apparent in their self-perceptions. It is also apparent in the perception of others. Within universities, for example, geography tends to be grouped in colleges of social science or behavioral science. The recent inclusion of geography in the Survey of the Behavioral and Social Sciences jointly sponsored by the National Academy of Science and the Social Science Research Council (Taaffe, 1970) is also of significance.

Nevertheless, for anyone contemplating, in an interdisciplinary context, an evaluation of geography's contribution to an understanding of American society, the roots of, and subsequent changes in, the discipline pose a number of problems. Critical here in the problem of identity. Partly as a result of changes in emphasis within the discipline there is a great deal of ignorance not only among the public at large but also within academia as to precisely what geographers are interested in, their modi operandi, etc. Consequently there is only a limited awareness of how geography could contribute to social knowledge both directly and also indirectly through its conceptual and methodological impact on other social sciences.

The paper commences, therefore, with a brief consideration of the nature of geography and its relation to social knowledge. We then move to a more lengthy description and explanation of the emergence of geography as a social science. The third major section describes the variety of understandings about American society which current social science geography is able to arrive at. The fourth and final section considers some of the limitations of this work and recent responses to those limitations.

The Nature of Geography and Its Relation to Social Knowledge

The most central concept of geography is that of geographic location. In addition to their substantive attributes objects have positions not only in time but also in geographic space. They therefore have locations relative to one another in terms of (e.g.) distance, direction, accessibility, and contiguity. When a set of objects—towns, households, individuals with different social characteristics, and the like—are considered with respect to their properties of relative location, it will be possible to characterize any locational order they have in terms of such concepts as localization, segregation, region, compactness, centrality, and density. These provide the necessary data with which all geographical theory must ultimately make contact.

In brief, the common denominators linking all geographic work concern locational description and explanation of those locations. Despite changing emphases in the discipline—geography as a discipline in distance (Watson, 1955), geography as the study of spatial organization (Abler, Adams and Gould, 1971), geography as the study of man-environment relations (Burton, Kates and Kirby, 1974), geography as the study of spatial interaction (Ullman, 1954), geography as the study of culture areas (Sauer, 1941)—the fundamental locational question is the one to which the discipline always returns. Few geographers now, or in the past, for example, would dispute that their field is about maps.

The formal study of geography, therefore, may be regarded as a response to a more generalized "geographical imagination" (Harvey, 1973: 24). Both disinterested intellectual curiosity and the imperatives of survival (Kirk, 1963) result in attempts to develop a conceptual structure by means of which one can begin to relate to location. Such a conceptual structure may take the form of some cognitive mapping of the places important to individual welfare or a more general classification of places—such as suburb vs. inner city—providing a degree of predictive ability. Alternatively people develop conceptions of spatial processes, such as that of racial invasion, having clear implications for their own behavior.

To the extent that geographers limit themselves to the geographical manifestations of social life (in contrast to physical geographers whose major concern is with the geographical expression of physical processes) they have a view of society which is complementary to that of other social scientists. Geographers have the same objects of study as economists, sociologists, and other social scientists: people, groups, societies, firms, etc. They tend to examine them, however, with a different criterion of significance in mind. A sociologist may examine a society from the viewpoint of group structure, classifying individuals into mutually exclusive, overlapping, or hierarchically organized groups. The geographer on the other hand, will be more concerned with the locational correlates of group membership: to what extent are particular groups localized in space and to what extent are different groups spatially exclusive or interpenetrating, for example? Likewise, in the examination of processes, disciplinary viewpoints are evident. In attempting to explain the spread of innovations or social values, a sociologist may look at socially constrained contact processes in which the item tends to diffuse within social classes rather than between. A geographer, on the other hand, is more sensitive to the implications for contact processes of relative location.

This is not to say that locational considerations are entirely absent from the work of other social scientists. Just as geographers may have to consider the role of market processes in locational choice, so economists will include distance relations in their labor market models. Nevertheless disciplinary biases tend to limit involvement in the concepts and theories central to other fields. Generally one limits oneself to an assumption of exogeneousness. Social science models, therefore, tend to assume a given set of spatial relations which affect the unfolding of an economic or social process but which are, in their turn, unaffected by that unfolding. While such assumptions may be operationally convenient, it seems a frustrating road to follow if one is interested in developing predictively-useful theory for a locationally differentiated world. Geography as a social science, therefore, seems a worthwhile endeavor.

The Emergence of Geography as a Social Science

As an academic field of study geography has a relatively short history. The first separate department of geography offering graduate work was founded in 1903 at Chicago; and a year later the major professional organization, the Association of American Geographers, was established. In a very real sense, therefore, academic geography in the U.S. is a creation of the twentieth century.

Despite this recency there have been substantial changes in conceptual and methodological apparati. In addition the period has witnessed a growing dominance of human as opposed to physical geography. The increasing correspondence of geography with human geography goes far to explain the emergence of the idea of geography as a social science.

In characterizing the history of concept and method in American geography a number of dichotomies are useful: (1) idiographic vs. nomothetic; (2) site vs. situation; (3) man-environment vs. man-man; and (4) maps vs. models. The terms in each dichotomy allow one to characterize different phases in the development of geography as a social science. This assumes, however, that one can come to conclusions as to which term was dominant in a particular time period. The basis for our evaluation here is a content analysis of the abstracts of papers presented at the annual meetings of the Association of American Geographers from 1911 to 1970; these abstracts are published yearly in the Annals of the Association of American Geographers. For each of the six decades included in this period three years were randomly selected. Each abstract was evaluated from the viewpoint of our four dichotomies and results aggregated by decade to provide some idea of trend (see Table 1). However, since the word "model" and model-related terms only found their way into the literature in the last two decades, references to the map-model dichotomy have not been tabulated. Details of the procedures adopted can be found in Appendix A. We now consider each dichotomy in turn, both from a historical standpoint and from a definitional viewpoint. We will then turn to a consideration of three distinct periods in the development of American geography.

TABLE 1
Shifts in the Conceptual Emphases of American Geography,
1911-1970, in Percents (N's in Parentheses)

	1911-1920	1921-1930	1931-1940	1941-1950	1951-1960	1961-1970
Idiographic	11	83	79	83	73	48
	(2)	(20)	(23)	(25)	(22)	(13)
Nomothetic	89	17	21	17	27	52
	(16)	(4)	(6)	(5)	(8)	(14)
Site	94	72	70	83	69	47
	(17)	(18)	(21)	(25)	(22)	(14)
Situation	6	28	30	17	31	53
	(1)	(7)	(9)	(5)	(10)	(16)
Man-Environment	100	86	87	52	55	19
	(17)	(18)	(20)	(12)	(12)	(4)
Man-Man	0	14	13	48	45	81
	(0)	(3)	(3)	(11)	(10)	(17)

(a) Details of construction are provided in Appendix A.
(b) Percentages sum vertically *within* the horizontal lines.

DISTINCTIONS OF CONCEPT AND METHOD

The idiographic vs. nomothetic distinction has provided food for a long-standing debate in geography (e.g., Hartshorne, 1959: Ch. 10). Is geography concerned with the unique or is it concerned with the orderly? Is it possible to develop laws of location in geography or are locations so unique that geographic work must stop short at some rational description of what exists? As the first two rows of Table 1 indicate, emphasis has shifted substantially. Up until the early 1920's the nomothetic view was dominant, the belief being that location did have some regularity that was subsumable under certain empirical generalizations and ultimately, under more all-embracing laws. For reasons to be explored later this belief faded in the 1920's and 1930's. The character of place was then believed to be intrinsically resistant to scientific analysis. Only since the 1950's has the nomothetic concern for generalization, laws, and geography as the science of location broken through in full vigor (Kohn, 1970).

Distinctive site and situation viewpoints can also be distinguished. The basis of the site viewpoint is that locations can be described and understood in terms of their in situ attributes rather than in terms of their relations with other locations. The basis of the situation viewpoint is that relative location is the critical consideration or, at the very least, the consideration which makes the work intrinsically geographic (Schaefer, 1953: 228). Thus, to illustrate these diverse approaches, one might explain agricultural location patterns in terms of such "site" variables as climate, soil fertility, farm size or technology; alternatively a situation viewpoint would emphasize such variables as access to markets, economies of agglomeration, and the movement of information regarding farming options or techniques from one farmer to another (Spencer and Horvath, 1963). The dichotomy is also reflected in more purely descriptive work. A description of the U.S., for example, might emphasize "site" variables producing such categories as the Corn Belt, the South or the Great Plains. A more situation-dependent viewpoint on the other hand, might classify places according to their nearness to major metropolitan centers (Huff, 1973), or according to their links to major metropolitan centers (Borchert, 1972).

Up until the 1950's (see rows 3 and 4 of Table 1) site viewpoints clearly dominated. Since then more situation-dependent approaches have gained an ascendancy. It would be untrue to say, however, that site variables have been discarded. Rather they appear to have been assimilated as special cases of situation-dependent approaches to form what has been called the spatial viewpoint (Taaffe, 1974). Situation-dependent approaches, for example, focus upon relationships of events which are locationally displaced with respect to each other: relationships of X and Y which are dependent upon (e.g.) their accessibility or direction with respect to each other, or perhaps upon the distance intervening between events. Site-dependent approaches, on the other hand, may be said to focus upon locational correspondence relationships: relationships between X and Y which are dependent upon their locational correspondence. The case of locational correspondence of events, of course, represents the special case of a locational displacement of events relative to each other with the value of zero.

The third dichotomy is that between man-environment and man-man approaches to the behavioral assumptions necessary for analysis in human geography. Given the attempt to explain the locations of man, his attributes and his works, some assumptions about choice mechanisms clearly become important. The locations dealt with in human geography and which make it of interest to social science in general, are at origin the result of human choice. Explaining geographic patterns, therefore, requires some set of ideas on the generation of those choices—the choices of migrants, commuters, businessmen, farmers, etc. Initially in American geography behavioral assumptions were provided by a simplistic stimulus-response model in which the natural environment provided the stimulus and human choice was the response. In this vision of man, human activity with respect to space was dictated by imperatives of soil, climate, bedrock, etc. This (1900-1920) was the era of the so-called environmental determinists. Some feeling for the type of assumptions made can be gathered from a brief perusal of Semple (1903) and Huntington and Cushing (1934).

The excesses of environmental determinism provoked their own reaction in the late 1920's and early 1930's. Ideas of "adjustment to the environment" replaced concepts of "environmental control"; the more cautious "environmental influence" replaced "environmental determination." More generally there was the behavioral assumption of possibilism (Tatham, 1967). The basic idea here was that human activities and the geographic patterns they formed were not determined by natural environmental forces; rather nature was seen as providing a set of alternatives between which men might choose: a variety of locational patterns, therefore, might be compatible with an existing set of environmental constraints. Quite obviously, therefore, debate over behavioral assumptions continued within the same man-environment framework, a number of workers, such as Sauer (1956), indicating the significance of cultural processes for adjustment to such alternatives.

Since 1940 and particularly since the late 1950's (see rows 5 and 6 of Table 1) the problem of behavioral assumptions for geographic analysis has been liberated from this framework. Decisions concerning the ways in which men relate to space are now seen more and more as structured by a set of social constraints socially created. However illusory this particular framework may ultimately prove to be, it has at least served to bring geography closer to the social sciences.

Finally there is the methodological dichotomy. Traditionally the map has been the geographer's methodological crutch: it served not only descriptive purposes, i.e. where it was, it also helped to explain why it was where it was. This was achieved through the comparison of map patterns (Kirk, 1963): if X appeared on the map in positions similar to those occupied by Y and both variables absented themselves from other locations then presumably there was a relationship between the two. Not surprisingly this technique, if it can be so termed, proved very restrictive. Not only did the subjectivity of map comparison impose problems of replication (McCarty and Salisbury, 1961), it was also limited to the bivariate case: while a relationship between X and Y might be evident there was (e.g.) no way of estimating the degree to which X was related to Y when holding Z constant. Even in the bivariate case the technique could not handle curvilinear relationships (Muller, 1975).

Despite these obvious drawbacks the widespread use of mathematical models in geography and the consequent transformation of map analysis is very recent indeed. In the content analysis I found no references to "model" before 1960. Since then the term has become widespread. In the abstracts for the 1971 meetings of the Association of American Geographers, for instance, 60 percent of all abstracts in human geography contained references to "model" or to model-related terms such as "regression," and "correlation."

While other social sciences have had their quantitative movements it is unlikely that the rupture with the past has been quite so sharp as in geography. There was, for instance, no transition between the analytic crudity of traditional map analysis and the widespread adoption of multivariate analysis. In other fields, such as sociology, the methodological transformation has been more evolutionary than revolutionary. Long before the advent of techniques such as regression, factor analysis, and information theory, cross tabulation provided an analytic tool that was far superior to traditional map analysis. Sociologists were therefore able to develop more reliable generalizations and a far stronger empirical basis for inductive theory development than was true of geographers working with traditional map analysis.

Such approaches as cross tabulation would have been perfectly feasible in geography. Continuous variables such as distance could have been converted into discrete variables with a limited number of classes along with such discrete variables as soil type or region and cell entries examined for evidence of trends. In fact no such transitional stage occurred. Some light is shed on this, however, when we look at the recent history of American geography not in terms of our four dichotomies but in terms of periods each of which was characterized by certain combinations of terms from these dichotomies.

A THUMBNAIL HISTORICAL SKETCH

The history of modern American geography can be divided into three periods: (1) the period from 1900 to 1920, which will be called "The False Start"; (2) the period from 1920 to about 1956 which we will call "The Reaction"; and (3) the period from 1956 on, which will be called "The Scientific Revolution." Like all classifications in the history of ideas these categories are somewhat caricatures; there were changes occurring in the 1920-1956 period, for example, which clearly anticipated the revolution in geographical thinking occurring after 1956. Nevertheless there is a good deal of empirical support for this characterization and it is consistent with the reactions of geographers themselves to the ideas dominant in their respective periods.

The "False Start" can be regarded as a start because it did attempt to arrive at generalizations regarding location. Decidedly for the founding fathers of American geography the field did not represent a study of the unique. Typically studies emphasized site variables, assumed a man-environment model of behavior and were nomothetic in their goals. Attempts to explain North American agricultural patterns, therefore, might be in terms of the natural areas or regions constituted by climatic zones; attempts to explain the location of towns would reduce to questions of the location of natural routes (gaps in mountain ranges were favorites), the dryness of soils and the availability of water.

However, the start was undoubtedly false and precipitated a reaction from which geography was unconscionably slow in recovering. Problems related largely to interpretation of the man-environment relationship. There was an inferential problem: a tendency to impute cause and effect relationships—involving the influence of climate, of soil fertility, etc.—to what were, at best, structural regularities. There was also an operational issue. The man-environment idea presumed that variables could be isolated as natural or non-natural. Yet only the vaguest familiarity with the impact of technology on nature—fertilizers, soil erosion, for instance—was enough to convince as to the difficulty of making this distinction. And there was a problem at the conceptual level: the transformation of the idea of environmental influence from what was at best a useful working assumption into a doctrine of infallibility. This, of course, served to close enquiry. Once the appropriate environmental influences had been identified, there was nothing else to discover.

The reaction during the 1920's and 1930's took a number of forms. Debate, however, remained centered on the man-environment framework. There was first a rejection of the idea of unidirectionality in man-environment relations. Geography, it was declared, was concerned with the *mutual* relations of man and environment. This view first received explicit articulation in an address to the Association of American Geographers by Harlan Barrows (1923). It was also strongly apparent in the views of a major figure in American geography at this time—Carl Sauer (1925). By stressing the role of man in reshaping the physical environment, Sauer thought that he could provide a positive alternative to environmental determinism. The second response was to reject the idea of developing laws of location. As we indicated above, one reaction to environmental determinism was the notion of possibilism in which, in the extreme case at least, anything was possible so how could it be predicted? This lengthy interim period, therefore, was marked by a rejection of generalization and by an interest in the geographically unique. In this sense it received its best expression in the views of Hartshorne who wrote both during (1939) and after (1959) the fact.

On the other hand it would be wrong to infer that there was any great feeling of satisfaction with the new paradigm. A significant minority of geographers, including some of the better known of the time, were never very satisfied with it. There was therefore a noticeable searching for new and alternative approaches. These probings anticipated much of what was to come later. There were, for instance, anticipations of the spatial approach and, significantly, these were associated with geographers who attained a good deal of distinction in the field. Sauer (1936) was one of the first American geographers to examine pattern from a diffusion standpoint while Platt (1928; 1946) pioneered in conceptualizing space in terms of linkage rather than in terms of site differences. There were also suggestions of behavioral assumptions that clearly did not conform to the prevalent man-environment notion. Whittlesey (1945) in a presidential address in 1944 clearly understood the notion of cognitive map well before it blossomed forth as a major research theme in human geography. And it was during this period that the applicability of quantitative methods was first mooted (Rose, 1936; Wright, 1937).

All these random probings came together in the period beginning sometime during the 1950's that I have called "The Scientific Revolution." Initially this was a quantitative revolution (Burton, 1963; Gould, 1969). Papers on "The Application of Game Theory to Geographic Problems" or on "The Use of Markov Chains in Map Analysis" initially dominated the field and generated intense debate on the merits of such rigor (Spate, 1960). Careful observation, classification and rigorous testing of hypotheses, however, assumed the existence of some body of theory. For many geographers this came second as the initial flurry of conclusions yielded by correlational analysis were scrutinized and found difficult to relate one to another. The ensuing emphasis on theory, laws of location and the development of a cumulative body of knowledge—something "The False Start" had not begun to produce—developed its own imperative: one for more adequate behavioral assumptions than those provided by the man-environment framework.

All this has served to bring geography closer to the social sciences. Not only are the mathematical models often the same—Markov chains, factor analysis, graph theory, etc.—but so are the behavioral assumptions and even some of the basic concepts. As Bunge (1966) has shown, many of the fundamental descriptive concepts in geography are simply geographical expressions of more general social science concepts. The concepts of region and regional system, for instance, reduce to the more general concepts of class and classification; a regional boundary is equivalent to a class interval; and the geographic center of some distribution is equivalent to the social scientist's mean.

Underlining this convergence between geography and social science, however, has been another change within geography as a whole: the shift in emphasis from physical to human geography. In the 1911-1920 decade, for example, 48 percent of the abstracts of papers presented at the annual meetings of the Association of American Geographers were physical in emphasis; by the 1961-1970 decade this figure had dwindled to 19 percent.[2] Quite why this occurred is not readily apparent. But the end result was that combined with the scientific revolution in geography it facilitated the emergence of the field as a social science.

Despite its short history, therefore, academic geography has witnessed substantial change in its conceptual filters and kitbag of tools. To some degree it is tempting to try to relate some of these changes to overall changes in American society as a whole. Consider, in this light, the demise of the man-environment framework and the emergence of the spatial viewpoint.

Is it reasonable to say, for example, that the role of nature in American society has been weakened so that the plausibility of the man-environment framework has been eroded? Accelerated technological change has likely had an impact on the American consciousness such that man is seen more as creating his own environment rather than as being created by it. This could conceivably account for the emergence of a viewpoint corresponding to that of Sauer, for instance, where the man-environment relationship was mutual rather than unidirectional.

It would not account, however, for a shift to a man-man behavioral viewpoint in which men relate not to a spatially differentiated nature but to a spatially differentiated society. Presumably this is a reflection of the fact that more and more people live in an urban environment in which the critical locational patterns have been socially created and owe little or nothing to variations in soil, slope, or climate. Indeed, to the extent that the geographer confines his attention to patterns within cities or to relationships between cities, natural environmental variation seems remarkably unimportant compared to the role of the economic system. Once indirect relationships to the natural environment are considered, of course, then the falsity of this consciousness becomes apparent. This helps to account for a continuing minority interest in contemporary geography in man-environment frameworks (Manners and Mikesell, 1974).

A similar logic may be applied in an attempt to understand the emergence of the spatial viewpoint emphasizing relative location and the assimilation of site variables. Spatial interdependence is certainly not something new. Even the frontier farmer of the nineteenth century depended on some links with the outside world for tools, and perhaps a little trade. But the pervasiveness of spatial interdependence is today categorically different. Division of labor and the development of national, not to say international, markets mean that livelihood is dependent on events at a distance in some other city or in some other region. This is in sharp contrast to the nineteenth century pioneer whose dependence on trade was very limited and who always had his land and, compared to today, relatively generalized farming skills to fall back on. These facts of social life, of course, are reflected in location. Locations of cities, agricultural land uses, social groups within cities, industries, yield to explanation only with resort to notions of interregional linkage, spatial interdependence and the like.

Both the emergence of the spatial viewpoint and the replacement of a man-environment framework by a man-man framework, then, can be related to broad social and economic changes and their reflection in the patterns confronted by American geographers. They also fed off each other, however. Man-environment viewpoints, for example, stressed site variables: the slope on which man walked directly, the rocks he removed from his land to build his house, and the soil and climate constraining his farming options. Appropriately enough, therefore, the man-environment viewpoint was accompanied by a site-dependent viewpoint: a commitment to natural regions, distinctive with respect to their soil, climate or vegetation. In a world of spatial interdependence, on the other hand, such locally experienced environmental dependencies lose their rationale: men relate less and less to the land on which they stand and more and more to socially-created geographical patterns over a much wider area.

Geography as a Social Science

Consider now the contribution of geography to social knowledge. Distinctive contributions of any social science to an understanding of American society fall into two major categories: those describing whatever order happens to exist; i.e. the isolation of predictabilities or descriptive regularities; and those which address themselves to the development of theory to account for whatever descriptive regularities have been isolated. Understandings, therefore, can come in the area of both pattern and process and in geography these patterns and processes concern the locational manifestations of social life. Given the recency of geography's emergence as a social science, however, many of the references made will be to rather recent work—in fact to work completed in the last three decades.

GEOGRAPHICAL PATTERN

Some idea of the geographer's work on pattern[3] can be gleaned from
a brief consideration of three ideas: (1) localization; (2) trend; and
(3) spatial periodicity.

Attributes of social and economic life tend to cluster in space: i.e.
they tend to be localized. In terms of the social and economic attributes of people located there, therefore, places close together tend to
be similar; places further apart tend to be dissimilar. This is true
whether one considers social segregation across census tracts in cities,
population densities by state or the agricultural specialization of different regions in the U.S. This suggests some elementary order in the
arrangement of things over space: given (e.g.) the race of a family
occupying a particular housing unit one can provide a pretty reliable
prediction as to the race of the family next door.

On the other hand, localization is not always that local. Variation
over space occurs at a variety of geographic scales—neighborhood, district, region, etc.—and theoretically, at least, it is possible to apportion
the total variance to each of those scales (Moellering and Tobler, 1972).
Where, for example, regional components tend to be rather large relative to local components, places at considerable distances apart may
be quite similar in their attributes.

Some sense of the scale of variation idea can be gained by varying
the scale of data-collecting units with respect to a given geographical
distribution. Examination of the population density distribution of the
U.S. as portrayed by variation across the states, for example, brings
out broad regional contrasts between a relatively densely populated
Midwest and Northeast, a less densely populated South, a sparsely
populated West and a somewhat more densely settled Pacific coast.
Examination of the same pattern at the level of counties, however,
would show that this regional pattern is superimposed upon smaller
scale variations distinguishing between more urban counties and their
rural hinterlands and linear patterns linking up major metropolitan
centers. Larger scale data-collecting units, therefore, tend to filter out
smaller scale variations which, presumably, are attributable to processes
operating at smaller geographic scales.

When directional relationships are taken into consideration as well
as distance, geographical trends (Chorley and Haggett, 1965) become
evident. A spatial diffusion of innovations, for example, may be characterized in terms of a map of dates of adoption. Such map patterns
can often be broken down into trends of either a radial or linear character. Dates of adoption tend to increase with distance from some point
or line that is presumably the locus of origin of the diffusion. Trends

may occur at both large and small scales. In one case the spread of tractor adoption from state to state in the central U.S. has been isolated as a spatial trend phenomenon centered somewhere in North Dakota (Casetti and Semple, 1969). Evidence from the diffusion of other agricultural innovations suggests the possibility of similar, though smaller-scale, trends within states (Johansen, 1971; Bowden, 1965).

Finally there is the concept of periodicity in geographical arrangement. Just as the attributes of points arranged in time exhibit some recurrent or cyclical patterns so do attributes of points arranged in space. In the case of a time series cycles may be characterized according to the length of temporal interval; conversely in the case of a spatial series cycles are characterized according to spatial interval. Some geographic theories, for example, predict a good deal of regularity in the spatial interval separating cities of a given size; or of shopping centers of a given size within cities. Scale variation is again apparent, however, shorter intervals separating, say, smaller cities and longer intervals separating larger cities (Tobler, 1969).

In fact, in the U.S. there is a good deal of evidence for precisely such periodicity. Larger cities do tend to be spaced further apart than smaller cities. They tend to provide a greater variety of retail services for their rural hinterlands and to serve larger trade areas (Berry, 1967).

GEOGRAPHICAL PROCESS

Consider now the origins of such patterning. At one level of explanation a set of geographic processes can be defined: diffusions, migrations, colonizations and shifts in business location which result in a sequence of slowly changing geographies like succeeding frames in a movie (Tobler, 1970). In such a view geographical pattern is one cross-section of an ongoing geographic process.

At the origin of geographic processes of residential movement, industrial location, and the like are locational decisions: decisions which discriminate between alternative locations according to some criterion and, by altering geographical pattern, transform the pattern of locational alternatives between which future locators will choose. A useful distinction here is that between competitive and agglomerative locational decisions. Decisions may be competitive with respect to each other in which case a class of locators may be characterized as attempting to get as far away from each other as possible; such decisions tend to exercise dispersing effects on geographic pattern. Or decisions may be agglomerative in which case locators can be described as attempting to get as close to each other as possible; these decisions tend to exercise concentrating effects on geographic pattern. Claval's statement that pattern represents an equilibrium between processes of dispersion and processes of concentration, therefore, has a certain heuristic value (Claval, 1970).

In order to employ such concepts of locational decision-making in theory building, however, a set of assumptions regarding decision processes is required. In this regard most of the inspiration of location theory is microeconomic in character (e.g., Smith, Taaffe, and King, 1968). However, there has been some reaction to this more recently in the form of what has been described as "The Behavioral Revolution" (Golledge, Brown and Williamson, 1972). We therefore discuss, successively, mainstream location theory and the behavioral revision of that theory.

Mainstream Location Theory. For much of contemporary location theory the assumptions are microeconomic in character. According to this conception locational decisions are the market decisions of men working with an assumed utility function with respect to location; with perfect information about locational alternatives; and within the constraints of a competitive market process in which locational choices are interdependent.

Space is costly because it poses barriers to movement: to the assembly of raw materials, to migration, to the distribution of finished products, etc. However, space can be manipulated to the locator's advantage. Where the locator's interests are complementary to those of others, for example, there are clear advantages to minimizing movement costs with respect to them; and where one can assume a strict linear relationship between movement cost and distance this will produce a locational pattern in which locators maximize their nearness with respect to each other. Locators may be complementary because they supply each other with necessary inputs (e.g. the relationship of the supplier to the consumer of either a finished or an intermediate product); or because they require certain common services in the provision of which there are economies of scale. Obviously these so-called economies of agglomeration are a fundamental force in processes of urban concentration, and a variety of scales also. They may act to increase the size of an individual city. And at a larger, regional scale economies of agglomeration may make smaller cities close to larger cities attractive as locations. Such agglomerative processes may therefore help to explain extensively urbanized regions such as that described as Megalopolis (Gottman, 1961) or even the American Manufacturing Belt (Harris, 1954; Ullman, 1958).

On the other hand the barrier effect of space may bestow benefits rather than disadvantages. As a result of its implications for movement costs, inaccessibility tends to protect from competition. By locating as far away from competitors as possible a degree of monopoly power and, hence, leverage over price may be attained. By locating too close together, for example, neighborhood grocery stores will be competing for the same neighborhood market; by locating further apart, and assuming consumers will patronize the nearest neighborhood grocery store, some discretion over pricing may be attained. Interregional migration can also be interpreted in this light. Migration typically takes place from low wage to high wage areas; it is therefore, a movement from labor surplus to labor deficit areas and hence an attempt on the part of individual migrators to locate so as to minimize labor market competition.

Clearly space-dispersing effects tend to co-exist with space-concentrating effects. To the extent that towns are retailing centers they may be regarded as competing with each other for a rural retail market and hence locate so as to maximize their distances from each other. Since larger towns require larger markets they will tend to be spaced further apart than smaller towns producing the types of spatial periodicities discussed above. On the other hand towns as retail centers will also tend to concentrate in areas where rural population densities are higher.[4] At any one time, therefore, locational pattern represents the results of a tradeoff between propensities to maximize nearness to complementary locators and propensities to minimize nearness to competitors. An attractive feature of such a pattern is that, ceteris paribus, it tends to be movement-minimizing.

Behavioral Revision. While micro-economic assumptions have provided the basis for a reasonably plausible and effective location theory there has also been some criticism of them and a feeling that the predictive power of current location theory would benefit from the incorporation of more realistic behavioral assumptions.

In a locational context the assumption of perfect information appears particularly vulnerable: spatial barriers will likely result in a variety of misperceptions and lacunae in the locator's knowledge. Certainly the results of studies of the spatial diffusion of innovations suggest spatially correlated imperfections in information; the spread of many innovations, for example, appears to be consistent with a distance-constrained contact process in which adoption is a function of information and information is a function of proximity to those who have already adopted (Brown, 1968).

The attempt to specify the nature of such spatially correlated imperfections in knowledge, in a way that allows them to be related to locational processes, has taken the form of identifying what can best be called processes and patterns of spatial cognition (Downs and Stea, 1973). The critical questions here are: what are the cognitive maps of their world which people develop as a result of their spatial experiences and what are the bases of these maps?

In order to survive in a geographical world individuals must navigate; and in order to navigate they must have some conception of the relative locations of the places important to them—home, work, school, and shops, for example. This conception takes the form of classification of places according to relative location and those attributes critical to individual utility; such conceptions have been variously called mental maps, spatial schemata and cognitive maps.

Obviously we cannot expect such cognitive maps to be facsimiles of reality. Of some assistance in understanding the underlying forces, however, is the fact that distortions tend to be shared—for example, short distances tend to be overestimated relative to longer distances (Briggs, 1973)—and groups of people with similar absolute locations tend to have very similar cognitive maps (Horton and Reynolds, 1971). Generally speaking it would seem that they are the outcome of a spatial learning process (Golledge, 1969). Knowledge about places critical to individual utility is acquired gradually, much of it by trial and error. As a consequence we would expect navigational abilities to improve with length of residence in a particular area and the individual's movements to increasingly approach optimality. Intuitively perhaps we can all recognize this recalling that a move to a new city is often followed within a short space of time by residential relocation within the city, presumably as a response to some learning process.

Current Limitations of Geography as Social Science

A concern of major proportions in American geography today is that of relevance. The view among many is that for all the achievements of the last two decades, recent theoretical advances in geography really have not helped much in understanding problems of individual social existence. More specifically the view is that a focus on geographical pattern and geographical relationships has become an end in itself irrespective of its social value. In diffusion research, for example, interest has been mainly in the spatial process of diffusion rather than in the socially inequitable nature of such processes.

Much of the responsibility for this can be traced to geography's relationships with the other social sciences. In the last 20 years or so these have been overwhelmingly with economics. The major institutionalized interdisciplinary forum in which geographers participate, for example, is the Regional Science Association; the other major disciplines represented there are economics and city planning. Relationships with sociology, political science and anthropology have been much weaker.[5] For most geographers, therefore, the space they deal with is economic in character.

The legacy of economics for the geographer's view of the world can be reduced to a simple idea: that of an equilibrium in a system of interrelationships to which institutional, political and social considerations are exogenous rather than endogenous. The adaptation of this view to a spatially differentiated world has had impacts on both the welfare implications geographers have chosen to draw from their work and also upon the conceptual frameworks they have adopted to explain geographic pattern.

In economics the concept of equilibrium has an attractive welfare attribute: net benefits to society are maximized and, therefore, the allocation of resources is an efficient one. The concept of equilibrium can be translated into a geographic framework as spatial equilibrium. There is a similar welfare implication: the geographical pattern of activities is an efficient one. This is a welfare implication commonly drawn from location theory: the predicted pattern of retail outlets is efficient in the sense that it minimizes consumer travel.

Equilibrium assumptions, however, have tended to induce a neglect of distributional questions. To some degree this is due to the equation of equilibrium with efficiency. It is also due however, to the emphasis of equilibrium concepts on self-correcting negative feedbacks. These, it is argued, will tend to mitigate, rather than exacerbate, inequalities and eliminate distributionally distasteful monopolies. In a strictly locational context, for instance, it is argued that labor mobility from low wage to high wage regions, motivated by the wage differential, will serve to equilibrate wages in the two regions by increasing the labor supply in the high wage region and decreasing it in the low wage region.

Turning from welfare implications to conceptual frameworks it is clear that emphasis in both economics and geography has been upon the playing out of limited sets of relationships; these relationships are seen as depending to a large degree upon the nature of social and institutional constraints which lie outside the model. An institutional context, for example, is assumed as necessary for the space economy, but the space economy merely reacts *to* it rather than *upon* it. From a viewpoint of individual social existence, therefore, the dominant emphasis in current geographic theory is one in which individuals solve the problems confronting them by altering their locational relationships: substituting one set of locational relationships for another. Individual households migrate to escape their problems, therefore, business enterprises relocate, and small farmers supplement their incomes by commuting.

The theoretical fulcrum for this approach is the concept of spatial equilibrium. Some attractiveness gradient over space—that is assumed rather than explained—leads to a series of relocations that ultimately eliminate the gradient which called them into being. The interregional migration discussed above is prototypical but the same logic is apparent in explanations of neighborhood change or of the location of retail outlets. In the latter case, for example, location is interpreted as a response to variations in perceived profitability which are then eliminated by acts of location.

This is clearly a very partial view of reality. In terms of solving problems of individual social existence it is true that there are a variety of private behaviors with geographic correlates and which have an impact upon the overall geographic pattern of social and economic life. The private behaviors open to individuals, however, and their feasibility are just as clearly dependent upon the rules of the game defined by the political process. Alternative to some spatial adjustment within existing rules of the game therefore, is some attempt to alter the rules so that currently non-feasible locational adjustments will be brought within the realm of possibility. In short, individuals not only react to the existing institutional constraints but also upon them. The assumption of the exogenousness of social, political and institutional constraints is, therefore, absolutely fundamental to the types of spatial patterns deduced by current theory.

In a world of ecological crisis, urban riots and Third World poverty, a human geography equipped with such a conceptual framework has seemed more and more irrelevant. As David Harvey (1973: 128-129) has written:

> There is a clear disparity between the sophisticated theoretical and methodological framework which we are using and our ability to say anything really meaningful about events as they unfold around us. There are too many anomalies between what we purport to explain and manipulate and what actually happens. There is an ecological problem, an urban problem, an international trade problem, and yet we seem incapable of saying anything of depth or profundity about any of them. When we do say anything it appears trite and rather ludicrous. In short our paradigm is not coping well.

Reactions to this dilemma have been twofold. On the one hand there has been an essentially descriptive approach documenting geographical inequalities, relationships between accessibility and distribution, and testing hypotheses about these distributional outcomes. Among these have been studies of territorial social indicators—a transposition of the social indicator concept to a geographic context (Smith, 1973); studies of the relationship between transportation and poverty (Beder-

man and Adams, 1974; Davies and Huff, 1972); a variety of housing
market studies (Meyer, 1973; Rose, 1970); studies in the geographical
distribution of crime (Harries, 1974); and studies dealing with access
to health care facilities (Shannon and Dever, 1974; deVise, 1973). By
and large these researchers have not related their findings to any
broader body of theory.

On the other hand there have been attempts to develop new conceptual approaches in which political and social processes are assumed
as endogenous rather than exogenous. A group led by Julian Wolpert,
at the University of Pennsylvania, has attempted some reformulation
of location theory by incorporating conflict as a critical variable (Wolpert, 1970; Austin, Smith and Wolpert, 1970): locators, for example, are
deflected from areas where their activities would generate opposition
into areas where, for whatever reasons, resident reactions are more
acquiescent. Such considerations seem to play an important role in the
location of freeways, drug treatment centers, new bridges and a variety
of other "obnoxious" land uses.

A more comprehensive approach is represented by the attempt to
substitute a neo-Marxist location theory for the existing neo-classical
constructs. This is largely associated with the work of David Harvey
who has done a variety of work on the geographical structure of housing markets (Harvey, 1974) and written a well-received book in which
he traces his own personal intellectual odyssey from what he calls
liberal to socialist formulations (Harvey, 1973). The interest in the work
of Harvey and Wolpert among geographers is testimony to the growing
feeling that existing location theory is inadequate as a basis for understanding the relationships between location and current public problems.

Concluding Comments

Geography is a very young social science. Academic geography dates
only from the beginning of this century. As a self-conscious science
concerned with describing and explaining locational aspects of social
life it is even more recert, the major thrusts occurring within the last
two decades.

Major understandings of American society have concerned locational
questions. The locational arrangements of people, groups, firms, their
artifacts, etc., typically show a good deal of predictability. This is
apparent in such obvious features of American society as segregation.
It is also apparent in less widely-recognized features such as the tendency for larger cities to be spaced further apart than smaller cities.

Locational pattern may be regarded as the outcome of an equilibrium between space-concentrating forces resulting in localizations, agglomerations of population and activities; and space-dispersing forces creating periodicities in geographical arrangement. Locational decisions underlying these processes can be regarded as agglomerative in which case complementary locators try to get as close to one another as possible; or competitive in which case competitive locators try to get as far away from each other as possible. Theory for understanding these decisions has been couched largely in microeconomic terms and has served to produce overlaps with economics in the urban and regional economics literature. More recently this theory has been called into question as a result of scrutiny of its underlying behavioral assumptions.

Reliance upon microeconomic assumptions, modified or not by behavioral revision has, however, tended to produce its own problems. In particular reliance on the economist's conception of reality as a self-equilibrating system to which political and social considerations are exogenous rather than endogenous has tended to induce a neglect of distributional issues and the forces producing those issues. Recent work responding to this relevancy problematic points in directions which should certainly result in geography being a more critical social science and possibly a more effective one too.

Appendix A

The content analysis is based on an evaluation of a sample of abstracts of papers delivered at the annual meetings of the Association of American Geographers. For each decade three years were randomly selected. For each of the three years a random sample of 10 abstracts dealing with the human geography of the U.S.A. was selected. Each abstract was classified as to the implicit goals of the paper: idiographic or nomothetic; as to the behavioral framework adopted: man-environment or man-man; and as to the site or situation bias of the conceptual framework. Frequencies within each of the classes were then aggregated by decade and form the immediate basis of Table 1.

One caveat is necessary. Given the procedure adopted it is reasonable to expect the absolute frequencies within columns and between the horizontal lines to sum, in each case, to 30. In actual fact this is a rarity, and for a variety of reasons. In the earlier years of the Association of American Geographers, abstracts were few in number and samples were often less than 10 and, therefore, equivalent to the populations being sampled. In addition some abstracts had no clear behavioral assumptions and received no classification according to the man-environment/man-man distinction. The same is true with respect to the idiographic-nomothetic distinction. Finally in some cases, abstracts had to be classified as both site- and situation-dependent in their emphases.

Sources for the data discussed above, therefore, are volumes of the Annals, Association of American Geographers as follows: 2(1912): 105-118; 6(1916): 121-132; 10(1920): 153-157; 11(1921): 119-136; 17(1927): 21-38; 18-(1928): 44-72; 22(1932): 44-87; 23(1933): 33-57; 30(1940): 44-80; 31-(1941: 55-75; 32(1942): 98-115; 36(1946): 79-109; 41(1951): 158-181; 46(1956): 237-284; 48(1958): 250-299; 52(1962): 318-372; 54(1964): 412-443; 55(1965): 603-660.

Notes

1. The author would like to acknowledge helpful comment on an earlier draft of this paper from Edward J. Taaffe, Department of Geography, The Ohio State University.

2. These statistics are byproducts of the content analysis referred to earlier and therefore describe samples rather than populations. For the 1911–1920 decade the years sampled were 1912, 1916 and 1920; while for the 1961–1970 decade the three years included were 1962, 1964 and 1965.

3. A particularly useful selection of readings on this topic can be found in Berry and Marble (1968).

4. This very cursory discussion hardly begins to do justice to what is a highly coherent body of theory with both explanatory and aesthetic appeal. See, for example, Berry (1967).

5. In this context Yi-Fu Tuan's (1972) statement seems reasonable: "Geography is by now an established branch of the social sciences, yet it remains curiously outside the mainstream of social science thinking; only economics can be said to have made a major impact on contemporary geography."

References

Abler, R., J. S. Adams and P. R. Gould. 1971. Spatial Organization (Englewood Cliffs, N.J.: Prentice-Hall).

Austin, M., T. E. Smith and J. Wolpert. 1970. "The Implementation of Controversial Facility-Complex Programs," Geographical Analysis, 2(October): 315-329.

Barrows, H. H. 1923. "Geography as Human Ecology," Annals, Association of American Geographers, 13: 1-14.

Beredman, S. H. and J. S. Adams. 1974. "Job Accessibility and Underemployment," Annals, Association of American Geographers, 64(3): 378-386.

Berry, B. J. L. 1967. Geography of Market Centers and Retail Distribution (Englewood Cliffs, N.J.: Prentice-Hall).

Berry, B. J. L. and D. F. Marble, eds. 1968. Spatial Analysis (Englewood Cliffs, N.J.: Prentice-Hall).

Borchert, J. R. 1972. "America's Changing Metropolitan Regions," Annals, Association of American Geographers, 62(2): 352-373.

Bowden, L. W. 1965. Diffusion of the Decision to Irrigate (Chicago: Department of Geography Research Papers).

Briggs, R. 1973. "Urban Cognitive Distance," in R. M. Downs and D. Stea, eds., Image and Environment (Chicago: Aldine): 361-388.

Brown, L. A. 1968. Diffusion Processes and Location (Philadelphia: Regional Science Research Institute).

Bunge, W. 1966. "Gerrymandering, Geography and Grouping," Geographical Review, 55(April): 256-263.

Burton, I. 1963. "The Quantitative Revolution and Theoretical Geography," Canadian Geographer, 7(Winter): 151-162.

Burton, I., R. W. Kates, and A. Kirkby. 1974. "Interdisciplinary Environmental Approaches, Theory by Discipline: Geography," Natural Resources Journal, 14.

Casetti, E. and R. K. Semple. 1969. "Concerning the Testing of Spatial Diffusion Hypotheses," Geographical Analysis, 1(3): 254-259.

Chorley, R. J. and P. Haggett. 1965. "Trend-Surface Mapping in Geographical Research," Transactions and Papers of the Institute of British Geographers, 37: 47-67.

Claval, P. 1970. "L'Espace en Géographie Humaine," Canadian Geographer, 14(Summer): 110-124.

Davies, C. S. and D. L. Huff. 1972. "Impact of Ghettoization on Black Employment," Economic Geography, 48(October): 421-427.

Downs, R. M. and D. Stea, eds. 1973. Image and Environment (Chicago: Aldine).

Fielding, G. J. 1974. Geography as Social Science (New York: Harper and Row).

Golledge, R. G. 1969. "The Geographical Relevance of Some Learning Theories," in K. R. Cox and R. G. Golledge, eds. Behavioral Problems in Geography: A Symposium (Evanston, Ill.: Northwestern University, Department of Geography, Research Paper 17): 101-145.

———, L. A. Brown and F. Williamson. 1972. "Behavioral Approaches in Geography: An Overview," Australian Geographer, 12(March): 59-79.

Gottman, J. 1961. Megalopolis (Cambridge, Mass.: MIT Press).

Gould, P. R. 1969. "Methodological Developments Since the Fifties," in C. Board et al., eds., Progress in Geography, 1(London: Edward Arnold): 1-49.

Harries, K. D. 1974. The Geography of Crime and Justice (New York: McGraw-Hill).

Harris, C. D. 1954. "The Market as a Factor in the Localization of Industry in the United States," Annals, Association of American Geographers, 44: 315-348.

Hartshorne, R. 1939. "The Nature of Geography: A Critical Survey of Current Thought in the Light of the Past," Annals, Association of American Geographers, 29: 173-658.

———. 1959. Perspectives on the Nature of Geography (Chicago: Rand Mc-Nally).

Harvey, D. 1973. Social Justice and the City (Baltimore: The Johns Hopkins University Press).

———. 1974. "Class-Monopoly Rent, Finance Capital and the Urban Revolution," Regional Studies, 8(3/4): 239-255.

Horton, F. E. and D. R. Reynolds. 1971. "Effects of Urban Spatial Structure on Individual Behavior," Economic Geography, 47(January): 36-48.

Huff, D. L. 1973. "The Delineation of a National System of Planning Regions on the Basis of Urban Spheres of Influence," Regional Studies, 7(September): 323-329.

Huntington, E. and S. W. Cushing. 1934. Principles of Human Geography (New York: Wiley).

Johansen, H. E. 1971. "Diffusion of Strip Cropping in Southwestern Wisconsin," Annals, Association of American Geographers, 61(4): 671-683.

Kirk, W. 1963. "Problems in Geography," Geography, 47(November): 357-371.

Kohn, C. F. 1970. "The 1960's: A Decade of Progress in Geographical Research and Instruction," Annals, Association of American Geographers, 60(2): 211-219.

McCarty, H. H. and N. E. Salisbury. 1961. Visual Comparison of Isopleth Maps as a Means of Determining Correlations Between Spatially Distributed Phenomena (Iowa City: University of Iowa, Department of Geography Publication No. 3).

Manners, I. R. and M. W. Mikesell, eds. 1974. Perspectives on Environment (Washington, D.C.: Association of American Geographers).

Meyer, D. R. 1973. "Interurban Differences in Black Housing Quality," Annals, Association of American Geographers, 63(3): 347-352.

Mikesell, M. W. 1974. "Geography as the Study of Environment: An Assessment of Some Old and New Commitments," in I. R. Manners and M. W. Mikesell, eds., Perspectives on Environment (Washington, D.C.: Association of American Geographers): 1-23.

Moellering, H. and W. Tobler. 1972. "Geographical Variances," Geographical Analysis, 4(1): 34-50.

Morrill, R. L. 1974. The Spatial Organization of Society (North Scituate, Mass.: Duxbury).

Muller, J-C. 1975. "Associations in Chloropleth Map Comparison," Annals, Association of American Geographers, 65(3): 403-413.

Platt, R. S. 1928. "A Detail of Regional Geography: Ellison Bay Community as an Industrial Organism," Annals, Association of American Geographers, 18(June): 81-126.

Platt, R. S. 1946. "Problems of Our Time," Annals, Association of American Geographers, 36(March): 1-43.

Rose, H. M. 1970. "The Development of an Urban Subsystem: The Case of the Negro Ghetto," Annals, Association of American Geographers, 60(1): 1-17.

Rose, J. K. 1936. "Corn Yield and Climate in the Corn Belt," Geographical Review, 26(January): 88-102.

Sauer, C. O. 1925. "The Morphology of Landscape," University of California, Publications in Geography, 2(2): 19-54.

———. 1936. "American Agricultural Origins: A Consideration of Nature and Culture," in Essays in Anthropology Presented to A. L. Kroeber in Celebration of His Sixtieth Birthday, June 11, 1936, (Berkeley: University of California Press): 279-297.

———. 1941. "Foreword to Historical Geography," Annals, Association of American Geographers, 31 (March): 1-24.

———. 1956. "Agency of Man on Earth," in W. L. Thomas, ed., Man's Role in Changing the Face of the Earth (Chicago: University of Chicago Press): 49-60.

Schaefer, F. K. 1953. "Exceptionalism in Geography: A Methodological Examination," Annals, Association of American Geographers, 43(September): 226-249.

Semple, E. S. 1903. American History and Its Geographic Conditions (New York: Houghton Mifflin).

Shannon, G. W. and G. E. A. Dever. 1974. Health Care Delivery: Spatial Perspectives (New York: McGraw-Hill).

Smith, D. M. 1973. The Geography of Social Well-Being in the United States (New York: McGraw-Hill).

Smith, R. H. T., E. J. Taaffe and L. J. King. 1968. Readings in Economic Geography (Chicago: Rand McNally).

Spate, O. H. K. 1960. "Quantity and Quality in Geography," Annals, Association of American Geographers, 50(September): 377-394.

Spencer, J. E. and R. J. Horvath. 1963. "How Does an Agricultural Region Originate," Annals, Association of American Geographers, 53(1): 74-92.

Taaffe, E. J. 1970. Geography (Englewood Cliffs, N.J.: Prentice-Hall).

———. 1974. "The Spatial View in Context," Annals, Association of American Geographers, 64(1): 1-16.

Tatham, G. 1967. "The Rise of Possibilism," in F. E. Dohrs and L. M. Sommers, eds., Introduction to Geography: Selected Readings (New York: Thomas Crowell): 130-138.

Tobler, W. R. 1969. "The Spectrum of U.S. 40," Papers and Proceedings of the Regional Science Association, 23: 45-52.

———. 1970. "A Computer Movie Simulating Urban Growth in the Detroit Region," Economic Geography, 46(2 Supplement): 234-240.

Tuan, Y-F. 1972. Review of R. E. Murphy, The Dialectics of Social Life, Annals, Association of American Geographers, 62 (September): 507-509.

Ullman, E. L. 1954. "Geography as Spatial Interaction," (abstract) Annals, Association of American Geographers, 44(September): 283.

———. 1958. "Regional Development and the Geography of Concentration," Papers and Proceedings of the Regional Science Association, 4: 179-198.

de Vise, P. 1973. Misused and Misplaced Hospitals and Doctors (Washington, D.C.: Association of American Geographers).

Watson, J. W. 1955. "Geography: A Discipline in Distance," Scottish Geographical Magazine, 71(April): 1-13.

Whittlesey, D. 1945. "The Horizon of Geography," Annals, Association of American Geographers, 35(March): 1-36.

Wolpert, J. 1970. "Departures from the Usual Environment in Locational Analysis," Annals, Association of American Geographers, 60(2): 220-229.

Wright, J. K. 1937. "Some Measures of Distributions," Annals, Association of American Geographers, 27(December): 177-211.

The Social Sciences in America:

Some Comments on Past, Present and Future[1]

LOUIS SCHNEIDER

The University of Texas at Austin

The foregoing essays on the social sciences in America suggest a certain restraint on the part of their authors with respect to what those disciplines can accomplish. The authors do report a number of successes, but the general tone is hardly one of unqualified celebration. One would not expect, to be sure, the high optimism of a Condorcet expressed nearly two centuries ago nor the later vast (some would say insane) hopes of an Auguste Comte for either the future of humanity or the role of social science in bringing that future about. And there are no metaphysics of the historical process of the kind that presumes a crypto-rational working of the process so that it will ultimately produce out of its own heavings that which is in accord with the canons of reason and morality, while social science lays bare the laws of this development and thereby consoles and inspires through exhibition of the secretly operative rationality which is in the end due to overcome wretched intermediate conditions.

There is at the most a qualified optimism here about history and society and economy and about what the social sciences can do about them. It is perhaps better to speak frankly of a strain of uncertainty about the social world and of discernible dissatisfaction with the social sciences, granted that we must take care not to exaggerate either of these.[2] The several essays do not show or suggest this strain in equal degree, but we shall shortly review the main specific dissatisfactions they exhibit and subsequently rely on the statements of these for aid in ascertaining what matters would seem likely to be problematic or "interesting" for the social sciences in the near future.

A Backward Glance

Before turning to an array of dissatisfactions that can be drawn from the essays it is well to provide a bit of historical perspective for the present symposium by a brief look backward to another, not entirely dissimilar one published over 50 years ago. This will suggest that the tone about the social sciences expressed by social scientists in America today is, if anything, rather more cautious in respect of optimism than it was some 50 years ago.

It would far transcend the scope of these comments to attempt anything remotely like a history of American social scientists' attitudes toward social science (and toward society in the light of what the social sciences might accomplish). The evidence relating to those attitudes we draw on in referring to older symposium material is most limited, but we go on the general presumption that the attitudes expressed by leading scholars in such older symposia (as in the present one) are in some important sense representative and suggest central biases prevalent in the scholars' fields.

In 1925 Harry Elmer Barnes issued a large, ambitious book on the social sciences under his editorship.[3] Barnes thought he saw in his day "a social order which is becoming more and more evidently and certainly dependent upon social science for adequate and intelligent control, direction and reorganization." He also drew a somewhat naive contrast (in its way reminiscent of the simplistic rationalism of Condorcet) between what he evidently thought was the much that could be done for the guidance of human conduct by social scientists on the one hand and the very little that could be done for it by "metaphysicians and theologians" on the other. Barnes in 1925 quoted at great length from a speech, made shortly before he wrote, on the subject of the discovery of truth in universities by Walter Dill Scott (then president of Northwestern University). Scott asserted that "the most fruitful researches during the twentieth century will probably be conducted not in the natural sciences but in the social sciences," that "we are at last coming to see that the proper study of mankind is man" and that "all our human relations will be improved as rapidly as we make progress in the social sciences, and I am convinced that our universities will make as great a contribution here during the twentieth century as they did by the discovery of truth in the natural sciences during the nineteenth century" (Barnes, 1925; Scott, 1924).

The other contributions to the Barnes-edited volume do not indicate any great optimism about the prospects of the social sciences in cognitive or in problem-solving respects. Barnes himself contributed the article on history and came out for pragmatic use of that discipline in the line of lessening the influence of the "dead hand" of the past "over those who today must plan a more efficient and happy future for the race." In his chapter on sociology Frank H. Hankins merely allowed himself a final, perhaps defensive observation that the time was fast coming when it would be wrong to designate the sociologist as "the fake professor of a pretended science." Karl Worth Bigelow, the economist, foresaw no great prospects for institutional economics. Walter J. Shephard, discussing political science, predicted changes for his discipline which might mean "progress" but he did not think they meant "a new heaven and a new earth." "Optimism" and "pessimism" about social science and the social world are simply not relevant categories for the chapters on geography by Jean Brunhes and anthropology by Alexander Goldenweiser.[4]

With these various indications that optimism about social science (and, for that matter, about the social order) was not "excessive" in the mid-20's, Barnes still showed traces of an older greater optimism. And even if we should concede that Walter Dill Scott's address may be regarded as hopeful rhetoric on the part of a vigorous academic leader in a prosperous time, he was still, one may suppose, decidedly more hopeful in expression than one would expect a university president to be today. The social sciences in America were not in a boundlessly self-confident phase a half century ago; yet one has the impression that there was a somewhat more optimistic tone about them than there is today. It is not (if we are right) that there were no unhappy things in American (and non-American) experience to look back to in 1925, but the character of the intervening 50 years has surely been such as to induce new caution in hopes about man and society and what man's cognitive achievements may do for him. Perhaps it is not amiss to suggest again that this does not imply a mood drenched in pessimism, but significant dissatisfactions in the social sciences do obtrude themselves. We turn to such dissatisfactions, expressed by the authors of the foregoing essays either as their own or as those of others in their respective fields.

Current Dissatisfactions

Goetzmann refers to new radicals determined to examine history in the light not of "consensus" but of "confrontation." The radicals see an American historical record replete with "contradictions, crimes and absurdities." For them, traditional consensus historians are mere glorifiers of America. And the radicals have insisted that the historian make use of his endeavors in order to right past and present wrongs. Value "neutrality" is in the radical view an indefensible stance. The "radical" phenomenon is clearly not confined to the field of history.

Spengler notes dissatisfaction with economics in the latest period of 1920–1925, referring to Veblen's fear of "obsolete preconceptions" that would impair analysis and to misgivings expressed by Paul Homan in his book on contemporary economic thought in 1928. (Homan, Spengler notes, wrote of "the present impasse" and of "diversity of thought and method.") Spengler also refers to reflections on theoretical uncertainty and lack of definitive authority for assertions in economics (even when backed by "consensus") on the part of John Maurice Clark (in the mid-30's) who voiced fear lest economists become imprisoned by their own devices, as did Wassily Leontief some four decades later. It is also true that Spengler sees economists living in a world that exhibits its own irrationalities and its own areas of ignorance, not necessarily easily responsive to such illumination as the economists may bring. The concluding section of Spengler's paper is quite emphatic on this point. He sees "the pandering of economically undertrained legislators . . . to the self-serving demands of special interest groups," is aware that economists may flatly *fail* to bring light, and is wary of an older tradition in economics that does not adequately face up to "the shrinking dowry of nature at man's disposal"—thereby inviting disastrous consequences for the human future.

More or less paralleling Spengler's suggestions about environing circumstances and groups in the larger society into which economic knowledge intrudes are some observations by Robin Williams on the line that "social sciences necessarily are received with sharply different and ambivalent appraisals by various audiences even within a generally permissive society." So true is it that social-science knowledge falls into a complex, conflict-filled social environment, inhabited by agents with different interests and motivations, that Williams feels constrained to say that "sheer knowledge alone, or 'disinterested search for truth,' will never be determinative and often may be of minor significance." To be sure, the extraneous limitations upon social science which Spengler and Williams both note in this connection refer (for they are indeed extraneous) not to the social sciences themselves but to their larger social ambiance.

Williams, for his part, does not seem especially alarmed that sociology may be, for the forseeable future, "a multiple paradigm science." Competitive approaches evidently may be disturbing to social scientists in varying degrees, this being perhaps partly contingent on what particular social science is involved. Although Williams and some other outstanding sociologists have not seemed greatly agitated by diversity of paradigms within their field (see particularly Merton, 1975), I may be allowed to add that such diversity or multiplicity of paradigms does seem (justifiably or not) to engender or support a sense of "crisis" among a number of sociologists. The relatively "easy" stance, in this connection, of Williams, Merton and others (with Merton, for one, observing that premature imposition of a supposedly definitive paradigm would merely induce stagnation) does not prevent "deepened tension and sometimes abrasive conflict" (Merton, 1975) among sociologists. There is a certain sensitivity about "politically" motivated conflict among cultivators of different paradigms. I may venture the guess that there is a strong sense of malaise in, and feeling of dissatisfaction about, social science today (beyond the ranks of sociologists alone) because of the sheer character that book reviews often show when books happen to fall into the hands of the "wrong" paradigmatists.

Since Eulau exhibits what he regards as the showpiece of his field, his own dissatisfactions, at least, as he proceeds, must have a somewhat subdued and incidental expression. But despite his gratification with the

subfield of American politics, Eulau sustains his judgment of the field of
political science as a whole of some two decades ago that if political scientists are agreed on anything, "it is probably the muddled state of their
science"—a science whose representatives were going off in numerous
directions, "evidently on the assumption that if you don't know where
you are going any road will take you there."

Goldschmidt is plainly dissatisfied with the theoretical achievement of
anthropology. He writes of "the failure to consolidate the theories of culture into some coherent and integrated whole" and avers that "those who
perceive a model of man . . . see it at best in a glass darkly." He also asserts early in his paper that "if anthropology ceases to be the study of
man it will dissolve into the meaningless examination of trivia—a danger
by no means remote, as a sampling of its literature will reveal."

Despite these strictures, Goldschmidt has some hope for his field. In
expressing that hope at the end of his paper, he argues critically that public policy is "in the hands of the economists," who hold a view of man as
"dominated by rationality and greed," and of the political scientists, whose
own vision is one of a human being "dominated by practicality and lust
for power." One might argue about this critical judgment as to who guides
public policy (depending on precisely what Goldschmidt here means).
And one might raise questions about whether economists and political
scientists are really confounding conveniently abstracted features of human beings with the concrete totality of these beings. But if Goldschmidt
entertains the notion that anthropology (for all its limitations) can bring
resources to the understanding of humanity which economics and political
science (and presumably some other disciplines) cannot, he nevertheless
of course hereby expresses dissatisfaction with at least certain aspects of
the standing of anthropology within the social sciences.

The geographer, Cox, believes his discipline needs more realistic behavioral assumptions than those it has worked with recently. The reliance
of geography on microeconomics has produced not only advances but also
distinctive problems, particularly as the notion of a self-equilibrating system ("to which political and social considerations are exogenous rather
than endogenous") has operated to induce neglect of questions of social
justice. Cox evidently hopes for the emergence of a social science of geography that shall be more critical and in so being shall be more attuned
to the solution of social problems to which geography has relevance. Plainly, Cox, too, suggests the urgency of value problems, and he would presumably be alert to a social science that would allow room for something
on the order of "evolutionary" assumptions transcending premises about
strongly stabilized or self-equilibrating systems.

To allow these various dissatisfactions or representations thereof to
tempt one into donning the mantle of the prophet would be foolish and
presumptuous. Yet there are suggestions as to some of the things the so-

cial sciences in America are likely to have to confront soon that are rather
readily derived from the above array when one stays modestly close to
the array itself. At the same time, in speculating on the future, I do allow
myself a measure of leeway in determining what is "bothersome" to numbers of social scientists today, even if it is not altogether explicit in the
foregoing items.

Things of the Future

It hardly seems farfetched to suggest, for one thing, that problems of
ethics, of distribution of various goods in a society and among societies,
of justice, of the value stance of social scientists, will soon become even
more urgent than they appear at present. There may be much disagreement about theories of justice, but such theories are bound to preoccupy
American social scientists (among others). Few would presumably want
to dissolve hard-won gains in social science in an unqualified ethical subjectivity working to subvert reliable knowledge, but a distinction between
what we would like to see and what actually prevails is utterly elementary. The pertinent references by Goetzmann to the radical historians, by
Spengler to dissipation of a heritage of natural resources, by Cox to problems of distribution that some geographers are unhappy to see neglected
—these alone suggest the urgency of the problems referred to and of the
need for going beyond what are by now near-banalities about how the
social scientist may relate himself to values.

The historical time of Max Weber, for instance, is gone. If we profit
still by his insights on values and social science, it may be contended
that they should indeed not be forgotten but also that they are no longer
adequate to present urgencies faced by social scientists. One possible line
of action is far more engagement in social science with the relevant work
on ethics of philosophers (*both* past and present). At least, many of the
ethical questions which philosophers have posed are quite unavoidable
even if the answers of various philosophers prove unsatisfactory. The record of the social sciences in dealing with ethical issues is hardly always
intellectually edifying or even barely defensible. Anthropology notoriously
presented us with the absurdities of that bent in "cultural relativism"
which strained toward the assertion that all cultures represent equally
valid ways of life or are equally good, and which repeatedly broke down
because those who adhered to it did not (to their credit) really believe it.[5]

Normative or ethical conclusions still require normative premises somewhere along the line, as welfare economists have inevitably again ascertained. But it is precisely the "normative" questions that call for much
more investigation, and our suggestion is that social scientists will increasingly come to regard it as futile, from the point of view of imperatives

forced on them by their own disciplines, to relegate such questions to philosophers or to anyone else.[6]

All this also has its bearings on the matter of the ambiance or larger social environment of the social sciences, ignorant or recalcitrant or arbitrary as various agents in that environment may be. (We here recall Spengler and Williams.) The problems that the ambiance raises are obviously very large and I must be content with quite general statements here. The deep ethical probing that may be in prospect is relevant to the ambiance. Given a generally high valuation of health, the tasks of physicians are evidently easier than they otherwise would be: "everyone" wants to be well. (For present purposes, this is not too radical a simplification.) A genuine ethical universalism may base itself on efforts to find human agreement on values lying well below superficial levels where disagreement prevails. This points to old but exceedingly important issues that one can readily imagine social science taking up with renewed interest once more.

Again, there is plainly no escaping the challenges to various representations of the economic, political and social world rendered by radical views. It may be well off the mark to see modern and contemporary society as "a theatre of a mad struggle for power, of a war of each against all, saved from absolute chaos by fear and repression," as Shils (1962) puts the matter, but this sort of contention (and in less blatant forms) will inevitably continue to demand critical consideration. "Conflict," "power," and the like are terms that lend themselves to facile ideological uses but they also point to realities whose dimensions and significance cannot be assessed by mere rhetoric, pro or con. Shils makes a useful (and easily refinable) classification of social science attitudes toward the social order as manipulative, alienated, and consensual—and social science attitudes toward the ambiance have an importance of their own.

Aside from matters bearing on ethics and the environment, the shape of the near future of social science may be affected by an evident, rather pervasive dissatisfaction with explanatory strategies and models that rely on the ascertainment of stable parameters. "Unfortunately," Boulding (1973: 275–276) comments, "in real social systems," parameters ascertained are "very rarely stable." Indeed, it may be "that there are no stable parameters in social systems." Boulding asserts, then, that we have to fall back on evolutionary theory (although that, too, may fail to bring "salvation" to economics). Old institutionalism, indeed, is likely to appear today in the garb of evolutionary economics.

Major structural change—"morphogenesis"—is already of considerable interest among social scientists who wish to go beyond consideration of system-preserving or -maintaining processes in a time that does seem peculiarly changeful. The geographer Cox, as we have suggested, appears in his dissatisfaction with certain traditional economic analyses at least potentially to be open to "evolutionary" ideas. Williams notes for sociology that "among many sociologists throughout the world, the formulations of T. Parsons and R. K. Merton are necessary referent points for any critical development of theory." And in recent years, of these two men, Parsons (particularly 1966) has been greatly interested in developing evolutionary theory. Anthropology of course has kept alive an evolutionary interest through the work of such men as Leslie White and Sahlins and Service (1960).

The word "evolution" is multi-valued enough. In sociology, the Lenskis (1974) are not quite the same sort of evolutionists as Parsons; and there are differences in the biases of the new evolutionary institutionalists in economics and of such a long-time and distinctively oriented student of evolutionary thought (particularly that of Mandeville and the Scottish moralists) as Hayek (for example, 1959, 1973). The near future, we would venture, will see new efforts to be precise and rigorous about the concept of evolution itself and to cast significant studies in social science within some evolutionary framework in more than a loose or perfunctory sense.

There are indications of the importance of mathematical work in the social sciences not touched on up to now which certainly merit at least concise statement and may give occasion for another line of observation about the future. The science-aspiration of the social sciences remains strong and the application of mathematics to their problems has plainly had appeal as a resource that might increase analytical power and social utilizability. The field of history witnesses the phenomenon of cliometrics, even if historians are not invariably happy with cliometric products. There is not only the much discussed sort of work of Fogel and Engerman but also a quantitative approach to historical data that has some clear inspiration from sociological orientations in particular, such as Thernstrom's (1973) study of social mobility in Boston over the course of almost a century. The future may well see the emergence of considerably more cross-disciplinary scholars such as Shorter and Tilly (1974) vitally concerned with both sociology and history and—for this is to the fore for the moment—also quantitatively oriented. The quantitative bias of sociologists is well known. Both sociology and economics have influenced political science in the way of stimulating quantitative work and suggesting the heuristic value of mathematical formulations. Anthropology and geography have been touched by the mathematical impulse.

Certainly, there is good reason to think that a variety of mathematical procedures will continue to be exploited and explored in the social sciences in the near future. But there are also reasons to think that a note of reservation about mathematics, long present, will continue and on some fronts become stronger than it is now. In the crucially important area, for mathematical reasoning in social sciences, of economics, numerous economists are evidently far from complacent about mathematics. There are frequent expressions of discontent of the type found in one of the forceful papers Spengler refers to in his exposition. Worswick (1972) sees branches of abstract economic analysis scarcely distinguishable from pure mathematics and so developed that one might almost say of them that their content is merely weakly reminiscent of what were once genuine economic questions. Econometricians forge "pretend-tools" that might be quite powerful if by chance empirical problems susceptible of their application should appear. Worswick does not mean to slight theory. Nor does he seek to depreciate the genuine contributions of econometricians, but the predictive power of their work has remained notably very low, at least if one uses natural science as criterion.

Worswick thinks progress in economics possible but likely to be slow, and mathematics in economics does not inhibit his saying that "we must reconcile ourselves to being inexact scientists." If various kinds of mathematical endeavor are likely to continue, it seems as safe a guess as any we can make that there will be contingents of social scientists who will look persistently (as some obviously already do) for inspiration to other disciplines for a variety of theoretical and "methodological" leads.

A more particular guess one might make here is that a number of social scientists will show much more interest than we have seen in the past in literature and certain branches of philosophy. Goetzmann refers to a theme of paradox in American historiography and mentions Niebuhr's *The Irony of American History*. C. Vann Woodward, Goetzmann intimates, was alert to "the irony and tragedy of history itself"; and irony and tragedy powerfully inform the history of the black in America as elsewhere. Robin Williams has a sense of the same things, and a feeling for the circumstance, important in this connection, that social arrangements often have counter-intuitive outcomes. We soon reach into an area, stretching beyond history and sociology, where we see (often even tragically or ironically) unforeseen outcomes of action and where social scientists may well find appeal and cogency in the work of outstanding literary critics (and other men and women of letters) without giving up scientific aspiration but while conceiving it in fresh, distinctively open-minded ways.

The last observations easily lead us to think "across the social sciences." It is really one of the salient points in our essays, as emphasized in the Introduction, that the social sciences have generally had a great deal of influence upon one another. There are good reasons for this, not the least being that, as Williams writes, "in terms of concepts, assumptions, explanatory paradigms and logic of investigation there are striking commonalities across cultural and social anthropology, welfare and developmental economics, social and cultural history, political science, social psychology and sociology."

A rich field for inquiry is thus suggested. Interpenetrations or certain kinds of duplications are simply inevitable. Let us note merely one instance, perhaps not quite so immediately evident as some others might be. When Goetzmann tells us of the work of Henry Nash Smith (and its apparent emphasis on "an image of the West" as impelling settlers to westward movement) and refers to the argument in his own work that "explorers, scientists and artists were 'programmed' to interpret what they saw in terms largely fashioned in Eastern cultural centers," he points to a feature of human motivation which, however much it may be obtruded upon the historian by reflection upon his own problems, is also obtruded upon social scientists by reflection upon theirs. Goetzmann writes in this connection that the early impressions upon "explorers, scientists and artists who went West" (in "terms largely fashioned in Eastern cultural centers") "largely governed the later course of Western development in a self-fulfilling prophecy." One is hardly surprised by this sociological language and would not have been surprised to find Goetzmann, in the course of his references to Smith's work and his own, taking up the well-known theme of William I. Thomas that if men define situations as real they are real in their consequences.

I would venture no particular prediction here, in respect of this matter of commonalities across the social sciences. But it may not be amiss to observe that, as far as I can tell from these essays and from some of the resources they draw upon, a great or spectacular breakthrough for the social sciences is not in the offing. They do not appear to be about to "discover the cure for cancer" or some equally intriguing analogue in their realm. In the presumptive absence of such achievement one may hope, if one dare not predict, that in the near future they will generate deeper reflection about their own content and seek to fashion a pervasive generalized mode of social science thought which will draw upon their various divisions without necessarily seeking to move toward the perhaps quite impossible goal of "one big social science" but while effectively undermining a number of residual provincialisms and silly misunderstandings. If this should all come about, relief might be forthcoming for some of the dissatisfaction regarding anthropology and other social sciences which Goldschmidt (who is surely not unique among anthropologists in this respect) expresses.

One may also hope that the developments for the near future here envisaged, if indeed they occur, will also help in other ways to relieve current dissatisfaction in the social sciences and enhance their beneficient and fruitful effect on their ambiance. I am well aware that the contributors to this symposium were asked not only to assess their fields but to relate the accomplishment of those fields to the character of American life. But since I have chosen in these few comments to remain so close to the fields themselves, it may be permissible, finally, to draw attention again to a rather immediate and pressing dissatisfaction, previously mentioned, to be found in them. This is the dissatisfaction arising from considerable conflict within a field, as among supporters of different paradigms in sociology.

Encountering abrasiveness and even downright injustice for one's own best work is surely no pleasure. Ideas and concepts—even paradigms and significant theories—impermanent beasts that they are, come and go, however, in the social sciences as elsewhere. It will hardly do to be flippant about them but it is notorious that they have to live dangerously if they are to live at all. There are today a number of interesting observations made by students of the history and sociology of science that may help to put some of our current pains over abrasive intradisciplinary conflicts in better perspective. There is a remarkable and especially "alleviating" anticipation of such observations made by an unusually acute writer two and a half centuries ago (who was not even thinking of the social sciences in particular, and who was certainly unfamiliar with our sense of "paradigm" or "model").[7] Mandeville (1730: 125-126) writes thus:

> An Hypothesis, when once it has been a little while establish'd, becomes like a Sovereign and receives the same Homage and Respect from its Vassals, as if it was Truth itself. This continues till Experience or Envy discovers a flaw in it: Yet unless it be a great man indeed, that finds fault first, his Discovery is only answered with Contempt for a while: But when another Hypothesis is broach'd (which is commonly soon after) that not having the fault of the former, and being likewise well contriv'd, gets a considerable number of Followers: Then you see all that fought under the Banners of the old Hypothesis bristle up, and every Man of Note among them thinks himself personally injured, and in Honour obliged to stand by it with his life and Fortune. Now all Arts and Sciences are ransack'd, and whatever can be drawn from Wit, Eloquence, or Learning, is produced to maintain their own Leige Hypothesis, and destroy the upstart one; and the whole Party is alarm'd with as much concern as they are in a Man of War, when they have receiv'd a shot under Water: In the mean time they that have lifted themselves under the new Hypothesis are not idle, and thus both Parties enter into a perfect state of war; the better sort fighting with Arguments, the rest with personal Reflections. This Play is generally continued for a considerable time with a great deal of Violence. . . .
>
> If the new Hypothesis is continually supplied with Men of Sense that zealously espouse its Cause, and keeps the Field till some of its chief Enemies, and those that first opposed it, are dead, it daily gets ground

till it triumphs at last, and ascends to the throne of the poor old one that
. . . is laid by among the rest of the maim'd Hypotheses. . . .

Mandeville had rather too strong an empiricist tendency and did not
quite see the importance of "hypothesis" and theory in science. But to
dwell on this failing of his would, in the light of present concerns, be too
much like quibbling. Given current agitations in the social sciences, it is
well to have before us this particular specimen of his robust good sense
and irony.

NOTES

1. I have benefitted from conversation on the subject of these comments
with Charles Bonjean and Walter Firey.

2. We do not find, for example, that special sort of pessimism about social
science which is marked by the notion that, in application to social problems,
it will merely aggravate them. Something apparently not far from this view is
suggested by the political scientist, Edward Banfield (1974: ix), who conjec-
tures that "owing to the nature of man and society (more particularly, American culture and institutions) we cannot 'solve' our serious problems by rational
management. Indeed, by trying we are almost certain to make matters worse."
One is rather reminded of the stance of William Graham Sumner expressed in
his title, "The Absurd Effort to Make the World Over,"–the title of an essay
published in the magazine *Forum* in 1894. (It should nevertheless be noted
that the sort of pessimism here intimated might still theoretically be connected
with a certain optimism about social science in particular respects—as in its
capacity sheerly to "reveal" things about the social order—and with a certain
optimism about society itself.)

3. In this volume the social sciences were conceived broadly indeed to include history, human geography, biology (with a long section on "biology and
some social problems"), social psychology, cultural anthropology, sociology,
economics, political science, jurisprudence and ethics. All chapters were written
by American scholars except for that on geography by Jean Brunhes of the
Collège de France.

4. Together with William F. Ogburn, Goldenweiser edited a symposium entitled *The Social Sciences and Their Interrelations*, which appeared in 1927,
two years after the Barnes volume. (Most of the articles were disappointingly
brief.) The two editors themselves stated that "both man and history . . . are
relatively impervious to the concept of law and but poorly subject to control."
The sociologist Pitirim A. Sorokin quoted a statement from F. H. Giddings to
the effect that data which the social sciences were making known "should en-
able us to diminish human misery and to live more wisely than the human race
has lived hitherto." Morris R. Cohen, the philosopher, referred a bit bitingly
to "those romantic souls who cherish the persistent illusion that by some new
trick of method the social sciences can readily be put on a par with the physi-

cal sciences in regard to definiteness and universal demonstrability." Cohen, an influential scholar in his time, was not the man to tolerate *hubris* in social scientists. (See also his comments relating to generalization in the social sciences in the relevant section of Louis Wirth, 1940: 227-273.) Cohen's views especially invite consideration of the small volume addressed to the question, *Can Science Save Us?* which George Lundberg published a generation ago in 1947).

5. Note, in this connection, the excellent critical remarks by William T. Couch (1974) on Ruth Benedict's *Patterns of Culture*, which presented this element in cultural relativism at its eloquently stated worst. [The very last sentence of *Patterns of Culture* referred to "the coexisting and *equally valid* patterns of life which mankind has created for itself from the new material of existence" (italics supplied). See Benedict, 1946: 257.] Ruth Benedict came to hold a different position, as have numerous other anthropologists; nor has anthropology been the only social science to "sin" in this way: American sociology was long haunted by Sumner's views on the relations of the folkways, mores and force with "right"—views that combined valid and invalid empirical observations with ethical blindness.

6. I am well aware that not all contributors to this very symposium would be free of qualms about such a bias as this. It is a bias which one may still regard as already in being, as due to be reinforced, and as desirable.

7. Mandeville thus does not discuss such a matter as the significant possibility that different paradigms may actually be appreciably complementary, but the statement that follows retains its considerable point today.

References

Banfield, E. 1974. The Unheavenly City Revisited (Boston: Little, Brown and Co.).

Barnes, H. E., ed. 1925. The History and Prospects of the Social Sciences New York: Alfred A. Knopf).

Benedict, R. 1946. Patterns of Culture (New York: Penguin Books).

Blau, P. M., ed. 1975. Approaches to the Study of Social Structure (New York: The Free Press).

Boulding, K. 1972. "Toward the Development of a Cultural Economics," Social Science Quarterly, 53 (September): 267–284.

Couch, W. T. 1974. The Human Potential (Durham: Duke University Press).

Hayek, F. 1959. The Constitution of Liberty (Chicago: University of Chicago Press).

———. 1973. Law, Legislation and Liberty (London: Routledge and Kegan Paul).

Lenski, G. and J. Lenski. 1974. Human Societies (New York: McGraw-Hill).

Mandeville, B. 1730. A Treatise of the Hypochondriack and Hysterical Diseases. (2nd ed.; London: J. Tonson in the Strand).

Merton, R. K. 1975. "Structural Analysis in Sociology," in P. M. Blau, ed., Ap-

proaches to the Study of Social Structure (New York: The Free Press):
21–52.

Ogburn, W. F. and A. A. Goldenweiser, eds. 1927. The Social Sciences and
their Interrelations (Boston: Houghton Mifflin).

Parsons, T. 1966. Societies: Evolutionary and Comparative Perspectives (Englewood Cliffs, N.J.: Prentice-Hall).

Sahlins, M. D. and E. R. Service, eds. 1960. Evolution and Culture (Ann Arbor:
University of Michigan Press).

Scott, W. D. 1924. "Discovery of Truth in Universities," The Century Magazine, 108 (August): 556–560.

Shils, E. A. 1962. "The Calling of Sociology," in T. Parsons, E. Shils, K. D.
Naegele, and J. R. Pitts, eds., Theories of Society (New York: The Free
Press), Vol. 2.

Shorter, E. and C. Tilly. 1974. Strikes in France, 1830–1968 (London: Cambridge University Press).

Thernstrom, S. 1973. The Other Bostonians: Poverty and Progress in the American Metropolis, 1880–1970 (Cambridge: Harvard University Press).

Wirth, L., ed. 1940. Eleven Twenty-Six: A Decade of Social Science Research
(Chicago: University of Chicago Press).

Worswick, G. D. N. 1972. "Is Progress in Economic Science Possible?" Economic Journal, 82 (March): 73–86.